The World of Kabbalah

Cover Art: *The Breath*
Michael Ellowitz, watercolor on Arches rough paper,
USA, 2016

Printed in the United States of America
© Copyrighted and Published 2023
by The Rohr Jewish Learning Institute
832 Eastern Parkway, Brooklyn, NY 11213

718-221-6900
WWW.MYJLI.COM

The World of Kabbalah

COURSE

TEXTBOOK

Revealing How Its Mystical Secrets Relate to You

The Rohr Jewish Learning Institute
gratefully acknowledges the pioneering
and ongoing support of

George and Pamela Rohr

Since its inception, the Rohr JLI has been
a beneficiary of the vision, generosity, care,
and concern of the Rohr family.

In the merit of the tens of thousands of hours
of Torah study by JLI students worldwide,
may they be blessed with health, *Yiddishe
nachas* from all their loved ones, and
extraordinary success in all their endeavors.

Citation Types

SCRIPTURE

The icon for Scripture is based on the images of a scroll and a spiral. The scroll is a literal reference; the spiral symbolizes Scripture's role as the singular source from which all subsequent Torah knowledge emanates.

SCRIPTURAL COMMENTARY

Throughout the ages, Jews have scrutinized the Torah's text, generating many commentaries.

TALMUD AND MIDRASH

The Talmud and Midrash record the teachings of the sages—fundamental links in the unbroken chain of the Torah's transmission going back to Mount Sinai.

TALMUDIC COMMENTARY

The layers of Talmudic teaching have been rigorously excavated in each era, resulting in a library of insightful commentaries.

JEWISH MYSTICISM

The mystics explore the inner, esoteric depths. The icon for mystical texts reflects the "*sefirot* tree" commonly present in kabbalistic charts.

JEWISH PHILOSOPHY

Jewish philosophic texts shed light on life's big questions and demonstrate the relevance of Jewish teachings even as the sands of societal values continuously shift.

JEWISH LAW AND CUSTOM

The guidance that emerges from Scripture and the Talmud finds practical expression in Jewish law, known as *Halachah* ("the way"), alongside customs adopted by Jewish communities through the generations.

CHASIDUT

Chasidism's advent in the eighteenth century brought major, encouraging changes to Jewish life and outlook. Its teachings are akin to refreshing, life-sustaining waters from a continuously flowing well of the profoundest insights.

LITURGY

The texts of the Jewish prayer book burst with the full spectrum of human emotion, from joy to longing to contrition and to hope. They all share the authentic search for a meaningful encounter with G-d.

PERSPECTIVES

Personal, professional, and academic perspectives, expressed in essays, research papers, diaries, and other works, can often enhance appreciation for Torah ideas and the totality of the Jewish experience.

Contents

Foreword — X

Endorsements — XI

Course Map — XII

LESSON 1
**THE EVOLUTION
OF EGO**   **1**

LESSON 2
**THE DAWN
OF LIMITATION**   **37**

LESSON 3
**THE INFINITE
LIGHT**   **73**

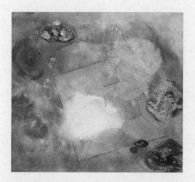

LESSON 4
**THE WORLD
OF CHAOS**   **109**

LESSON 5
**THE GREAT
CONCEALMENT**   **141**

LESSON 6
**THE ESSENCE
OF EVERYTHING**   **175**

Acknowledgments — 212

JLI Chapter Directory —218

Foreword

IN THE SIXTH CENTURY OF THE SIXTH MILLENNIUM, THE SUPERNAL GATES OF WISDOM WILL BE OPENED AS WILL THE WELLSPRINGS OF WISDOM BELOW. THIS WILL PREPARE THE WORLD FOR THE SEVENTH MILLENNIUM, JUST AS WE PREPARE OURSELVES ON FRIDAY, AS THE SUN BEGINS TO WANE, FOR SHABBAT.
—*ZOHAR* 1, 117A

For the majority of the three and a half millennia of Jewish history, it was unanimously accepted that the Torah's esoteric and mystical insights could only be appreciated by our nation's most outstanding scholars—those with broad minds and sensitive souls, who also lived particularly sacred lifestyles. Given the complex and nuanced nature of these teachings, there was a genuine fear that the mystical could easily be misunderstood and misapplied by the uninitiated. As a result, Judaism's mystical library was inaccessible to the average Jew. Those privy to this branch of wisdom had to be instructed directly by a seasoned master, and for that reason, the wisdom gained the moniker "kabbalah"—the "received tradition."

That protective shell cracked around the year 1570, when perhaps Judaism's most famous kabbalist, Rabbi Yitzchak Luria (the "Arizal," 1534–1572), arrived in the Holy Land and began teaching kabbalah to a group of scholars in the city of Safed. He not only revolutionized the understanding of kabbalah, revealing entirely fresh layers of Divine knowledge, but—uniquely—he promoted the teaching of kabbalah to the masses. The Arizal argued that this wisdom had the power to awaken and nourish the Jewish soul, empowering its students to withstand the trials and overcome the troubles of those harsh times.

Since then, society has undergone radical changes in every area of life, and today there is widespread public thirst for all things kabbalistic.

Rising to the occasion, the Rohr Jewish Learning Institute (JLI) is excited to present *The World of Kabbalah: Revealing How Its Mystical Secrets Relate to You*. This six-part course offers an unprecedented opportunity to immerse in the study of kabbalah, to encounter secrets that were safeguarded for centuries, and to explore the mysteries of Creation.

A primary focus within kabbalah is knowledge of the many descending levels that stretch between the Divine will to create the universe and its actual Creation. *The World of Kabbalah* explains this metaphysical system as a six-step journey that begins with the lower rungs of existence and progressively climbs to higher realities within this hierarchy—and beyond.

Furthermore, the kabbalists, and especially the masters of Chasidism, revealed in detail how this supernal system is mirrored within each individual. *The World of Kabbalah* draws on this profound branch of relatable kabbalah to provide opportunities for self-reflection and self-awareness. Spiritual secrets of the loftiest nature are shown to play out within each individual's personal life. Consequently, each lesson in this series concludes with mystically-based guidance on living happier, more productive, and more meaningful lives.

Endorsements

"Science shows us that we all are built with an innate 'neural docking station' for a sacred, transcendent awareness. We are inherently born to see relational spirituality with Hashem and His magnificent presence in our love for fellow human beings and living beings. However, this gift is one-third innate and two-thirds environmentally formed, which means we must always continue to learn—to foster our own birthright of spiritual awareness. Foremost we must prepare ourselves to serve as spiritual ambassadors of our children, to embrace their natural core for spiritual formation."

DR. LISA MILLER

Professor of Psychology, Columbia University

Founder, *Spirituality Mind Body Institute*

Author, *The Awakened Brain: The New Science of Spirituality and Our Quest for an Inspired Life*

"This course sets the groundwork for leading a more authentic and meaningful life. Merging together religious philosophy and existential psychology, this course provides valuable lessons that lead to self-actualization while recognizing the subjective journey that each person is on. I highly recommend this course for anyone looking to grow as a human being and live a life of authenticity and purpose, while gaining a deep level of empathy and understanding for those we share this world with."

DR. LINDSEY A. HARVELL-BOWMAN

Associate Professor, James Madison University

Director, Terror Management Lab

Treasurer and Board Member, International Society for the Science of Existential Psychology

"For millennia, kabbalah remained a secret teaching, but in the eighteenth century, the Baal Shem Tov and his disciples disclosed kabbalah to the Jewish people. What prompted the Chasidic masters to make such a fateful decision? The best explanation was given by Rabbi Shneur Zalman of Liadi, the founder of Chabad, in the form of a parable:

> The son of the king fell ill and was about to die. The doctors told the king that the only way to save his son was to grind the most precious stone of his crown, put it into the water, and give it to the son to drink. The courtiers tried to convince the king not to do it, but he answered: 'Why do I need the stone if my beloved son is dying?'

"This course, offered by JLI, is long overdue. The material is authentic, written in a language fully accessible to our contemporaries. In a reasonably concise way, the course conveys the main principles and ideas of kabbalah. I strongly recommend taking JLI's *The World of Kabbalah*, which, I am convinced, will be a great success."

DR. EDUARD SHYFRIN

Author, *From Infinity to Man: The Fundamental Ideas of Kabbalah within the Framework of Information Theory and Quantum Physics*

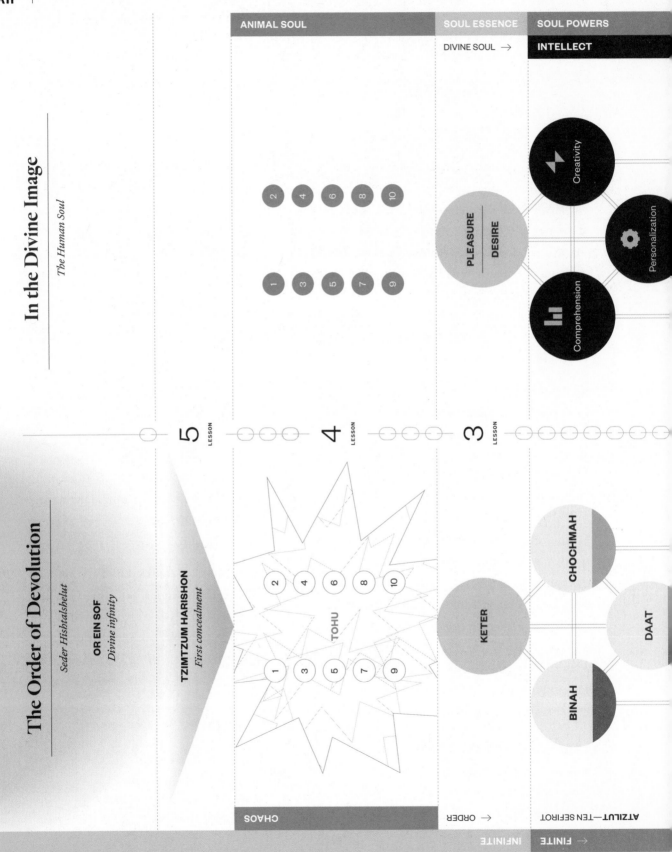

The Order of Devolution

Seder Hishtalshelut

OR EIN SOF
Divine infinity

TZIMTZUM HARISHON
First concealment

TOHU

KETER

BINAH — CHOCHMAH — DAAT

ATZILUT—TEN SEFIROT

ORDER →

CHAOS

FINITE → INFINITE

In the Divine Image

The Human Soul

ANIMAL SOUL

SOUL ESSENCE

SOUL POWERS

DIVINE SOUL →

INTELLECT

PLEASURE / DESIRE

Creativity

Personalization

Comprehension

LESSON 5

LESSON 4

LESSON 3

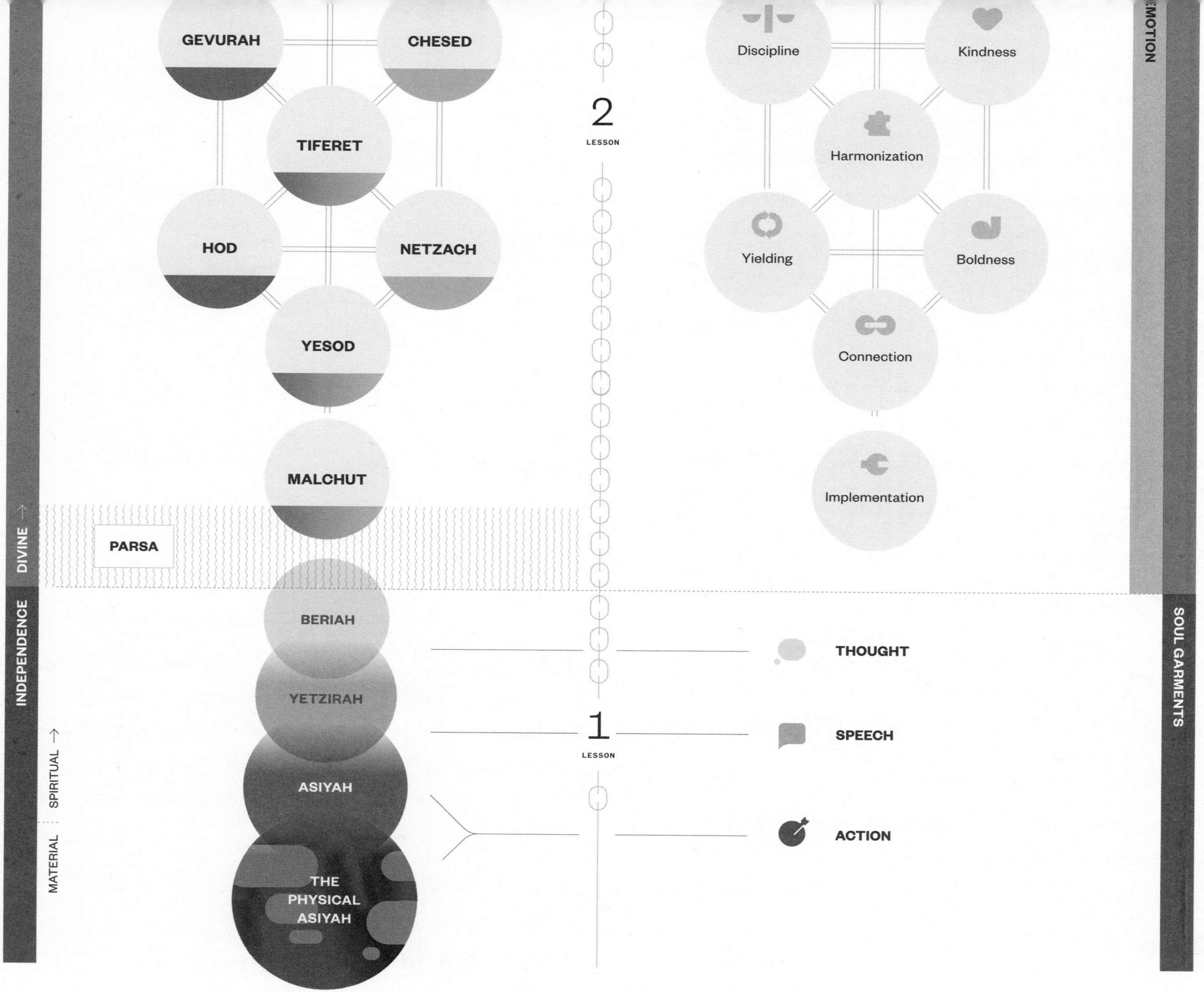

SOUL GARMENTS

EMOTION

Kindness

Boldness

Harmonization

Connection

Implementation

Discipline

Yielding

THOUGHT

SPEECH

ACTION

LESSON 2

LESSON 1

CHESED

NETZACH

TIFERET

YESOD

GEVURAH

HOD

MALCHUT

BERIAH

YETZIRAH

ASIYAH

THE PHYSICAL ASIYAH

PARSA

INDEPENDENCE

← DIVINE

← SPIRITUAL

MATERIAL

1

IN THE BEGINNING
Jane Kamentser, oil on
canvas, 2015, Los Angeles

THE EVOLUTION OF EGO

Our mystical journey is initiated by an overview of three unique spiritual worlds that precede the physical cosmic system within which we exist. These three realms correspond to three strata within the individual human experience—namely, thought, speech, and action. The insights from this awareness will become practical empowerment for personal growth.

I. INTRODUCTION

Welcome to *The World of Kabbalah: Revealing How Its Mystical Secrets Relate to You.* This course provides a journey into the fascinating yet mysterious realm of kabbalah, genuine Jewish mysticism.

The intellectual bridge that facilitates this journey is an analysis of a fascinating hierarchy present within the human soul. That hierarchy is a reflection of a far higher cosmic order referred to as *seder hishtalshelut,* the magnificent sequence of spiritual evolution that stretches from G-d's* infinite desire to create the world all the way down the Divine pipeline until the final, finite product. This order gave rise to the curious-looking charts that appear in kabbalistic works, and it is key to the present study.

---

* Throughout this book, "G-d" and "L-rd" are written with a hyphen instead of an "o" (both in our own translations and when quoting others). This is one way we accord reverence to the sacred Divine name. This also reminds us that, even as we seek G-d, He transcends any human effort to describe His reality.

FIGURE 1.1

Driving Questions

1. What is kabbalah?

2. What are its central teachings?

3. What is the significance of some of its key terms, like *sefirot*?

4. How are these teachings relevant to my everyday life?

KABBALAH
Bracha Lavee, felt on canvas, Israel, 2021

Kabbalah Diagram

FIGURE 1.2

Rabbi Moshe Cordovero, *Pardes Rimonim* (Koretz, 1786), p. 32b

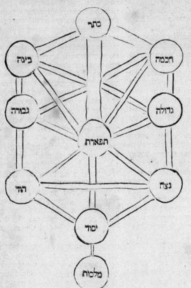

Prominent kabbalist. Ramak belonged to the circle of Jewish mystical thinkers who flourished in 16th-century Safed. The name Cordovero indicates that his family originated in Córdoba, Spain. His most famous kabbalistic work is *Pardes Rimonim*.

Kabbalah Diagram

FIGURE 1.3

Rabbi Shabtai Sheftel Halevi Horowitz,
Shefa Tal (Hanau, 1612), p. 5a

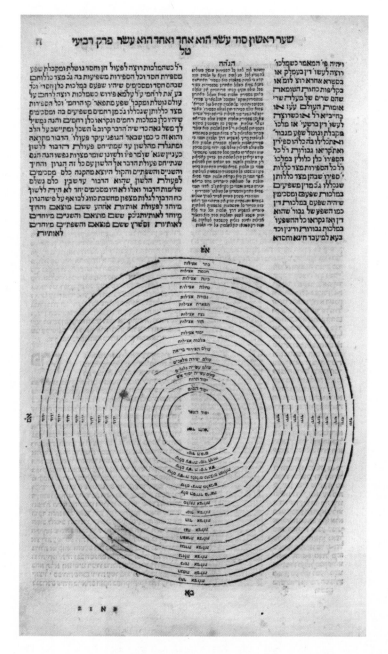

The Mortal Mirror

Rabbi Meir ibn Gabai, *Tolaat Yaakov, Sod Hamilah*

כִּי הָאָדָם דְּגְמָא עֶלְיוֹנָה. וְכָל מָה שֶׁבָּעֶלְיוֹנִים
וְתַחְתּוֹנִים כָּלוּל בּוֹ. וְהוּא סוֹד "צֶלֶם אֱלֹקִים"
(בְּרֵאשִׁית א, כז), בִּהְיוֹתוֹ בְּדֻגְמַת הַדְּבָרִים הָאֱלֹקִים,
בְּסוֹד "וּמִבְּשָׂרִי אֶחֱזֶה אֱלוֹקַהּ" (אִיּוֹב יט, כו).

A mortal is a mirror for the supernal reality. All that exists in both higher and lower realms is present in microcosmic form within the human. This is the deeper significance of the Torah's statement that the human was created "in the Divine image" (GENESIS 1:27). And this is why we say, "From my flesh, I envision G-d" (JOB 19:26).

RABBI MEIR IBN GABAI
1480–AFTER 1540

Kabbalist and author. Ibn Gabai was born in Spain, from which he emigrated during the 1492 expulsion. Eventually he settled in Egypt. He authored three books in which he elucidates many basic mystical concepts, which have become kabbalistic classics: *Tolaat Yaakov* (which he authored at the age of 26), *Derech Emunah*, and *Avodat Hakodesh*.

JACOB'S LADDER
Lesley Friedmann, acrylic on board, on permanent display, Chabad of Vancouver Island synagogue foyer, Victoria, BC, Canada, 2017

TEXT 2

Divine Ladder

Rabbi Moshe Alshich, Genesis 1:26

מָה עָשָׂה הוּא יִתְבָּרַךְ? עָשָׂה "סֻלָּם מֻצָּב אַרְצָה וְרֹאשׁוֹ מַגִּיעַ הַשָּׁמָיְמָה" (בְּרֵאשִׁית כח, יב), לְמַעַן עַל יְדֵי מַדְרֵגוֹת הַסֻּלָּם יִשְׁתַּלְשֵׁל שֶׁפַע עֶלְיוֹן, קַו לָקַו יוֹרֵד וּמִתְעַבֶּה, עַד יוּכַן לְהִתְקַבֵּל עַד מַטָּה מַטָּה.

G-d fashioned "a ladder planted on the earth, whose top reaches into the heavens" (GENESIS 28:12). This ladder's rungs serve as channels through which the flow of Divine energy can devolve degree after degree, in a constant pattern of progressive coarsening, until the flow can be received at the lowest extreme of existence.

RABBI MOSHE ALSHICH
1508–1593

Biblical exegete. Rabbi Alshich was born in Turkey and moved to Safed, Israel, where he became a student of Rabbi Yosef Caro, the preeminent codifier of Jewish law. Alshich's commentary to the Torah, titled *Torat Moshe*, remains popular to this day. His students included Rabbi Chaim Vital and Rabbi Yom Tov Tzahalon. He is buried in Safed.

KEY TERM 1.1

HEBREW TERM	סֵדֶר הִשְׁתַּלְשְׁלוּת
TRANSLITERATION	*seder hishtalshelut*
LITERAL MEANING	**system of devolution**
DEFINITION	the many degrees of systematic descent that stretch between G-d's desire to create the universe and the tangible result of that goal

Word of Caution

Rabbi Shneur Zalman of Liadi, *Likutei Torah*, Vayikra 51c

אָמַר קְדוֹשׁ ה' הָרַב יִשְׂרָאֵל בַּעַל שֵׁם טוֹב
נִשְׁמָתוֹ עֵדֶן: אֲשֶׁר בְּלִמּוּד סִפְרֵי הַקַּבָּלָה יֵשׁ
לְהִזָּהֵר שֶׁלֹּא יְדַמֶּה הַדְּבָרִים כִּפְשׁוּטָתָן.

The saintly Rabbi Yisrael Baal Shem Tov taught that when studying works of kabbalah, we must be careful not to perceive the kabbalistic ideas as literal, physical concepts.

THE WAGON OF THE BESHT
Shoshannah Brombacher,
oil pastel on paper,
Brooklyn, 1995

RABBI SHNEUR ZALMAN OF LIADI (ALTER REBBE) 1745–1812

Chasidic rebbe, Halachic authority, and founder of the Chabad movement. The Alter Rebbe was born in Liozna, Belarus, and was among the principal students of the Magid of Mezeritch. His numerous works include the *Tanya*, an early classic containing the fundamentals of Chabad Chasidism; and *Shulchan Aruch HaRav*, an expanded and reworked code of Jewish law.

RABBI YISRAEL BAAL SHEM TOV (BESHT) 1698–1760

Founder of the Chasidic movement. Born in Slutsk, Belarus, the Baal Shem Tov was orphaned as a child. He served as a teacher's assistant and clay digger before founding the Chasidic movement and revolutionizing the Jewish world with his emphasis on prayer, joy, and love for every Jew, regardless of his or her level of Torah knowledge.

II. THE THREE WORLDS

The *Zohar* discusses the existence of three spiritual worlds that precede our physical universe. Their titles in Jewish mysticism reflect the varying degrees to which they are endowed with a sense of partial independence from G-d. The greater the sense of self, the greater the loss of an empowering surrender to G-d.

TEXT 4

Beriah, Yetzirah, Asiyah

Zohar 2, 155a

דְּאִית בֵּיהּ אוּף הָכִי בְּרִיאָה, וְעַל דָּא בְּרָאתִיו.

בְּהַהוּא כָּבוֹד עִלָּאָה אִית בֵּיהּ יְצִירָה, וְעַל דָּא יְצַרְתִּיו . . .

בְּהַהוּא כָּבוֹד עִלָּאָה אִית בֵּיהּ עֲשִׂיָּה, וְעַל דָּא אוּף הָכִי בְּבַר נַשׁ כְּתִיב עֲשִׂיתִיו.

לְמִהֱוֵי אִיהוּ כְּגַוְנָא דְּהַהוּא כָּבוֹד עִלָּאָה.

G-d's glory includes *Beriah*, and G-d bestowed this unto the human.

G-d's glory includes *Yetzirah*, and G-d bestowed this unto the human. . . .

G-d's glory includes *Asiyah*, and G-d bestowed this unto the human.

Thus, the human is rendered in the image of the supernal glory.

ZOHAR

The seminal work of kabbalah, Jewish mysticism. The *Zohar* is a mystical commentary on the Torah, written in Aramaic and Hebrew. According to the Arizal, the *Zohar* contains the teachings of Rabbi Shimon bar Yocha'i, who lived in the Land of Israel during the 2nd century. The *Zohar* has become one of the indispensable texts of traditional Judaism, alongside and nearly equal in stature to the Mishnah and Talmud.

HEBREW TERM	בִּי"עַ
TRANSLITERATION	*BiYA*
LITERAL MEANING	**created, shaped, made**
DEFINITION	acronym for the grouping of the three spiritual words, **B**eriah, **Y**etzirah, and **A**siyah

HEBREW TERM	יְשׁוּת
TRANSLITERATION	*yeshut*
LITERAL MEANING	**existence**
DEFINITION	existence with a sense of self-awareness and independence

ILAN SEFIROT
(*SEFIROT* TREE)
Yehoshua Wiseman,
acrylic on canvas, Israel

FIGURE 1.4

Names of *BiYA*

NAME OF WORLD	TRANSLATION	IMPLICATION	DEGREE OF SELF-AWARENESS
BERIAH	Created	The initial appearance of a novel entity	Minimal
YETZIRAH	Shaped	Supplying form to a preexisting entity	Intermediate
ASIYAH	Made	Completion of an entity's production	Maximal

An introductory page of the *Zohar* from the first printed edition, Mantua (in modern-day Italy), 1558. Numerous handwritten notes of an unknown author fill the margins of this particular copy. (JTS Library, New York)

TEXT 5

Decisive Factor: Closeness

Rabbi Shalom Dovber Schneersohn,
Sefer Hamaamarim 5662, pp. 357–358

RABBI SHALOM DOVBER
SCHNEERSOHN
(RASHAB)
1860–1920

Chasidic rebbe. Rabbi
Shalom Dovber became
the 5th leader of the
Chabad movement
upon the passing
of his father, Rabbi
Shmuel Schneersohn.
He established the
Lubavitch network
of *yeshivot* called
Tomchei Temimim. He
authored many volumes
of Chasidic discourses
and is renowned for
his lucid and thorough
explanations of
kabbalistic concepts.

וְהֵן ג׳ מַדְרֵגוֹת: בְּרִיאָה, יְצִירָה, עֲשִׂיָּה.

דִּבְרִיאָה הוּא רֵאשִׁית הִתְחַדְּשׁוּת הַיֵּשׁ . . . אֶלָּא
שֶׁאֹפֶן הִתְהַוּוּתוֹ עַד שֶׁנַּעֲשָׂה בִּבְחִינַת יֵשׁ מַמָּשׁ, דְּהַיְנוּ
הִתְגַּלּוּת יְשׁוּתוֹ בְּפֹעַל מַמָּשׁ, הוּא בְּג׳ מַדְרֵגוֹת . . .

וְהַטַּעַם מָה שֶׁהִתְהַוּוּת הַיֵּשׁ הוּא בְּאֹפֶן כָּזֶה שֶׁאֵינוֹ
נַעֲשֶׂה בִּבְחִינַת יֵשׁ מַמָּשׁ בִּתְחִלַּת הִתְהַוּוּתוֹ . . . לְפִי
שֶׁבַּתְּחִלַּת וְרֵאשִׁית הִתְהַוּוּת הַיֵּשׁ הֲרֵי הוּא קָרוֹב עֲדַיִן
אֶל הָאַיִן הָאֱלֹקִי וּמֵאִיר בּוֹ בְּחִינַת הָאַיִן . . . וְלָכֵן אִי
אֶפְשָׁר שֶׁיִּהְיֶה בִּבְחִינַת מְצִיאוּת יֵשׁ מַמָּשׁ.

כִּי אִם כַּאֲשֶׁר יֵרֵד מִמַּדְרֵגָה לְמַדְרֵגָה, וְהַיְנוּ
שֶׁמִּתְעַלֵּם הָאוֹר וְאֵינוֹ מֵאִיר בּוֹ בְּגִלּוּי.

עַד בְּחִינַת עֲשִׂיָּה, שֶׁהָאוֹר מֻסְתָּר לְגַמְרֵי,
אָז דַּוְקָא נַעֲשָׂה בִּבְחִינַת יֵשׁ מַמָּשׁ.

There are three rungs: *Beriah*, *Yetzirah*, and *Asiyah*.

Beriah is the first introduction of *yeshut*, an
independent self-concept. . . . However,
existence only develops into a complete
yesh when it reaches the third stage. . . .

The reason *yeshut* develops gradually . . . is because the initial stage of existence remains close to G-d, and His presence is very much sensed at this level.

Then *Beriah* devolves into *Yetzirah*, where the presence of G-d is somewhat concealed.

Finally, *Yetzirah* devolves into *Asiyah*, where G-d is *completely* concealed. At this point, existence becomes a true *yesh* and gains a complete sense of selfhood.

KEY TERM 1.4

HEBREW TERM	בִּטּוּל
TRANSLITERATION	*bitul*
LITERAL MEANING	**surrender, suspension, nullification**
DEFINITION	a subdued sense of self due to being absorbed by something overwhelmingly impressive, and the desire to become one with it

Does *bitul* (surrender) harm one's self self-esteem? **Rabbi Shais Taub** responds: **myjli.com/kabbalah**

III. THE HUMAN EXAMPLE

An analysis of mortal thought, speech, and action that identifies the distinctions unique to each of these functions provides an analogy through which to understand the nature of *BiYA* and the distinctions between these worlds.

KEY TERM 1.5

HEBREW TERM	לְבוּשֵׁי הַנֶּפֶשׁ
TRANSLITERATION	*levushei hanefesh*
LITERAL MEANING	**the soul's garments**
DEFINITION	Thought, speech, and action—the soul's behaviors, which are external to the soul itself

Title page of *Sefer Yetzirah*, an early kabbalistic work, from the first printed edition, Mantua, 1562. (Scholem Collection, National Library of Israel, Jerusalem)

TEXT 6A

Removable

Rabbi Shneur Zalman of Liadi,
Maamarei Admur Hazaken 5567, p. 414

שֶׁבְּחִינַת בְּרִיאָה יְצִירָה עֲשִׂיָּה הֵם עַל דֶּרֶךְ מָשָׁל כְּמוֹ
לְבוּשׁ גַּשְׁמִי, שֶׁיָּכוֹל לִפְשֹׁט אוֹתוֹ וְלִלְבֹּשׁ לְבוּשׁ אַחֵר,
לְפִי שֶׁהַלְּבוּשׁ אֵינוֹ נוֹגֵעַ לְעַצְמוּתוֹ . . . כְּמוֹ מַחֲשָׁבָה
דִּבּוּר וּמַעֲשֶׂה לְעַצְמוּת הַנֶּפֶשׁ, הֵם רַק בְּחִינַת לְבוּשִׁים.

Beriah, *Yetzirah*, and *Asiyah* are comparable to
physical garments. We can always remove our
garments and dress in alternative garments because
garments are not part of our essential selves. . . . In
the soul's experience, this correlates to thought,
speech, and action, which are not relevant to the
core of the soul, but serve only as its garments.

Handwritten correspondence
by Rabbi Shneur Zalman
of Liadi, dated 1811.
(Library of Agudas Chasidei
Chabad, Brooklyn, N.Y.)

TEXT 6B

Triple Correspondence

Rabbi Shneur Zalman of Liadi, ibid.

בְּרִיאָה הוּא בְּחִינַת מַחְשָׁבָה, וִיצִירָה הוּא בְּחִינַת
דִּבּוּר, וַעֲשִׂיָּה הוּא בְּחִינַת מַעֲשֶׂה בְּגַשְׁמִיּוּת.

Beriah corresponds to thinking; *Yetzirah*, to
speaking; and *Asiyah*, to physical action.

Kabbalistic diagram in the first
printed edition of *Shefa Tal* by
Rabbi Shabtai Sheftel Halevi
Horowitz, Hanau (in modern-
day Germany), 1612. (National
Library of Israel, Jerusalem)

Watch "Do Your Thoughts
Matter?" by **Mrs. Sara
Esther Crispe:**
myjli.com/kabbalah

FIGURE 1.5

Degrees of Separation

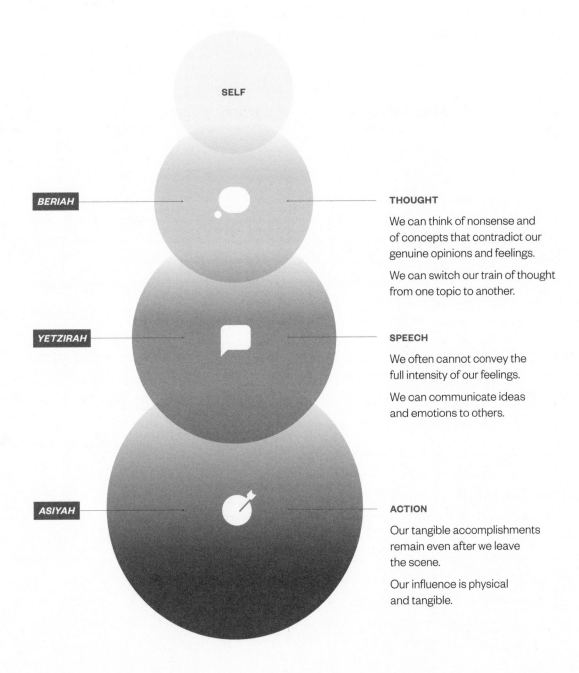

SELF

BERIAH

THOUGHT

We can think of nonsense and of concepts that contradict our genuine opinions and feelings.

We can switch our train of thought from one topic to another.

YETZIRAH

SPEECH

We often cannot convey the full intensity of our feelings.

We can communicate ideas and emotions to others.

ASIYAH

ACTION

Our tangible accomplishments remain even after we leave the scene.

Our influence is physical and tangible.

Souls in the Spiritual Worlds

The spiritual worlds of *Beriah* and *Yetzirah* are home to souls due to descend to, or that have already returned from, our physical world—*Asiyah*. Even while a soul is installed in a human body in *Asiyah*, it nevertheless retains a connection with its source in the higher, spiritual worlds.

The following collection of texts chart the soul's journey from the spiritual worlds to our physical world and back.

SPIRITUAL ORIGINS

Rabbi Moshe Cordovero, *Pardes Rimonim* 1:7

The world of *Beriah* is referred to as the Divine Throne. It is the World of Souls, as per the *Zohar*'s (3:29b) teaching: "Souls are hewn from beneath the Divine Throne." The original source of souls is actually far higher than *Beriah*, but *Beriah* is the realm within which souls emerge as distinct entities.

Rabbi Shmuel Schneerson, *Likutei Torah: Torat Shmuel* 5635:2, p. 3017

In our Morning Blessings, we turn to G-d and exclaim, "My G-d! The soul You placed into me is pure. *Atah Beratah*—You created it! *Atah Yetzartah*—You formed it! And You breathed it into me."

The significance of this prayer is that it depicts the path through which a soul descends into a human body. The soul's earliest origin is described as "pure," indicating that it is within pristine Divinity. In order to descend into our world, the soul must travel through the realms referred to as *Beratah*, "You created it"— the world of *Beriah*, and then *Yetzartah*, "You formed it"—the world of Yetzirah, and finally, "You have breathed it into me"—the soul's installation within a human body, here in the world of *Asiyah*.

RESIDUAL SPIRITUALITY

The Rebbe, Rabbi Menachem Mendel Schneerson, *Likutei Sichot* 9, p. 25

A number of Talmudic statements inform us that heavenly voices regularly call upon us to better our ways. This is rather puzzling. What could be the point of issuing calls that people fail to hear?

The answer is that part of us indeed hears these calls. For part of our soul remains on high and does not descend into the body. This part of the soul, which resides in the spiritual realms, clearly hears the heavenly voices—and its reaction stirs the part of the soul that is installed within the body.

The result of this process is discernable in individuals who suddenly feel inspired to become more connected with G-d—even though they did nothing at all to invite such spiritual feelings. Rather, their inspiration is the trickle-down effect of a heavenly call that is heard by the part of the soul that resides in Heaven.

SPIRITUAL RETURN

Rabbi Shneur Zalman of Liadi, *Torah Or*, *Miketz* 32d

Our sages taught that "in the afterlife, there is no eating, drinking, procreation, business dealings, jealousy, hatred, or competition. Rather, the righteous sit with crowns on their heads and enjoy the splendor of the Divine presence" (Talmud, Berachot 17a).

What is the splendor of the Divine presence that the souls enjoy in Paradise? It is a radiance of G-d's infinite light that the souls in Paradise are capable of perceiving.

There are two general levels within Paradise: Higher Paradise is located in the spiritual world of *Beriah*, while Lower Paradise is located in the spiritual world of *Yetzirah*. Within these two divisions, however, there exist infinite sublevels.

Souls in Paradise constantly advance. They rise from one level to the next, as they refine their capacity to perceive the radiance of the Divine Light. When a soul desires to graduate to the next level, it must first immerse in *nahar di'nor*, the "fiery river," an experience that allows it to erase its memory of its previous understanding of the Divine. This is necessary because the perception attained on any given level is insignificant compared to the perception available on the next level and disturbs the absorption of the advanced understanding.

The Rebbe, Rabbi Menachem Mendel Schneerson, *Likutei Sichot* 14, pp. 34–35

The Talmud (Berachot 64a) states that "the righteous have no rest—not in the present world, nor in the next, as it is stated, 'They will go from strength to strength'" (Psalms 84:8).

While the soul of the deceased constantly ascends within Paradise, it experiences a quantum leap on each anniversary of its passing (*yahrtzeit*). That is because the death of the body allowed the soul to undergo its first quantum leap, releasing it from the physical world to the spiritual realm. Similarly, within Paradise, each major ascent of the soul requires "death," a release from its previous level within Paradise. That is precisely what occurs on each anniversary of the soul's departure from this world, allowing the soul to experience another quantum leap within Paradise.

For that reason, we recite the Kaddish prayer on each anniversary of passing, and observe related practices—for at that time, the soul experiences a similar propulsion to the day of mortal demise.

Rabbi Menachem Mendel of Lubavitch, *Likutei Torah, Bamidbar* 2b, note

A soul's post-life experience in the lower Gan Eden is far more profound than its pre-life experience in the higher Gan Eden.

Three Types of Angels

Isaiah and Ezekiel frequently encountered angels in their prophetic visions. They employed rich and detailed metaphors to describe them.

The angels of Heaven are divided into three general categories, each occupying a distinct spiritual realm.

The following texts are selections from the prophetic visions that describe the various forms of angels, together with explanatory texts that highlight the unique qualities of each particular form.

ANGEL ABOVE THE SHTETL (DETAIL)
Ksenija Pecaric. acrylic on canvas, New Jersey, 2009

BERIAH
Seraphim: Flaming Entities

Isaiah 6:1–4

In the year that King Uziah died, I saw the L-rd sitting on a high and exalted throne, and His lower extremity filled the Temple. Above Him stood Seraphim, each with six wings: with two wings they covered their faces, with two they covered their feet, and with two they would fly.

The Seraphim were calling to one another: "Holy, holy, holy is the L-rd of Hosts! The entire earth is filled with His glory!"

At the sound of their voices the doorposts shook, and the house was filled with smoke.

Rabbi Shneur Zalman of Liadi, *Likutei Torah, Emor* 32b

Seraphim reside in *Beriah*, the realm in which there is a high degree of comprehension of G-d's infinite light. The angels of this world perceive G-d as He transcends the entire process of Creation. For that reason, they proclaim, "Holy!" (*Kadosh*)—because the term *kadosh* connotes something entirely separate and distinct.

As a result of their mental concentration and their comprehension of this aspect of G-d, the Seraphim burn with passion to fully perceive G-d's glory.

YETZIRAH
Chayot: Holy Animals

ASIYAH
Ofanim: Wheeling angels

Ezekiel 1:13–14

The appearance of the living creatures was like burning coals of fire, like torches. The fire moved back and forth among the creatures; it was bright, and lightning flashed out of it. The creatures rushed back and forth like flashes of lightning.

Ezekiel 1:16

This was the appearance and function of the wheels: They had the appearance of crystal, and all four looked alike. Each appeared and functioned like a wheel within a wheel.

Rabbi Shneur Zalman of Liadi, *Tanya, Likutei Amarim*, ch. 39

The holy *Chayot* reside in the world of *Yetzirah*, while the *Seraphim* dwell in Beriah.

Beriah is a world of intellectual revelation of G-d, and the *Seraphim* are therefore in a constant state of *bitul*, standing in the same spot without change.

By contrast, in the world of *Yetzirah,* G-d's emotive attributes—Divine love and awe, etc.—are revealed. The angels of this realm are referred to as *Chayot*, "animals," because like animals, they experience emotions rather than intellect. Being primarily emotional creatures, the *Chayot* of *Yetzirah* are highly excitable, and as they experience the revelations of *Yetzirah*, they rush back and forth.

Rabbi Menachem Mendel of Lubavitch, *Or HaTorah, Shemot* 5, pp. 1467–1468

Ofanim reside in the spiritual layer of the world of *Asiyah* (as opposed to the material layer of *Asiyah* that mortals inhabit). *Asiyah* is a world of action, devoid of the depth of understanding and profundity of feeling available in the higher realms. Consequently, the *Ofanim's* perception of G-d takes the form of uncomplicated acknowledgment and straightforward acceptance.

Due to their lack of intellectual understanding, the *Ofanim* are incapable of distinction and complexity. This is why they are described as round like a wheel, without a particular beginning or conclusion, and within which no position carries uniqueness over any other.

Therefore, whereas the *Chayot* express their emotional perception of G-d in rushing movements, racing upward, then racing back down, the *Ofanim* express their acknowledgment of G-d as a steady, simple motion, like the unfluctuating turning of a wheel.

IV. LESSONS

Several insights emerge from an analysis of *BiYA*: Firstly, *BiYA*'s sense of independence from G-d implies that humans are endowed with the ability to control their actions, speech, and even thoughts, irrespective of one's internal makeup. Furthermore, the existence of *BiYA*'s three rungs and their specific hierarchy imparts insight into human planning, consulting, and implementation. In addition, it is possible to begin each day with a *BiYA*-exercise to facilitate an adequate sense of grounding that is coupled with spiritual focus.

EXERCISE 1.1

Peruse the following list, and mentally identify one trait that does *not* pose a challenge for you. Then mentally identify one that *does*.

Anger	Extravagance	Jealousy
Arrogance	Fickleness	Laziness
Crassness	Flakiness	Pessimism
Cynicism	Frivolity	Pettiness
Dishonesty	Greed	Selfishness
Disloyalty	Insensitivity	Stinginess
Disorganization	Intrusiveness	Timidity

TEXT 7

In Control

The Rebbe, Rabbi Menachem Mendel Schneerson,
Torat Menachem: Sefer Hamaamarim Melukat 3, p. 382

מַחֲשָׁבָה דִבּוּר וּמַעֲשֶׂה הֵם לְבוּשֵׁי הַנֶּפֶשׁ. וְלָכֵן כְּמוֹ
שֶׁלְּבוּשֵׁי הַגּוּף . . . בִּיכָלְתּוֹ לְפוֹשְׁטָם, וּמִכָּל שֶׁכֵּן
שֶׁאֵינוֹ מֻכְרָח בִּלְבוּשִׁים אֵלּוּ (שֶׁלּוֹבֵשׁ עַכְשָׁו) וּבִיכָלְתּוֹ
לְהַחֲלִיפָם בִּלְבוּשִׁים אֲחֵרִים, עַל דֶּרֶךְ זֶה הוּא בִּלְבוּשֵׁי
הַנֶּפֶשׁ, דְּהַלְּבוּשִׁים דִבּוּר וּמַעֲשֶׂה אֶפְשָׁר לְפוֹשְׁטָם. וְגַם
הַמַּחֲשָׁבָה שֶׁהִיא בִּתְמִידוּת, נֶחְלֶפֶת בְּמַחֲשָׁבָה אַחֶרֶת.

מַה שֶּׁאֵין כֵּן הַשֵּׂכֶל וְהַמִּדּוֹת הֲרֵי הֵם מַהוּת
הַנֶּפֶשׁ, וְלָכֵן בִּכְדֵי לְשַׁנּוֹתָם צָרִיךְ לִיגִיעָה.

Thought, speech, and action are merely garments to
the soul. Just as we are able to remove . . . the body's
garments, so we can remove the soul's garments of
speech and action by refraining from speaking or
acting. And just as we can exchange one article of
clothing for another, so can we switch our thought,
which constantly runs, from one subject to another.

This is in contrast to the intellect and emotion
that, as part of the actual soul, demand
much effort to effectively change.

RABBI MENACHEM
MENDEL SCHNEERSON
1902–1994

The towering Jewish
leader of the 20th
century, known as "the
Lubavitcher Rebbe," or
simply as "the Rebbe."
Born in southern
Ukraine, the Rebbe
escaped Nazi-occupied
Europe, arriving in
the U.S. in June 1941.
The Rebbe inspired
and guided the revival
of traditional Judaism
after the European
devastation, impacting
virtually every Jewish
community the world
over. The Rebbe often
emphasized that the
performance of just
one additional good
deed could usher in
the era of Mashiach.
The Rebbe's scholarly
talks and writings have
been printed in more
than 200 volumes.

Human = Thought, Speech, Action

Rabbi Shneur Zalman of Liadi, *Likutei Torah, Behaalotecha* 31c

HEBREW LETTER	ENGLISH	REPRESENTING THE WORD	MEANING	
א	**A**	*Alefcha*	Thought (lit., teaching/ learning)	
ד	**D**	*Dibur*	Speech	
מ	**M**	*Maaseh*	Action	

THE WISE SON
Joel ben Simeon Feibush, from *The Ashkenazi Haggadah,* an illuminated parchment manuscript from South Germany, c. 1460. (British Library, London)

Kabbalistic tips on how to control your mind and emotions:
myjli.com/kabbalah

TEXT 8

The Physiognomist

Rabbi Betzalel Ashkenazi, *Shitah Mekubetzet*, Nedarim 32b

מַעֲשֶׂה בְּחָכָם אֶחָד שָׁלַח דְּמוּת פַּרְצוּפוֹ לְחָכָם
אַחֵר שֶׁהָיָה מַכִּיר בִּדְמוּת הַפַּרְצוּפִין.

נִטְמַן פָּנֵי מִבִּיעֲתוּתֵיהּ דְּהַהוּא פַּרְצוּף.
לְסוֹף שָׁאַל לוֹ לָמָה נִטְמַן מִמֶּנּוּ.

וְעָנָה: אוֹתוֹ הַפַּרְצוּף מֵאָדָם רַע שֶׁאֵין כִּדְמוּתוֹ -
חַמְדָן וְנוֹאֵף וְלִסְטִים - וְאֵין לְהַבִּיט אֵלָיו.

וְהַמְבִיאוֹ נִתְיָרֵא מִלָּשׁוּב אֶל אֲדֹנָיו, עַד שֶׁשָּׁלַח
אֵלָיו שֶׁלֹּא יִירָא מִמֶּנּוּ. וְשָׁאַל לוֹ כָּל הָעִנְיָן, וְאָמַר
לוֹ כָּל מָה שֶׁשָּׁמַע וְלָכֵן יָרֵאתִי לָשׁוּב אֵלֶיךָ.

אָמַר: בְּוַדַּאי אֵין חָכָם כְּמוֹ אוֹתוֹ בַּעַל הַפַּרְצוּף, שֶׁמָּן
הַכֹּל אָמַר אֱמֶת - שֶׁיִּצְרִי מְגָרֶה בִּי וּמֵסִית אוֹתִי לַעֲשׂוֹת
כָּל זֹאת. אֲבָל הַחָכְמָה שֶׁבִּי מוֹנַעַת אוֹתִי מִכָּל זֶה.

There was once a sage who sent a drawing
of his face to a physiognomist—a master
who discerns temperament and character
from one's outward appearance.

When the master saw the drawing, he immediately
blocked his face in fright. The messenger who
brought the drawing asked him, "Why have you
blocked your face from looking at the drawing?"

RABBI BETZALEL ASHKENAZI C. 1520–1592

Rabbi and scholar; lived in Egypt and Israel. While in Egypt he studied under the Radvaz and, upon the latter's immigration to Israel, assumed leadership of the community. Later, he himself immigrated to Israel, where he became the leader of the Jerusalem community. He is best known for his *Shitah Mekubetzet*, an anthology of classical commentaries to the Talmud. His most important disciple was the famous kabbalist, Rabbi Yitzchak Luria.

The master replied, "I've never seen the face of such a horrible person before. I saw in him coveting, adultery, and robbery. One shouldn't gaze at the face of such evil."

The messenger was obviously terrified of bringing back this reading to the sage. However, the sage sent word that he should return without fear. Upon his return, the sage inquired about what had occurred. The messenger conveyed everything that he had heard, concluding, "That's why I was afraid to return to you."

The sage replied, "Surely, this physiognomist outshines all others. Everything he said about me is true. My internal inclination drives me and seduces me to commit all of the wrongdoing that the master saw. Yet, I use my wisdom to refrain from acting on it."

EXERCISE 1.2

Rate yourself in terms of the following three statements:

A. I strategize and plan well.   1 2 3 4 5

B. I solicit helpful advice from others.   1 2 3 4 5

C. I get the job done. I'm an implementer.   1 2 3 4 5

5 = very much
4 = pretty well
3 = average
2 = somewhat weak
1 = very weak

TYPES OF JEWS, JERUSALEM
James Tissot, ink on paper mounted on board, France, c. 1886 or 1889 (Brooklyn Museum, N.Y.)

TEXT 9

Plan, Consult, Act

The Rebbe, Rabbi Menachem Mendel Schneerson,
Sefer Hasichot 5750:2, pp. 464–467

דִי הַנְהָגָה פוּן אַ געזוּנְטְן אוּן פוּלְקָאמְעֶנְעֶם מֶענְטְשׁ (אַ בַּר
שֵׂכֶל) אִיז בַּאגְרִינְדֶעט אוּן וועֶרְט אָנְגעֶפִֿירְט דוּרְךְ דְרַיי זַאכְן
- מַחֲשָׁבָה דִבּוּר אוּן מַעֲשֶׂה: צוּם אַלעֶם עֶרְשְׁטְן טְרַאכְט עֶר;
דעֶרְנָאךְ בְּרעֶנְגְט עֶר אַרוֹיס זַיין מַחֲשָׁבָה אִין דִבּוּר צוּ אַנְדעֶרעֶ,
דעֶרְצֵיילְן זֵיי וואָס עֶר טְרַאכְט, זִיךְ בַּאראַטְן מִיט יְדִידִים
מְבִינִים (אִין דעֶם תְּחוּם מְסָיָם) בִּכְדֵי קְלָערעֶר אוּן רִיכְטִיקעֶר
פַֿארְשְׁטֵיין דִי זַאךְ; דעֶרְנָאךְ קוּמְט עֶר צוּ אַ מַסְקָנָא לְפֿעֹל,
אוּן בְּרעֶנְגְט אַרוֹיס זַיין מַחֲשָׁבָה וְדִבּוּר אִין מַעֲשֶׂה בְּפֿעֹל . . .

אַן אָדָם שָׁלֵם בַּאנוּגְעֶנְט זִיךְ נִיט מִיט מַחְשָׁבָה אַלֵיין, אָדעֶר
אֲפִֿילוּ מִיט מַחֲשָׁבָה אוּן דִבּוּר, נָאר עֶר בְּרעֶנְגְט אַרוֹיס
זַיינעֶ פְּלעֶנעֶר (בְּמַחֲשָׁבָה וְדִבּוּר) אִין מַעֲשֶׂה בְּפֿעֹל (דעֶר
עִנְיָן הַשְּׁלִישִׁי) . . . לְאִידָךְ גִיסָא: בִּכְדֵי דִי מַעֲשֶׂה זָאל זַיין
בִּשְׁלֵמוּת דַארְף זִיךְ אִין אִיר אָנְהעֶרן וְוִי זִי אִיז אַן עִנְיָן
שְׁלִישִׁי, וועֶלְכעֶר אִיז בַּאגְרִינְדעֶט אוּן קוּמְט נָאך מַחֲשָׁבָה
וְדִבּוּר: זַיין מַעֲשֶׂה זָאל נִיט זַיין סְתָם געֶכַאפְּט אוּן געֶטָאן,
נָאר זִי זָאל קוּמעֶן דַוְקָא נָאך דעֶם וואָס עֶר הָאט עֶס גוּט
דוּרְכְגעֶטְרַאכְט אוּן דוּרְכְגעֶרעֶדְט מִיט אַנְדעֶרעֶ . . .

אוּן כְּשֵׁם וְוִי שְׁלֵמוּת הָאָדָם בַּאשְׁטֵייט פֿוּן אַלעֶ דְרַיי עִנְיָנִים
פֿוּן מַחֲשָׁבָה דִבּוּר וּמַעֲשֶׂה, אוּן דַוְקָא אַלְס שְׁלֹשָׁה דַרְגוֹת
אוּן בְּסֵדֶר זֶה - אַזוֹי אִיז דָאס אוֹיךְ אִין עוֹלָם, אַז שְׁלֵמוּת
הִשְׁתַּלְשְׁלוּת הָעוֹלָמוֹת . . . וועֶרְט אוֹיפֿגעֶשְׁטעֶלְט דַוְקָא
דוּרְךְ דִי דְרַיי דַרְגוֹת הַנִזְכָּרוֹת לְעֵיל וּבְסֵדֶר זֶה דַוְקָא.

The behavior of properly functioning people is based on and guided by three things: thought, speech, and action. First comes thought. Those thoughts are then expressed via speech to others, such as when consulting friends who understand a specific field, for the sake of arriving at a clearer and more accurate picture of the matter. This allows a person to arrive at a practical conclusion, whereby their thoughts and discussions are translated into concrete action. . . .

Thought alone is insufficient. Similarly, contemplation with subsequent discussion is not enough. We must bring our plans to *action*. . . . At the same time, in order for an action to be complete, it must reflect the reality that it is simply the third link in a chain, following forethought and helpful discussion. Otherwise, our actions will be rash. . . .

When we engage all three (thought, speech, and action, and in that particular order), we can reach our full potential, just as the hierarchy of the worlds is complete . . . only with all three worlds present in their specific order.

TEXT 10

Daily Exercise

Rabbi Shneur Zalman of Liadi, *Shulchan Aruch HaRav,*
Mahadura Tinyana 1:4–6

וּמִיָּד שֶׁנֵּעוֹר מִשְׁנָתוֹ . . . יַחֲשֹׁב בְּלִבּוֹ לִפְנֵי מִי הוּא שׁוֹכֵב,
וְיֵדַע שֶׁמֶּלֶךְ מַלְכֵי הַמְּלָכִים הַקָּדוֹשׁ בָּרוּךְ הוּא חוֹפֵף
עָלָיו, שֶׁנֶּאֱמַר "מְלֹא כָל הָאָרֶץ כְּבוֹדוֹ" (יְשַׁעְיָה ו, ג) . . .

וְטוֹב לְהַרְגִּיל עַצְמוֹ לוֹמַר מִיָּד שֶׁנֵּעוֹר מִשְׁנָתוֹ
(מוֹדֶה אֲנִי לְפָנֶיךָ מֶלֶךְ חַי וְקַיָּם שֶׁהֶחֱזַרְתָּ בִּי
נִשְׁמָתִי בְּחֶמְלָה רַבָּה אֱמוּנָתֶךָ), וְעַל יְדֵי זֶה יִזְכֹּר
אֶת ה' הָעוֹמֵד עָלָיו, וְיָקוּם בִּזְרִיזוּת . . .

וּלְפִי שֶׁבְּנֻסַח זֶה אֵין בּוֹ שׁוּם שֵׁם מִז' שֵׁמוֹת שֶׁאֵינָם
נִמְחָקִין, אֵין אִסּוּר לְאָמְרוֹ קֹדֶם שֶׁנָּטַל יָדָיו.

As soon as we wake up . . . we should contemplate before Whom we are lying, and become aware that the King of kings is close at hand, as it is stated, "The entire earth is filled with His glory" (ISAIAH 6:3). . . .

It is best to habituate ourselves immediately upon waking to recite *Modeh Ani*—"I thank You, living and eternal King, for You have mercifully restored my soul within me. Great is Your faithfulness!" This will remind us of G-d's intimate presence and inspire us to rise energetically. . . .

Seeing that the *Modeh Ani* does not include
a Divine name, we are permitted to recite
it before ritually washing our hands.

Title page of *Seder Hayom*,
by Rabbi Moshe ben Machir
of Safed, from the first
printed edition, Venice, 1599.
This work is the first-known
source of the custom to
recite the Modeh Ani prayer.

KEY TERMS

1. Seder hishtalshelut

The many degrees of systematic descent that stretch between G-d's desire to create the universe and the tangible result of that goal

2. BiYA

Acronym for the grouping of the three spiritual worlds, **B**eriah, **Y**etzirah, and **A**siyah

3. Yeshut

Existence with a sense of self-awareness and independence

4. Bitul

A subdued sense of self due to being absorbed by something overwhelmingly impressive, and the desire to become one with it

5. Levushei hanefesh

Thought, speech, and action—the soul's behaviors, which are external to the soul itself

KEY POINTS

1   The study of Jewish mysticism is not simply
    a pursuit of fascination and mystique
    but is primarily geared to bear a positive
    effect on how we live our lives.

2   Kabbalah is largely an exploration of *seder
    hishtalshelut*. In addition to thereby advancing
    our knowledge of G-d, this material allows us
    to better understand many aspects of life.

3   Analyzing the human character and soul yields
    much insight into *seder hishtalshelut*, because
    the human is created in the Divine image.

4   When studying kabbalah, we must avoid
    perceiving spiritual ideas in a literal, physical sense.

5   Kabbalah teaches that the first existence with
    yeshut (independent sense of self) is the
    spiritual world of *Beriah*. However, because
    Beriah senses G-d acutely, it remains in a
    constant state of overwhelming *bitul*. By
    contrast, the subsequent worlds of *Yetzirah*
    and *Asiyah* sense G-d to far lesser degrees,
    resulting in more extreme degrees of *yeshut*.

6   We are able to tap into these higher worlds and reside in them temporarily during moments in which we sense G-d acutely and are overwhelmed by His presence.

7   Human thought, speech, and action correspond to *Beriah*, *Yetzirah*, and *Asiyah*. We can use these three areas of life to advance our understanding of *BiYA*. The same is true in reverse: studying *BiYA* produces numerous insights into living more effectively through thought, speech, and action.

KEY TAKEAWAYS

1   The disposition of our internal character need not automatically dictate what occurs in the realm of our thought, speech, and action. We can control our *levushim* irrespective of our personality.

2   Our actions should be preceded by proper planning (thought) and consultation (speech). On the other hand, we must make certain to graduate from planning and discussion to engage in concrete action.

3   We can begin each day with a motivational exercise that is a built-in feature of Jewish practice: to first *think* about the Creator, then *verbalize* our gratitude toward Him, and then *act* by ritually preparing our hands. This brief early morning tour through *BiYA* sets the appropriate tone for our entire day.

2

THE DAWN OF LIMITATION

This lesson delves into the realm of the Divine by examining G-d's ten sefirot *and their corresponding ten powers within the human being. Studying the distinct manifestation of the* sefirot *within each individual enables us to discern our unique soul root, thereby facilitating the optimization of our inherent strengths and weaknesses.*

GOLDEN TREE OF LIFE
Darius Gilmont, oil and gold
leaf on canvas,
S. Paulo, Brazil, 2013

I. INTRODUCTION

In this lesson, we advance on our kabbalistic journey into the exalted world of *Atzilut*. This supernal realm corresponds in the human sphere to the *kochot hanefesh*—the soul's ten internal attributes. Understanding these attributes is itself crucial for identifying our life's mission.

TEXT 1

Lost Souls

Rabbi Yanki Tauber, *Once Upon a Chassid*
(New York: Kehot Publication Society, 1994), pp. 157–158

A wealthy businessman and his coachman arrived in a city one Friday afternoon. The rich man was settled at the best hotel in town, and the coachman went off to his humble lodgings.

Both washed and dressed for Shabbos, and then set out for the synagogue for the evening prayers. On his way to *shul*, the businessman came across a large wagon that had swerved off the road and was stuck in a ditch. Rushing to help a fellow in need, the businessman climbed down into the ditch and began pushing and pulling at the wagon together with its hapless driver. But for all his finesse at handling the most challenging of business deals, when it came to extracting a wagon and a team of horses from a muddy ditch, our businessman was hopelessly out of his depth. After struggling for an hour in the knee-deep mud, he succeeded only in ruining his best

RABBI YANKI TAUBER
1965–

Chasidic scholar
and author. A native
of Brooklyn, N.Y.,
Rabbi Tauber is an
internationally renowned
author who specializes
in adapting the teachings
of the Lubavitcher
Rebbe. He is a member
of the JLI curriculum
development team and
has written numerous
articles and books,
including *Once Upon
a Chassid* and *Beyond
the Letter of the Law*.

suit of Shabbos clothes, amassing a most impressive collection of cuts and bruises, and getting the wagon even more impossibly embedded in the mud. Finally, he dragged his limping body to the synagogue, arriving a scant minute before the start of Shabbos.

Meanwhile, the coachman arrived early to the synagogue and sat down to recite a few chapters of Psalms. At the synagogue he found a group of wandering paupers and, being blessed with a most generous nature, the coachman invited them all to share his Shabbos meal. When the synagogue sexton approached the poor and homeless to arrange meal placements for them with the town's householders— as is customary in Jewish communities—he received the same reply from them all: "Thank you, but I have already been invited for the Shabbos meal."

Unfortunately, however, the coachman's budget was hardly equal to his generous heart. It would be most difficult to believe that his dozen guests left his table with more than a shadow of a meal in their hungry stomachs.

Thus the coachman, with his twenty years of experience in pulling wagons out of mud holes, took it upon himself to feed a small army, while the wealthy businessman, whose Shabbos meal leftovers could easily have fed every hungry man within a ten-mile radius, floundered about in a ditch.

The **Lubavitcher Rebbe** on discovering your personal mission: **myjli.com/kabbalah**

Rabbi Yosef Yitzchak of Lubavitch told this story and explained its lesson: "Every soul is entrusted with a mission unique to her alone, and is granted the specific aptitudes, talents and resources necessary to excel in her ordained role. One must take care not to become one of those 'lost souls' who wander haplessly through life, trying their hand at every field of endeavor except for what is truly and inherently their own."

KEY TERM 2.1

HEBREW TERM	כּוֹחוֹת הַנֶפֶשׁ
TRANSLITERATION	*kochot hanefesh*
LITERAL MEANING	**the soul's powers**
DEFINITION	the soul's ten attributes that are broadly divided into two categories: intellect (*sechel*) and emotion (*midot*)

TEXT 2

Ineffable

Rabbi Yosef Yitzchak Schneersohn, cited in *Hayom Yom,*
10 Cheshvan

דֶער רַבִּי (רַבֵּנוּ הַזָּקֵן) פְּלֶעגְט זָאגֶן אוֹיף אֲצִילוּת
"אוֹיבֶּען". מֶען דֶערצֵיילְט אַז אִין כְּתַב פְּלֶעגְט עֶר, פֿון
הִתְרַגְשׁוּת, מֶער וִוי "אַצִי" נִיט קֶענֶען אָנְשְׁרֵייבֶּען.

The Alter Rebbe, Rabbi Shneur Zalman of Liadi,
used to refer to *Atzilut* as "Above." It is said
that because of intense emotion when writing
the word, he could get no further than *Atzi.*

**RABBI YOSEF YITZCHAK
SCHNEERSOHN
(RAYATZ, FRIERDIKER
REBBE, PREVIOUS REBBE)
1880–1950**

Chasidic rebbe, prolific
writer, and Jewish
activist. Rabbi Yosef
Yitzchak, the 6th leader
of the Chabad movement,
actively promoted
Jewish religious practice
in Soviet Russia and
was arrested for these
activities. After his
release from prison
and exile, he settled in
Warsaw, Poland, from
where he fled Nazi
occupation and arrived
in New York in 1940.
Settling in Brooklyn,
Rabbi Schneersohn
worked to revitalize
American Jewish life.
His son-in-law Rabbi
Menachem Mendel
Schneerson succeeded
him as the leader of the
Chabad movement.

Kabbalistic diagram in
a Yemenite manuscript,
c. 1800. (Gross Family
Collection, Tel Aviv)

II. THE WORLD OF *ATZILUT*

The unique nature of *Atzilut* can be appreciated by way of a theological dilemma: biblical verses often portray G-d as bearing specific attributes, whereas the sages of the Talmud consistently refer to G-d as utterly transcending any attributes. The resolution: G-d chose to emanate specific and definable attributes, *sefirot*, from His infinite light that itself transcends attributes. The *sefirot* are a downgrade, relative to G-d's infinity, but remain within G-d's light.

TEXT 3

Three Attributes
Proverbs 3:19–20

ה' בְּחָכְמָה יָסַד אָרֶץ, כּוֹנֵן שָׁמַיִם בִּתְבוּנָה,
בְּדַעְתּוֹ תְּהוֹמוֹת נִבְקָעוּ.

G-d, with wisdom, founded the earth; with understanding, established the heavens; with His knowledge, the depths were split.

PROVERBS

Biblical book. The book of Proverbs appears in the "Writings" section of the Bible and contains the wise teachings, aphorisms, and parables of King Solomon, who lived in the 9th century BCE. The ethical teachings of Proverbs give counsel about overcoming temptation, extol the value of hard work, laud the pursuit of knowledge, and emphasize loyalty to G-d and His commandments as the foundation of true wisdom.

TEXT 4

Seven Attributes

I Chronicles 29:11

לְךָ ה' הַגְּדֻלָּה וְהַגְּבוּרָה וְהַתִּפְאֶרֶת וְהַנֵּצַח וְהַהוֹד,
כִּי כֹל בַּשָּׁמַיִם וּבָאָרֶץ. לְךָ ה' הַמַּמְלָכָה.

Unto You, G-d, is greatness, and power, and beauty, and triumph, and splendor; for all in heaven and on earth [is Yours]. Unto You, G-d, is kingship.

CHRONICLES

Biblical book. The book of Chronicles (Divrei Hayamim), commonly divided into two parts, is the concluding book of the Writings (*Ketuvim*) section of the Tanach. Chronicles contains a genealogical list from Creation until the establishment of the first Kingdom of Israel, and then it briefly surveys the history of the Davidic dynasty until the destruction of the First Temple. The book was written by Ezra the Scribe in the 4th century BCE. The book has been artificially divided into I Chronicles and II Chronicles, but it is essentially one book.

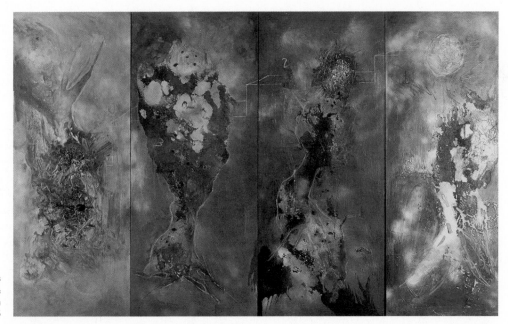

THE FOUR WORLDS
Bonita Helmer, acrylic and mixed media on canvas, 2002–2005

TEXT 5

Transcending Attributes

Rabbi Yehudah Loew, *Gevurot Hashem*, Second Introduction

הוּא יִתְבָּרַךְ שֶׁקְּרָאוּ רַבּוֹתֵינוּ זַ"ל בְּשֵׁם "הַקָּדוֹשׁ בָּרוּךְ
הוּא" וְלֹא נִקְרָא "הַשֵּׂכֶל בָּרוּךְ הוּא", כִּי אֲמִתַּת עַצְמוֹ לֹא
נוֹדַע, רַק שֶׁהוּא נִבְדָּל מִכָּל מִכָּל גֶּשֶׁם וְגוּף וּמִכָּל הַנִּמְצָאִים. וְעַל
זֶה נֶאֱמַר "קָדוֹשׁ בָּרוּךְ הוּא", שֶׁעִנְיָן קָדוֹשׁ נֶאֱמַר עַל מִי
שֶׁהוּא נִבְדָּל. כִּי הוּא יִתְבָּרַךְ פָּשׁוּט בְּתַכְלִית הַפְּשִׁיטוּת.

Our sages purposefully refer to G-d as *kadosh*—
"the *Holy* One, blessed be He"—as opposed to
"the *Intelligent* One, blessed be He." For G-d's
true self is unknowable. All that we know about
G-d is that He is detached from and beyond
every form of physicality and any existing entity.
It is, therefore, appropriate to refer to G-d as
the Holy One, for the term *kadosh* describes
an entity that is transcendent. Indeed, G-d is
peshitut, the ultimate abstract simplicity.

RABBI YEHUDAH LOEW (MAHARAL OF PRAGUE) 1525–1609

Talmudist and
philosopher. Maharal
rose to prominence
as leader of the famed
Jewish community
of Prague. He is the
author of more than a
dozen works of original
philosophic thought,
including *Tiferet Yisrael*
and *Netzach Yisrael*. He
also authored *Gur Aryeh*,
a supercommentary
to Rashi's biblical
commentary; and a
commentary on the
nonlegal passages of
the Talmud. He is
buried in the Old Jewish
Cemetery of Prague.

KEY TERM 2.2

HEBREW TERM	פְּשִׁיטוּת
TRANSLITERATION	*peshitut*
LITERAL MEANING	**simplicity**
DEFINITION	a state of abstractness in the sense of transcending definable qualities and specific attributes

TEXT 6

Two Truths

Tikunei Zohar, Introduction

דְּאַנְתְּ הוּא חַד וְלָא בְּחֻשְׁבָּן, אַנְתְּ הוּא עִלָּאָה עַל כָּל עִלָּאִין,
סְתִימָא עַל כָּל סְתִימִין, לֵית מַחֲשָׁבָה תְּפִיסָא בָּךְ כְּלָל.

אַנְתְּ הוּא דְּאַפֵּקַת עֲשַׂר תִּקּוּנִין, וְקָרִינָן לוֹן עֲשַׂר סְפִירָן,
לְאַנְהָגָא בְהוֹן עָלְמִין סְתִימִין דְּלָא אִתְגַּלְיָן וְעָלְמִין דְּאִתְגַּלְיָן.

You are One, but not in a numerical sense. You are exalted above all the exalted ones, hidden from all the hidden ones. No thought can grasp You whatsoever.

You are the One Who has brought forth ten "ornaments," which we call the ten *sefirot,* to direct concealed worlds and revealed worlds.

TIKUNEI ZOHAR

An appendix to the *Zohar,* the seminal work of kabbalah (Jewish mysticism). *Tikunei Zohar* consists mostly of 70 kabbalistic expositions on the opening verse of the Torah. It was first printed in Mantua in 1558.

TEXT 7

Number = Limitation

Rabbi Moshe Cordovero, *Pardes Rimonim, Shaar* 8, ch. 2

וְיֵשׁ שֶׁפֵּרֵשׁ מִלְּשׁוֹן מִסְפָּר: כִּי הַמִסְפָּר מִבַּעֲלֵי הַגְּבוּל.

Some have linked the word *sefirah* to the word *mispar*, number, which indicates a state of finitude.

RABBI MOSHE CORDOVERO (RAMAK) 1522–1570

Prominent kabbalist. Ramak belonged to the circle of Jewish mystical thinkers who flourished in 16th-century Safed. The name Cordovero indicates that his family originated in Córdoba, Spain. His most famous kabbalistic work is *Pardes Rimonim*.

KEY TERM 2.3

HEBREW TERM	סְפִירוֹת
TRANSLITERATION	*sefirot*
LITERAL MEANING	**numbered entities**
DEFINITION	ten specific, definable attributes that G-d manifested from His infinite Self

TEXT 8

True Infinity

Rabbi Meir ibn Gabai, *Avodat Hakodesh, Chelek Hayichud* 8

אֵין סוֹף הוּא שְׁלֵמוּת מִבְּלִי חִסָּרוֹן. וְאִם תֹּאמַר שֶׁיֵּשׁ לוֹ
כֹּחַ בְּלִי גְבוּל וְאֵין לוֹ כֹּחַ בְּגִבוּל, אַתָּה מְחַסֵּר שְׁלֵמוּתוֹ.

The Infinite One is perfect without any flaw. Should
you assert that He has infinite power but lacks
the power of finitude, you deny His perfection.

RABBI MEIR IBN GABAI
1480–AFTER 1540

Kabbalist and author.
Ibn Gabai was born in
Spain, from where he
left during the 1492
Expulsion. Eventually
he settled in Egypt. He
authored 3 books, in
which he elucidates many
basic mystical concepts,
and which have become
kabbalistic classics:
Tolaat Yaakov (which
he authored at the age
of 26), *Derech Emunah*,
and *Avodat Hakodesh*.

TEXT 9A

His Wisdom

Rabbi Menachem Mendel of Lubavitch, *Derech Mitzvotecha*,
Haamanat Elokut, ch. 6

שֶׁאֵין מַהוּת הַחָכְמָה עוֹלָה בְּשֵׁם בְּרִיאָה בִּפְנֵי עַצְמָהּ
חַס וְשָׁלוֹם, אֶלָּא שֶׁהִיא אֱלֹקוּת מַמָּשׁ, שֶׁהַחָכְמָה
הִיא חָכְמָתוֹ, וְכֵן בִּינָתוֹ וְדַעְתּוֹ וְחַסְדוֹ כוּ', דְּהַיְנוּ שֶׁהוּא
הַמְצַמְצֵם אוֹרוֹ לִהְיוֹת מֵאִיר בְּצִמְצוּם, עַד שֶׁיִּהְיֶה בְּחִינַת
חָכְמָה וּבְחִינַת חֶסֶד וְכוּ' מְאִירִים בְּגִלּוּי מִמֶּנּוּ יִתְבָּרֵךְ.

The first of the *sefirot, chochmah,* cannot be
termed a "creation," G-d forbid, because it is
literal G-dliness. Rather, G-d condensed His
light to the extent that He could manifest
Himself in *chochmah* and the other attributes.
The intellectual attributes are *His* attributes;
the kindness is *His* kindness, and so forth.

RABBI MENACHEM
MENDEL OF LUBAVITCH
(TZEMACH TZEDEK)
1789–1866

Chasidic rebbe and noted
author. The *Tzemach
Tzedek* was the third leader
of the Chabad Chasidic
movement and a noted
authority on Jewish law.
His numerous works
include Halachic responsa,
Chasidic discourses, and
kabbalistic writings. Active
in the communal affairs of
Russian Jewry, he worked
to alleviate the plight of the
cantonists, Jewish children
kidnapped to serve in the
czar's army. He passed
away in Lubavitch, leaving
7 sons and 2 daughters.

TEXT 9B

Etymology of *Atzilut*

Rabbi Menachem Mendel of Lubavitch, ibid.

וְלָכֵן נִקְרְאוּ הָעֶשֶׂר סְפִירוֹת אֲצִילוּת, וְלֹא בְּרִיאָה,
כִּי אֲצִילוּת נִגְזַר מִלָּשׁוֹן "וַיָּאצֶל מִן הָרוּחַ" (בַּמִּדְבָּר
יא, כה) . . . שֶׁכָּךְ הָאֲצִילוּת הֵמָה מִבְּחִינַת זִיו וְאוֹר
הָאֵין סוֹף, וְלֹא בְּרִיאָה לִהְיוֹת נִפְרָד חַס וְשָׁלוֹם . . .
וְלָכֵן נִקְרָא אֲצִילוּת גַּם מִלָּשׁוֹן אֵצֶל וְסָמוּךְ.

The *sefirot* are called *Atzilut*, not *Beriah*. The term *Atzilut* in the Torah (NUMBERS 11:25) means emanation . . . which indicates that the *sefirot* are an emanation from G-d's infinity, not an independent creation. . . . This provides us with a second reason for referring to the *sefirot* as *Atzilut*—from the etymological root *etzel*, meaning "together with" G-d.

Opening page to the Book of Numbers in the *Red Dragon Pentateuch*, copied in Germany in the late thirteenth century. The dragon motif shown within the large opening word, *Vayedaber*, can be found throughout the decorations in this unique manuscript. (Bavarian State Library, Munich)

KEY TERM 2.4

HEBREW TERM	אֲצִילוּת
TRANSLITERATION	*Atzilut*
LITERAL MEANING	**emanation; togetherness**
DEFINITION	G-d's emanation of the ten *sefirot*, attributes of Divine but finite expression

G-dliness

TEXT 9C

Rabbi Menachem Mendel of Lubavitch, ibid.

וְאַף עַל פִּי כֵן, לְגַבֵּי מַהוּתוֹ וְעַצְמוּתוֹ הֵם אֵין עֲרוֹךְ. וְזֶה פֵּרוּשׁ לָשׁוֹן אֱלוֹקוּת, גֶעטְלִיךְ, וְלֹא אֱלוֹקָה בְּעַצְמוֹ חַס וְשָׁלוֹם.

The *sefirot* are utterly incomparable to G-d's essence. For that reason, we refer to them as *Elokut*, G-dliness, as opposed to *Eloka*, G-d Himself.

KEY TERM 2.5

HEBREW TERM	אֱלוֹקוּת
TRANSLITERATION	*Elokut*
LITERAL MEANING	**G-dliness**
DEFINITION	an expression of G-d that is not G-d's essential self

The Ladder of Prayer

The kabbalists teach that the structure of Shacharit, the Morning Prayer, resembles a four-step ladder that carries us steadily upward, rung after rung. During each of the four rungs of Shacharit, we experience one of the four worlds (*Atzilut*, *Beriah*, *Yetzirah*, and *Asiyah*), and the prayers contained in that rung reflect the Divine attributes that shine in the corresponding world.

AMIDAH
עֲמִידָה

SHEMA
שְׁמַע

PESUKEI DEZIMRAH
פְּסוּקֵי דְזִמְרָה

BIRCHOT HASHACHAR—HODU
בִּרְכוֹת הַשַּׁחַר-הוֹדוּ

SOURCES:

Likutei Torah, Tzav, p. 12b; *Peri Etz Chayim, Shaar Hatefilah*, ch. 1;
Beshaah Shehikdimu 5672:1, pp. 619–621.

④ Amidah

WORLD *ATZILUT*
SEFIRAH *CHOCHMAH:*
INITIAL COGNITIVE FLASH

The pinnacle of prayer is the Amidah, at which point, we enter the world of *Atzilut*. In this realm, G-dliness is felt acutely, and everything else pales into utter insignificance, in a state of *bitul*—nullification. During the preceding sections of prayer, we spoke about G-d, but we are now ready to speak to G-d, directly. The Amidah prayer is recited while standing in a submissive pose, in a barely audible voice. Before beginning, we ask G-d to help us open our mouths and speak in His presence.

③ Shema

WORLD *BERIAH*
SEFIRAH *BINAH:*
INTELLECTUAL ANALYSIS

The emotional experience of Pesukei Dezimrah elevates us to the cognitive world of *Beriah*. The Shema and its related blessings are a contemplative exercise, during which we focus our minds on G-d's greatness and oneness.

② Pesukei Dezimrah

WORLD *YETZIRAH*
SEFIROT *CHESED, GEVURAH, TIFERET:*
EMOTIONS

After acknowledging G-d and expressing our appreciation for Him through the morning blessings and the recital of Hodu, we are able to ascend to the world of *Yetzirah* and experience G-d with our emotional attributes. This stage of the prayers is known as Pesukei Dezimrah, the Verses of Praise, in which we passionately sing the praises of our Creator.

① Birchot Hashachar—Hodu

WORLD *ASIYAH*
SEFIROT *NETZACH, HOD, YESOD:*
EXECUTIVE EMOTIONS

The morning prayers begin with the "Morning Blessings," in which we express our thanks to G-d for blessing us with a new day of life. We then recite Hodu, a prayer of acknowledgement and appreciation. As we begin our prayers, we are still firmly grounded in the world of action (*Asiyah*). Incapable of profound emotional experience or intellectual comprehension as of yet, we express our simple acknowledgment of G-d as our Creator and Ruler and declare our gratitude to Him.

III. EXPLORING THE *SEFIROT*

The Divine *sefirot* are ten traits enumerated in biblical verses. Three of these traits are *chesed*, *gevurah*, and *tiferet*. As the following texts demonstrate, the Talmudic sage Hillel was a living paradigm of *chesed* (love, kindness), while his colleague Shamai was a living paradigm of *gevurah* (restraint, severity). In fact, all things in our universe came about through the *sefirot*, which is why specific creations can be traced to specific *sefirot*.

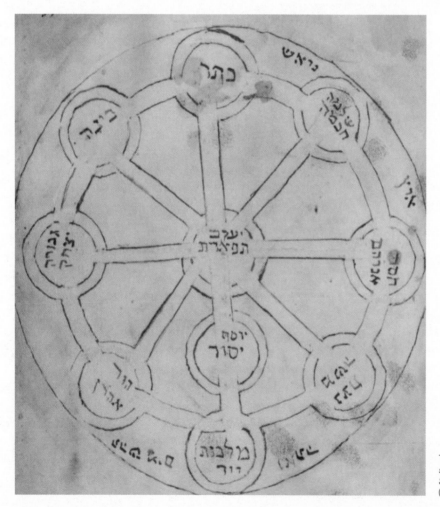

The earliest known diagram of the *sefirot* in a 1284 manuscript of *Sefer Yetzirah* produced in Rome (National Library of France, Paris)

FIGURE 2.1

The Ten *Sefirot*

Rabbi Meir ibn Gabai, *Avodat Hakodesh* 1:2

HEBREW NAME		LITERAL TRANSLATION	CORRESPONDING TERM IN PROVERBS 3:19	CORRESPONDING TERM IN I CHRONICLES 29:11
chochmah	חָכְמָה	wisdom	בְּחָכְמָה יָסַד אָרֶץ	
binah	בִּינָה	comprehension	כּוֹנֵן שָׁמַיִם בִּתְבוּנָה	
daat	דַעַת	knowledge	בְּדַעְתּוֹ תְּהוֹמוֹת נִבְקָעוּ	
chesed	חֶסֶד	kindness		הַגְּדֻלָּה
gevurah	גְּבוּרָה	strength		וְהַגְּבוּרָה
tiferet	תִּפְאֶרֶת	beauty		וְהַתִּפְאֶרֶת
netzach	נֶצַח	victory		וְהַנֵּצַח
hod	הוֹד	splendor		וְהַהוֹד
yesod	יְסוֹד	foundation		כִּי כֹל בַּשָּׁמַיִם וּבָאָרֶץ
malchut	מַלְכוּת	kingdom		הַמַּמְלָכָה

Three Columns

Rabbi Dovber of Lubavitch, *Bad Kodesh*, pp. 11–12

עֶשֶׂר סְפִירוֹת דַּאֲצִילוּת, שֶׁנֶּאֶצְלוּ מֵעַצְמוּת אוֹר
אֵין סוֹף בָּרוּךְ הוּא וְכוּ', וְיָדוּעַ שֶׁהֵם מְצֻיָּרִים בְּסִפְרֵי
הָאֱמֶת דֶּרֶךְ כְּלָל עַל פִּי הַלוּחַ בְּצִיּוּר ג' קַוִּין . . . וּבֵאוּר
עִנְיָנָם מְבֹאָר מְעַט בְּסִפְרֵי הַקַּבָּלָה: דְּקַו הַיָּמִין בִּכְלָל
מוֹרֶה עַל בְּחִינַת הַחֶסֶד, וְקַו הַשְׂמֹאל בִּכְלָל מוֹרֶה
עַל בְּחִינַת הַגְּבוּרָה . . . וְקַו הָאֶמְצָעִי בִּכְלָל הוּא
בְּחִינַת הַמְמֻצָּע הַכּוֹלֵל לְב' הַקַּוִּין דְּחֶסֶד וּגְבוּרָה.

The ten *sefirot* of *Atzilut*, which emanate from
the essence of the Divine infinity, are generally
depicted in kabbalistic works in a three-columned
chart. . . . Kabbalistic works explain that the
right column is associated with *chesed*, the
left column is associated with *gevurah* . . . and
the middle column is the bridge between the
two, comprising both *chesed* and *gevurah*.

**RABBI DOVBER
OF LUBAVITCH
(MITELER REBBE)
1773–1827**

Rabbi Dovber was
the eldest son of and
successor to Rabbi
Shneur Zalman of Liadi
and greatly expanded
upon and developed his
father's groundbreaking
teachings. He was the 1st
Chabad rebbe to live in
the village of Lubavitch.
Dedicated to the welfare
of Russian Jewry, at
that time confined to
the Pale of Settlement,
he established Jewish
agricultural colonies. His
most notable works on
Chasidic thought include
*Shaar Hayichud, Torat
Chayim,* and *Imrei Binah.*

Three Traits

TEXT 11

Rabbi Shneur Zalman of Liadi, *Tanya, Igeret Hakodesh* 15

מִדַּת הַחֶסֶד - לְהַשְׁפִּיעַ בְּלִי גְבוּל.

וּמִדַּת הַגְּבוּרָה - לְצַמְצֵם מִלְהַשְׁפִּיעַ כָּל כָּךְ, אוֹ שֶׁלֹּא לְהַשְׁפִּיעַ כְּלָל.

וּמִדַּת הָרַחֲמִים - לְרַחֵם עַל מִי שֶׁשַּׁיָּךְ לָשׁוֹן רַחְמָנוּת עָלָיו. וְהִיא מִדָּה מְמֻצַּעַת בֵּין גְּבוּרָה לְחֶסֶד, שֶׁהִיא לְהַשְׁפִּיעַ לַכֹּל, גַּם לְמִי שֶׁלֹּא שַׁיָּךְ לָשׁוֹן רַחְמָנוּת עָלָיו כְּלָל, מִפְּנֵי שֶׁאֵינוֹ חָסֵר כְּלוּם וְאֵינוֹ שָׁרוּי בְּצַעַר כְּלָל. וּלְפִי שֶׁהִיא מִדָּה מְמֻצַּעַת נִקְרֵאת תִּפְאֶרֶת, כְּמוֹ בִּגְדֵי תִפְאֶרֶת עַל דֶּרֶךְ מָשָׁל, שֶׁהוּא בֶּגֶד צָבוּעַ בִּגְוָנִים הַרְבֵּה מְעֹרָבִים, בְּדֶרֶךְ שֶׁהוּא תִפְאֶרֶת וְנוֹי.

RABBI SHNEUR ZALMAN OF LIADI (ALTER REBBE) 1745-1812

Chasidic rebbe, Halachic authority, and founder of the Chabad movement. The Alter Rebbe was born in Liozna, Belarus, and was among the principal students of the Magid of Mezeritch. His numerous works include the *Tanya*, an early classic containing the fundamentals of Chabad Chasidism; and *Shulchan Aruch HaRav*, an expanded and reworked code of Jewish law.

The attribute of *chesed* seeks to provide without limit, even if the recipient is in no need of pity, lacks nothing, and faces no difficulty.

The attribute of *gevurah* seeks to exercise restraint when providing to others or to refrain from giving altogether.

The attribute of compassion seeks to pity whomever is in need. It is the mediating attribute between *gevurah* and *chesed*. For that reason, it is called *tiferet*, beauty, akin to a multicolored garment that provides harmonious beauty.

TEXT 12

Hillel and Shamai

Talmud, Shabbat 31a

מַעֲשֶׂה בְּנָכְרִי אֶחָד שֶׁבָּא לִפְנֵי שַׁמַּאי. אָמַר לוֹ: גַּיְּרֵנִי עַל מְנָת שֶׁתְּלַמְּדֵנִי כָּל הַתּוֹרָה כֻּלָּהּ כְּשֶׁאֲנִי עוֹמֵד עַל רֶגֶל אַחַת.

דְּחָפוֹ בְּאַמַּת הַבִּנְיָן שֶׁבְּיָדוֹ.

בָּא לִפְנֵי הִלֵּל, גַּיְּרֵיהּ. אָמַר לוֹ: דַּעֲלָךְ סָנֵי לַחֲבֵרָךְ לֹא תַּעֲבֵיד. זוֹ הִיא כָּל הַתּוֹרָה כֻּלָּהּ וְאִידָךְ פֵּרוּשָׁהּ הוּא, זִיל גְּמֹר.

A non-Jewish man once approached Shamai and told him, "I would like you to convert me to Judaism on the condition that you teach me the entire Torah while I stand on one foot!"

Shamai used the builder's measuring tool he was holding to chase the fellow away.

The prospective convert then approached Hillel with the same request. Hillel converted him, telling him, "Whatever you hate being done to you, do not do to your fellow. That is the entire Torah—the rest is its commentary. Now, go and learn the rest!"

BABYLONIAN TALMUD

A literary work of monumental proportions that draws upon the legal, spiritual, intellectual, ethical, and historical traditions of Judaism. The 37 tractates of the Babylonian Talmud contain the teachings of the Jewish sages from the period after the destruction of the 2nd Temple through the 5th century CE. It has served as the primary vehicle for the transmission of the Oral Law and the education of Jews over the centuries; it is the entry point for all subsequent legal, ethical, and theological Jewish scholarship.

A thought-provoking lecture about love and awe of G-d:
myjli.com/kabbalah

KEY TERM 2.6

HEBREW TERM	חֶסֶד
TRANSLITERATION	*chesed*
LITERAL MEANING	**kindness**
DEFINITION	the disposition to give and share, irrespective of the recipient's state

KEY TERM 2.7

HEBREW TERM	גְּבוּרָה
TRANSLITERATION	*gevurah*
LITERAL MEANING	**strength**
DEFINITION	the disposition to restrain giving and sharing in order to provide only in proportion to what the recipient deserves

KEY TERM 2.8

HEBREW TERM	תִּפְאֶרֶת
TRANSLITERATION	*tiferet*
LITERAL MEANING	**beauty**
DEFINITION	the harmonization of opposites, such as *chesed* and *gevurah*, yielding a beautiful balance

FIGURE 2.2

Chesed and *Gevurah* in Our World

גְּבוּרָה	חֶסֶד
GEVURAH	**CHESED**
fire	water
darkness	light
bitterness	sweetness
gold	silver
meat	milk
ox	donkey
sadness	joy
linen	wool
red	white

The *Sarajevo Haggadah* was copied and illuminated on vellum in Barcelona, in approximately 1350 CE. It opens with thirty-four pages of illustrations that depict biblical scenes, including this spread, portraying the six days of Creation. (The National Museum of Bosnia and Herzegovina, Sarajevo)

IV. RELEVANCE

The origin of our souls is in the Divine sphere of *Atzilut*. More particularly, each soul is rooted in a specific *sefirah*, which is the source of our personalities. This is supposed to guide us toward determining the specific mitzvah that will become a focus of our extra time, energy, and resources. And yet, because each soul is generally linked to all *sefirot*, we possess the capacity to manifest any *sefirah* in our lives, just as Shamai was eventually able to teach and practice kindness.

TEXT 13

Pure Soul

Siddur, Morning Blessings

אֱלֹקַי, נְשָׁמָה שֶׁנָּתַתָּ בִּי טְהוֹרָה הִיא.
אַתָּה בְרָאתָהּ אַתָּה יְצַרְתָּהּ אַתָּה נְפַחְתָּהּ בִּי.

My G-d,

The soul You placed within me is pure.

You created it,

You formed it,

You breathed it into me.

SIDDUR

The siddur is the Jewish prayer book. It was originally developed by the sages of the Great Assembly in the 4th century BCE and later reconstructed by Rabban Gamliel after the destruction of the Second Temple. Various authorities continued to add prayers, from then until contemporary times. It includes praise of G-d, requests for personal and national needs, selections from the Bible, and much else. Various Jewish communities have slightly different versions of the siddur.

Soul Source

Rabbi Shalom Dovber Schneersohn,
Sefer Hamaamarim 5664, p. 31

וְכַיָּדוּעַ דְּהַנְּשָׁמוֹת מֻשְׁרָשִׁים בְּעֶשֶׂר סְפִירוֹת. וְיכוֹלִים
לֵדַע בָּזֶה שָׁרְשׁוֹ וּמְקוֹרוֹ בְּאֵיזֶה סְפִירָה הוּא.

כְּמוֹ שֶׁאָנוּ רוֹאִין בְּהַהֶאָרָה הִתְגַּבְּרוּת הַמֹחִין
בְּיוֹתֵר, אוֹ הִתְגַּבְּרוּת הַמִּדּוֹת כוּ'.

וּכְמוֹ כֵן בְּאֵיזֶה מִדָּה פְּרָטִית: שֶׁיֵּשׁ מִי שֶׁעִקָּרוֹ הוּא בְּמִדַּת
הַנִּצָּחוֹן עַל דֶּרֶךְ מָשָׁל. וְיֵשׁ מִבְּחִינַת הַחֶסֶד וְכַדוֹמֶה.

It is well-known that souls are rooted in the
ten *sefirot*. By examining our personalities, it
is possible to identify the individual *sefirah*
that serves as the root of each person's soul.

We readily observe that intellect is dominant in
some individuals, whereas emotions are dominant
in others. [This phenomenon indicates that
some souls are rooted in the intellectual *sefirot*
of *Atzilut*, and others in its emotive *sefirot*.]

As far as individual *sefirot* are concerned,
we notice that some individuals display a
dominating strain of *netzach*, and others a
dominating trait of *chesed*, and so on.

RABBI SHALOM DOVBER SCHNEERSOHN (RASHAB) 1860–1920

Chasidic rebbe. Rabbi
Shalom Dovber became
the 5th leader of the
Chabad movement
upon the passing
of his father, Rabbi
Shmuel Schneersohn.
He established the
Lubavitch network
of *yeshivot* called
Tomchei Temimim. He
authored many volumes
of Chasidic discourses
and is renowned for
his lucid and thorough
explanations of
kabbalistic concepts.

KEY TERM 2.9

HEBREW TERM	שֹׁרֶשׁ הַנְשָׁמָה
TRANSLITERATION	*shoresh haneshamah*
LITERAL MEANING	**the soul's root**
DEFINITION	the specific *sefirah* in *Atzilut* from which a particular soul derives

EXERCISE 2.1

Rate yourself using the following scale:

5 = very dominant

4 = somewhat dominant

3 = neutral

2 = somewhat weak

1 = very weak

CHESED		GEVURAH	
generous	1 2 3 4 5	frugal	1 2 3 4 5
kind	1 2 3 4 5	exacting	1 2 3 4 5
loving	1 2 3 4 5	respectful	1 2 3 4 5
extroverted	1 2 3 4 5	introverted	1 2 3 4 5
optimistic	1 2 3 4 5	realistic	1 2 3 4 5
forgiving	1 2 3 4 5	perfectionist	1 2 3 4 5

The Character of the *Sefirot*

Human beings are created in the Divine image. As a result, the ten Divine *sefirot* are reflected in the ten fundamental characteristics of the human soul.

The following chart presents the ten *sefirot* and specifies some of the human character traits associated with each of the *sefirot*.

The Cognitive Attributes

CHOCHMAH: WISDOM	*BINAH*: COMPREHENSION	*DAAT*: KNOWLEDGE
Creative	Analytical	Emotionally present
Original	Logical	Focused
	Organized	
	Studious	

 ## The Emotional Attributes

CHESED: KINDNESS	*GEVURAH*: STRENGTH	*TIFERET*: BEAUTY
Generous	Frugal	Balanced
Kind	Exacting	Compassionate
Loving	Respectful	Empathetic
Extroverted	Introverted	Sensitive
Optimistic	Realistic	
Forgiving	Perfectionist	

 ## The Executive-Emotional Attributes

NETZACH: VICTORY	*HOD:* SPLENDOR	*YESOD:* FOUNDATION	*MALCHUT:* KINGDOM
Bold	Devoted	Selfless	Leader
Competitive	Grateful	Altruistic	Communicator
Determined	Humble	Social Connection	Implementer
Gritty	Yielding		Receptive
Ambitious			

TEXT 15

Shining Particularity

Talmud, Shabbat 118b

אָמַר לֵיה רַב יוֹסֵף לְרַב יוֹסֵף בְּרֵיה
דְּרַבָּה: אֲבוּךְ, בְּמַאי זָהִיר טְפֵי?

Rav Yosef questioned Rav Yosef, son of Rabah,
"In which mitzvah was your father most careful?"

TEXT 16

Three Examples

The Rebbe, Rabbi Menachem Mendel Schneerson,
Sichot Kodesh 5734:2, p. 98

לְכָל אֶחָד וְאֶחָד עִנְיָנוֹ הוּא מָה שֶׁה' נָתַן לוֹ כֹּחוֹת
בְּאֹפֶן עֲבוֹדָתוֹ, וְהוּא צָרִיךְ לַעֲבֹד אֶת עֲבוֹדָתוֹ לְפִי
הַכֹּחוֹת וְהַחוּשִׁים שֶׁה' נָתַן לוֹ - שֶׁזֶּה הַחֵלֶק שֶׁלּוֹ.

וְעַל דֶּרֶךְ אֶחָד שֶׁה' נָתַן לוֹ כֹּחַ בְּשֵׂכֶל, צָרִיךְ הוּא לְנַצֵּל אֶת
שִׂכְלוֹ לְלִמּוּד הַתּוֹרָה, וּבְזֶה צָרִיךְ לִהְיוֹת כָּל חַיּוּתוֹ. אָמְנָם
הוּא צָרִיךְ לְקַיֵּם מִצְוֹת וְכָל הָעִנְיָנִים שֶׁתּוֹבְעִים מִכָּל אֶחָד
וְאֶחָד, מִכָּל מָקוֹם, כֵּיוָן שֶׁיֵּשׁ לוֹ חוּשׁ בְּלִמּוּד הַתּוֹרָה,
צָרִיךְ לִהְיוֹת לוֹ בָּזֶה זָהִיר טְפֵי, כֵּיוָן שֶׁיֵּשׁ לוֹ חוּשׁ לָזֶה.

וְעַל דֶּרֶךְ זֶה מִי שֶׁיֵּשׁ לוֹ חוּשׁ בְּעִנְיָן שֶׁל הֶרְגֵּשׁ הַלֵּב,
צָרִיךְ לְנַצֵּל אֶת זֶה לְעִנְיָן שֶׁל אַהֲבַת יִשְׂרָאֵל, לְקָרֵב יְהוּדִי
וּלְהַסְבִּיר לוֹ אֶת הָעִנְיָן שֶׁל אַהֲבַת ה' וְאַהֲבַת הַתּוֹרָה.

**RABBI MENACHEM
MENDEL SCHNEERSON
1902–1994**

The towering Jewish
leader of the 20th century,
known as "the Lubavitcher
Rebbe," or simply as "the
Rebbe." Born in southern
Ukraine, the Rebbe escaped
Nazi-occupied Europe,
arriving in the U.S. in June
1941. The Rebbe inspired
and guided the revival of
traditional Judaism after
the European devastation,
impacting virtually every
Jewish community the
world over. The Rebbe
often emphasized that
the performance of just
one additional good deed
could usher in the era of
Mashiach. The Rebbe's
scholarly talks and writings
have been printed in more
than 200 volumes.

וְגַם מִמֶּנּוּ תּוֹבְעִים לִמּוּד הַתּוֹרָה וְכָל הָעִנְיָנִים, אֶלָּא שֶׁעִקַּר
חַיּוּתוֹ צָרִיךְ לִהְיוֹת בָּזֶה, כֵּיוָן שֶׁיֵּשׁ לוֹ כֹּחוֹת מְיֻחָדִים לָזֶה.

וְעַל דֶּרֶךְ זֶה אֶחָד שֶׁהוּא בַּעַל פֹּעַל "אַ פְּרַאקְטִישֶׁער
מֶענְטְשׁ", שֶׁהוּא בַּעַל פֹּעַל, כְּשֶׁצָּרִיךְ לְהָקִים מוֹסָד הוּא רָץ
וְעוֹשֶׂה אֶת כָּל הַמַּאֲמַצִּים שֶׁיָּקֵם הַמּוֹסָד הַזֶּה. אוֹ כְּשֶׁצָּרִיךְ
לִרְאוֹת שֶׁבַּמּוֹסָד לֹא יִהְיֶה מִדַּי קַר וְלֹא מִדַּי חַם, כְּדֵי
שֶׁהַתַּלְמִידִים יוּכְלוּ לִלְמֹד מִתּוֹךְ הַרְחָבָה, אָז הוּא עוֹשֶׂה אֶת
זֶה. וְעַל דֶּרֶךְ זֶה "כִּי תִרְאֶה עָרֹם וְכִסִּיתוֹ", "וַעֲנִיִּים מְרוּדִים
תָּבִיא בָיִת". וּכְמוֹ כֵן אֶצְלוֹ גַּם כֵּן יֶשְׁנָם הָעִנְיָנִים שֶׁל לִמּוּד
הַתּוֹרָה וְהֶרְגֵּשׁ הַלֵּב, אֶלָּא הָעִקָּר עִנְיָנוֹ זֶה מַעֲשֶׂה בְּפֹעַל.

G-d provides each individual with a unique set of abilities. Each of us must pursue our Divine mission in accordance with our specific abilities and potentials—for they indicate our personal responsibilities in life.

Say, for example, that G-d gave you significant intellectual abilities. It is your duty to utilize those abilities to study Torah and to invest all your energy into this endeavor. True, you are required to observe the other *mitzvot* and to commit yourself to all obligations shared by all Jews. Nevertheless, since you have a unique aptitude for Torah study, you need to be extra particular and passionate about it.

Or, if you are graced with strong emotional sensitivity, it is your duty to utilize this sensitivity to show love and care to others. This includes sharing Judaism's rich heritage with Jews who never had the opportunity

to learn about it and inspiring them with love for
G-d and love for the Torah. Again, you are also
obligated to study Torah and observe the other
mitzvot, but your main passion should be reserved
for the above-stated activities—as indicated by the
very fact that you have unique abilities in this area.

Perhaps you are pragmatic by nature—you know
how to get things done. In that case, your duty is
to achieve practical projects. If there is a need to
establish an institution for Jewish education, for
example, it is your calling to put your abilities
into practice by actively pursuing every effort to
open the institution. If there is a need to solve a
particular challenge that inhibits the students'
performance—the building is too frigid, the dorm
requires cooling—make it your duty to solve
the challenge expeditiously. Or perhaps you can
effectively alleviate the plight of the poor and
homeless, and the like. Certainly, you must also
study Torah and act with emotional sensitivity, but
your overarching purpose is to get things done.

**Rabbi Lord Jonathan
Sacks** on finding purpose
as we advance in years:
myjli.com/kabbalah

TEXT 17

Displacing Divinity

Sefer Habahir (Jerusalem, 1951), p. 86

כָּךְ אָמְרָה מִדַּת הַחֶסֶד: כָּל יְמֵי הֱיוֹת אַבְרָהָם
בָּעוֹלָם, לֹא הִצְרַכְתִּי אֲנִי לַעֲשׂוֹת מְלַאכְתִּי, שֶׁהֲרֵי
אַבְרָהָם עָמֵד שָׁם בִּמְקוֹמִי וַיִּשְׁמֹר מִשְׁמַרְתִּי.

The attribute of *chesed* (kindness) declared, "For as
long as Abraham lived, I did not have to do my work,
for Abraham stood in my place and did my job."

SEFER HABAHIR

Kabbalistic work. *Sefer Habahir* is attributed to the 2nd-century Tannaic sage, Rabbi Nechunyah ben Hakanah. The book contains kabbalistic expositions about the creation of the world, the Divine attributes, and the Hebrew alphabet. In the early 13th century, *Sefer Habahir* was one of the first works of kabbalah to be publicly disseminated, and it had a strong influence on the development of this field.

TEXT 18

Shamai's Heroics

Mishnah, Avot 1:15

שַׁמַּאי אוֹמֵר: עֲשֵׂה תוֹרָתְךָ קֶבַע, אֱמֹר מְעַט וַעֲשֵׂה
הַרְבֵּה, וֶהֱוֵי מְקַבֵּל אֶת כָּל הָאָדָם בְּסֵבֶר פָּנִים יָפוֹת.

Shamai would say, "Make your Torah study
a permanent fixture of your daily schedule.
Say little and do much. And receive every
human with a pleasant countenance."

**AVOT
(ETHICS OF THE
FATHERS; PIRKEI AVOT)**

A 6-chapter work on Jewish ethics that is studied widely by Jewish communities, especially during the summer. The first 5 chapters are from the Mishnah, tractate Avot. Avot differs from the rest of the Mishnah in that it does not focus on legal subjects; it is a collection of the sages' wisdom on topics related to character development, ethics, healthy living, piety, and the study of Torah.

1. Consider an area of your life that can benefit from a stronger dose of *chesed*.

2. Consider an area of your life that can benefit from a stronger dose of *gevurah*.

KEY TERMS

1. Kochot hanefesh

The soul's ten attributes that are broadly divided into two categories: intellect (*sechel*) and emotion (*midot*)

2. Peshitut

A state of abstractness in the sense of transcending definable qualities or specific attributes

3. Sefirot

Ten specific, definable attributes that G-d manifested from His infinite self

4. Atzilut

G-d's emanation of the ten *sefirot*, attributes of Divine but finite expression

5. Elokut

An expression of G-d that is not G-d's essential self

6. Chesed

The disposition to give and share, irrespective of the recipient's state

7. Gevurah

The disposition to restrain giving and sharing in order to
provide only in proportion to what the recipient deserves

8. Tiferet

The harmonization of opposites, such as *chesed*
and *gevurah*, yielding a beautiful balance

9. Shoresh haneshamah

The specific *sefirah* in *Atzilut* from which a particular soul derives

KEY POINTS

1   We sometimes refer to G-d as "the Holy
    One." This refers to G-d in His state of infinite
    peshitut, devoid of specificity and limitation—
    exalted, hidden, and ungraspable.

2   True infinity includes the ability to be finite. G-d
    chose to project this potential by emanating ten
    specific *sefirot*. These traits remain G-dly, but
    they are inferior relative to His infinity.

3   G-d projected the *sefirot* because He desired to use
    specific traits—for example, unrestrained giving
    (*chesed*), proportionate giving (*gevurah*), and balanced
    giving (*tiferet*)—in creating and sustaining the worlds.

4   The *sefirot* enabled the creation of our finite and
    diverse universe. The ten *sefirot,* though limited in
    number, combine in a variety of ways to generate
    all that exists—both physical and spiritual. This
    is why we can identify dominant strains of *chesed*,
    gevurah, etc., in various entities around us.

5   All of our souls are rooted in *Atzilut*, but they are as
    diverse as the *sefirot* themselves. For example, the
    sage Hillel personified *chesed*—his soul was strongly
    rooted in *chesed*. His colleague Shamai personified
    gevurah—his soul was strongly rooted in *gevurah*.

KEY TAKEAWAYS

1 Reminding ourselves about our *Atzilut* origins provides us with durable confidence, teaches us that spiritual growth is always within reach, and inspires us to change our environment for the better.

2 It is important to identify the root of our soul by closely analyzing our personality. This will guide us in identifying the mitzvah that requires our special focus in terms of extra time, energy, and resources. The ideal goal would be for us to displace our root *sefirah*, so to speak, by fully utilizing our G-d-given potential in a positive way.

3 Part of our spiritual growth involves identifying a trait that is not revealed within us by default and working at utilizing that trait in productive and meaningful ways.

LESSON

3

HASHEM SOURCE OF ALL
Ariel Fabian Lijtmaer,
acrylic and mixed media on
canvas, Los Angeles, 2016

THE INFINITE LIGHT

This lesson studies the relationship between the Divine infinite light that surpasses all limitation and the sefirot *that facilitate finite creations. This knowledge is then unveiled as the key to human harmony and collaboration. Additionally, we explore the nature of human willpower as a reflection of the Divine infinite light and offer guidance for harnessing the willpower to surmount obstacles.*

I. REACHING FOR INFINITY

Today's lesson explores an idea touched on briefly in the previous class: G-d's higher state of transcendent simplicity. In Jewish mystical thought, this state is referred to as *or ein sof* (infinite light) and *sovev kol almin* (that which encompasses all worlds). It is a form of Divine self-expression that comes into sharp focus during our daily prayers when we recite a cryptic verse from the prophet Isaiah's mystical vision. The theme of this verse is the Heavenly angels' quest for Divine infinity.

TEXT 1

Isaiah's Vision

Isaiah 6:2–3

שְׂרָפִים עֹמְדִים מִמַּעַל לוֹ, שֵׁשׁ כְּנָפַיִם שֵׁשׁ כְּנָפַיִם
לְאֶחָד . . . וְקָרָא זֶה אֶל זֶה וְאָמַר: קָדוֹשׁ קָדוֹשׁ
קָדוֹשׁ ה' צְבָאוֹת, מְלֹא כָל הָאָרֶץ כְּבוֹדוֹ.

Seraphim stood above [to serve] Him; six wings, six wings to each one. . . . And one called to the other and exclaimed, "Holy, holy, holy is the G-d of hosts! The entire Earth is full of His glory!"

ISAIAH

Biblical book. The book of Isaiah contains the prophecies of Isaiah, who lived in the 7th–6th centuries BCE. Isaiah's prophecies contain stern rebukes for the personal failings of the contemporary people of Judea and the corruption of its government. The bulk of the prophecies, however, are stirring consolations and poetic visions of the future Redemption.

TEXT 2

In the Beginning

Rabbi Chaim Vital, *Etz Chayim, Derush Igulim Veyosher* 1:2

טֶרֶם שֶׁנֶּאֱצְלוּ הַנֶּאֱצָלִים וְנִבְרְאוּ הַנִּבְרָאִים, הָיָה אוֹר
עֶלְיוֹן פָּשׁוּט מְמַלֵּא כָּל הַמְּצִיאוּת . . . וְלֹא הָיָה לוֹ בְּחִינַת
רֹאשׁ וְלֹא בְּחִינַת סוֹף . . . וְהוּא הַנִּקְרָא "אוֹר אֵין סוֹף."

Before *Atzilut* was emanated, and before the
creations were created, a simple Divine light filled
all of reality. . . . It had no aspect of beginning or
end. . . . It is called *or ein sof,* the infinite light.

KEY TERM 3.1

HEBREW TERM	אוֹר אֵין סוֹף
TRANSLITERATION	*or ein sof*
LITERAL MEANING	**infinite light**
DEFINITION	G-d's infinite self-projection that is intimately connected with G-d's essence and that transcends definition, limitation, and specific attributes

**RABBI CHAIM VITAL
C. 1542–1620**

Lurianic kabbalist.
Rabbi Vital was born in
Israel, lived in Safed and
Jerusalem, and later lived
in Damascus. He was
authorized by his teacher,
Rabbi Yitzchak Luria,
the Arizal, to record his
teachings. Acting on this
mandate, Vital began
arranging his master's
teachings in written
form, and his many works
constitute the foundation
of the Lurianic school
of Jewish mysticism.
His most famous work
is *Etz Chayim.*

TEXT 3

Two Postures

Zohar 3, 225a

אִיהוּ סוֹבֵב עַל כָּל עָלְמִין . . . אִיהוּ מְמַלֵּא כָּל עָלְמִין.

He encompasses all worlds. . . . He fills all worlds.

ZOHAR

The seminal work of kabbalah, Jewish mysticism. The *Zohar* is a mystical commentary on the Torah, written in Aramaic and Hebrew. According to the Arizal, the *Zohar* contains the teachings of Rabbi Shimon bar Yocha'i, who lived in the Land of Israel during the 2nd century. The *Zohar* has become one of the indispensable texts of traditional Judaism, alongside and nearly equal in stature to the Mishnah and Talmud.

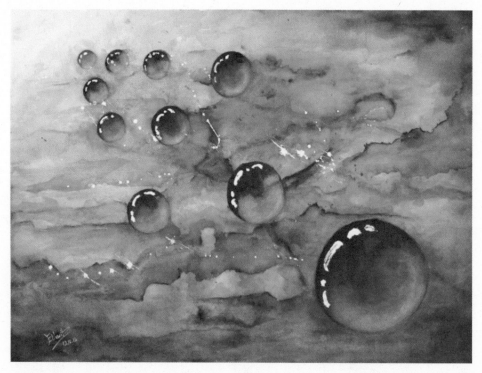

BINAH BIRTHS
Michael Ellowitz, watercolor on Arches paper, New York, 2016

KEY TERM 3.2

HEBREW TERM	סוֹבֵב כָּל עָלְמִין
TRANSLITERATION	*sovev kol almin*
LITERAL MEANING	**encompasses all worlds**
DEFINITION	G-d as He transcends the emanation of *sefirot* and the creation of *Beriah*, *Yetzirah*, and *Asiyah*

KEY TERM 3.3

HEBREW TERM	מְמַלֵּא כָּל עָלְמִין
TRANSLITERATION	*memalei kol almin*
LITERAL MEANING	**fills all worlds**
DEFINITION	G-d as He emanates the *sefirot* and actively creates *Beriah*, *Yetzirah*, and *Asiyah*

TEXT 4

The Seraphim's Desire

Rabbi Shneur Zalman of Liadi, *Likutei Torah*, Emor 32b

מַלְאָכִים עֶלְיוֹנִים שֶׁבְּעוֹלָם הַבְּרִיאָה . . . הֵם מִתְלַהֲבִים
וּמִתְלַהֲטִים בִּתְשׁוּקָה וְרִשְׁפֵּי אֵשׁ לְאִסְתַּכְּלָא בִּיקָרָא
דְמַלְכָּא, בִּבְחִינַת סוֹבֵב כָּל עָלְמִין, שֶׁהוּא קָדוֹשׁ
וּמֻבְדָל. וְלָכֵן נִקְרָאִים שְׂרָפִים, עַל שֵׁם הָרִשְׁפֵּי אֵשׁ
וְהַתְּשׁוּקָה הַנִפְלָאָה. וְזֶהוּ שֶׁאוֹמְרִים "קָדוֹשׁ".

The lofty angels of *Beriah* . . . are called "seraphim,"
from the word "to burn," due to their flaming
passion to gaze at the King's glory, at *sovev kol
almin* (the state of G-dliness that "encompasses
all worlds"), which is separate and transcendent
(*kadosh*). That is why they proclaim "*kadosh*."

**RABBI SHNEUR
ZALMAN OF LIADI
(ALTER REBBE)
1745–1812**

Chasidic rebbe, Halachic
authority, and founder of
the Chabad movement.
The Alter Rebbe was
born in Liozna, Belarus,
and was among the
principal students of the
Magid of Mezeritch. His
numerous works include
the *Tanya*, an early
classic containing the
fundamentals of Chabad
Chasidism; and *Shulchan
Aruch HaRav*, an
expanded and reworked
code of Jewish law.

KEY TERM 3.4

HEBREW TERM	שְׂרָפִּים
TRANSLITERATION	*seraphim*
LITERAL MEANING	**burning beings**
DEFINITION	angels of *Beriah* who experience a fiery passion to cleave to G-d as He transcends limitation

TEXT 5

Meaning of Wings

Rabbi Shmuel Schneersohn,
Likutei Torah: Torat Shmuel 5627, p. 334

הַשְׂרָפִים אוֹמְרִים "קָדוֹשׁ", שֶׁמַּשִּׂיגִים אֵיךְ שֶׁהוּא
יִתְבָּרֵךְ קָדוֹשׁ וּמֻבְדָּל . . . לָכֵן יֵשׁ בָּהֶם שֵׁשׁ כְּנָפַיִם,
לְפִי שֶׁהֵם בִּבְחִינַת הָעֲלָאָה מִלְמַטָּה לְמַעְלָה.

The seraphim say "*kadosh*" because they
comprehend G-d's transcendence. . . .
That's why they have six wings: they are
in a constant state of rising upward.

**RABBI SHMUEL
SCHNEERSOHN
(REBBE MAHARASH)
1834–1882**

Known by the acronym
"Maharash"; 4th Chabad
rebbe and leader of
Russian Jewry. Born in
Lubavitch, Russia, he was
the youngest son of Rabbi
Menachem Mendel of
Lubavitch (the *Tzemach
Tzedek*). Much of his
leadership was devoted
to combating anti-Jewish
policies. His discourses
have been collected and
published as *Likutei
Torah: Torat Shmuel*.

Jacob's vision of angels in the *Sister
Haggadah*, a heavily decorated
manuscript originating in Catalonia,
Spain in the mid-fourteenth century.
(Angels are spiritual beings, and
the physical attributes described
in Jewish texts and artwork
are employed as metaphors.)
(British Library, London)

Thirteen Attributes of Divine Mercy

Based on *Shaar Hakavanot, Derushei Vayaavor, Derush 3*

13	12	11	10	9	8

נֹצֵר חֶסֶד לָאֲלָפִים, נֹשֵׂא עָוֹן וָפֶשַׁע וְחַטָּאָה וְנַקֵּה.

and [He] < and sin, < transgression, < forgiving < for two thousand < preserving
cleanses.   iniquity,   generations,   kindness

After the debacle of the Sin of the Golden Calf and G-d's favorable reaction to Moses's intercession, Moses asked G-d to reveal His glory to him. In response, G-d delivered a proclamation regarding His great mercy, and told Moses that this proclamation of the "Thirteen Attributes of Mercy" is a key to Divine forgiveness.

Presented here is the Torah passage that records the thirteen attributes of Divine mercy, with subsequent explanations regarding the functioning of these Divine elements.

The Source of Mercy

Rabbi Shneur Zalman of Liadi, *Likutei Torah, Derushim LeShabbat Shuvah*, p. 67d

The Thirteen Attributes of Mercy are rooted in G-d's Desire. They therefore stand beyond all of the spiritual worlds, and beyond the standard Divine attributes known as the *sefirot*. For when we seek repentance for past transgressions, the Divine attributes that are revealed within the created worlds are insufficient to help us achieve repair. The spiritual worlds are part of a logically structured system; the first of all of the Divine attributes expressed in the worlds is *chochmah*, wisdom. Now, from the standpoint of logic, once the damage of a transgression has been inflicted, there is no way to erase it and wipe the slate clean. Cleansing can only arrive as a result of something beyond the logical system, and this is where the Thirteen Attributes of Mercy enter the picture. Rooted in G-d's simple desire, there are no barriers to constrain their application; they can cleanse us from any transgression, no matter how severe.

Repentance

Rabbi Shneur Zalman of Liadi, ibid.

In order to reach and activate the Thirteen Attributes of Mercy, we need to tap into a corresponding feature within our own soul. It is not enough to merely appreciate intellectually the error of our ways and to regret them. We must also return to G-d from the very depths of our soul, based on the knowledge that we have a G-dly core that cannot bear to be separated from our Divine Source. When we step beyond our intellectual and emotional attributes, and awaken the purest desire for G-d that lies at our core, G-d will respond in kind and grant us suprarational forgiveness and cleansing from the place of His greatest desire.

7	6	5	4	3	2	1

וַיַּעֲבֹר ה' עַל פָּנָיו וַיִּקְרָא: ה' ה' אֵ־ל רַחוּם וְחַנּוּן, אֶרֶךְ אַפַּיִם וְרַב חֶסֶד וֶאֱמֶת.

| and truth; | < | and abundant in kindness | < | to anger, | < | slow | < | and gracious | < | merciful | < | L-rd | < | G-d G-d | < | G-d passed before him and proclaimed: |

Humility

Rabbi Shmuel Schneersohn, *Likutei Torah: Torat Shmuel* 5637:2, p. 930

The actual Thirteen Attributes of Mercy are limitless. They can express themselves in any place and at any time. On our end, however, we need to be capable of receiving and assimilating their light. When we enter a state of *bitul*—humble submission and self-negation—we are capable of receiving this vast, unlimited light from beyond the spiritual cosmic system.

Communal Prayer

Rabbi Shmuel Schneersohn, ibid. 5627, p. 373

The Thirteen Attributes of Mercy can also be effectively invoked through the community gathering to pray together. G-d pledged that He will never reject our communal prayers (Job 36:5; Talmud, Berachot 8b); He is always fully accessible when we assemble to unite in prayer.

The High Holy Days

Rabbi Shneur Zalman of Liadi, *Likutei Torah*, *Nitzavim* 51a

The ten days that begin with Rosh Hashanah and end with Yom Kippur are known as the "Ten Days of Repentance." Regarding this auspicious time, we are told to "seek out G-d when He is present, call out to Him when He is near" (Isaiah 55:6; Talmud, Rosh Hashanah 18a). For the Thirteen Attributes of Mercy are revealed throughout these ten days, and they facilitate our repentance and atonement.

True, the Thirteen Attributes of Mercy can be accessed all year round via heartfelt repentance. Nevertheless, it requires great effort on our end to evoke this coveted Divine response. By contrast, during the Ten Days of Repentance, the Thirteen Attributes of Mercy are revealed and we can access them with less effort on our part. For that reason, we recite the Thirteen Attributes of Mercy repeatedly during our prayers on Rosh Hashanah and Yom Kippur.

The Call of the Shofar

Rabbi Shneur Zalman of Liadi, *Likutei Torah*, *Ki Tavo* 43d

The Thirteen Attributes of Mercy are rooted in G-d's deepest desire, and we can evoke them through arousing our own deep desire for closeness to G-d. Over the course of our day-to-day lives we are engaged in the pursuit of mundane needs and desires, which causes the profound spiritual desire that breathes at our core to be lulled into slumber. The sound of the shofar on Rosh Hashanah is intended to serve as a wakeup call, arousing our truest desire from its hibernation. Our freshly awakened boundless passion for G-d activates G-d's own limitless attributes of mercy in response, providing us with forgiveness and a clean slate for the new year.

II. SYNTHESIS

Kabbalah reveals that G-d's infinite light is crucial for generating "peace in the Heavens," that is, synthesis among the *sefirot*. This peace is also relevant to humans, especially in marriage.

TEXT 6

Divine Peace

Siddur, Kaddish, final stanza

עֹשֶׂה שָׁלוֹם בִּמְרוֹמָיו, הוּא יַעֲשֶׂה שָׁלוֹם עָלֵינוּ וְעַל כָּל יִשְׂרָאֵל, וְאִמְרוּ אָמֵן.

May He Who makes peace in His Heavens make peace for us and all of Israel, and say: Amen.

KEY TERM 3.5

HEBREW TERM	הִתְכַּלְלוּת
TRANSLITERATION	*hitkalelut*
LITERAL MEANING	**incorporation**
DEFINITION	the intermingling and harmonization of the G-dly *sefirot*

SIDDUR

The siddur is the Jewish prayer book. It was originally developed by the sages of the Great Assembly in the 4th century BCE and later reconstructed by Rabban Gamliel after the destruction of the Second Temple. Various authorities continued to add prayers, from then until contemporary times. It includes praise of G-d, requests for personal and national needs, selections from the Bible, and much else. Various Jewish communities have slightly different versions of the siddur.

TEXT 7

Parable of Ministers

Rabbi Shneur Zalman of Liadi, *Siddur Im Dach*, p. 261d

דְּשֹׁרֶשׁ בְּחִינַת הַהִתְכַּלְלוּת דְּעֶשֶׂר סְפִירוֹת,
וּבִפְרָט בְּב' הֲפָכִים חֶסֶד וּגְבוּרָה, הוּא בָּא מִצַּד
בְּחִינַת הַמְשָׁכַת אוֹר הָעֶלְיוֹן אֲשֶׁר נַעֲלֶה מִשְּׁנֵי
הַהֲפָכִים, עַל כֵּן יִתְבַּטְּלוּ מְצִיאוּתָם וְיִתְכַּלְלוּ.

עַל דֶּרֶךְ מָשָׁל ב' שָׂרִים מְנֻגָּדִים שֶׁבָּאִים לִפְנֵי הַמֶּלֶךְ,
שֶׁמִּתְבַּטְּלִין מִמְּצִיאוּתָם וְיִתְחַבְּרוּ לְדֵעָה אַחַת מַמָּשׁ,
(דְּהַיְנוּ שֶׁכָּל אֶחָד סוֹבֵל דַּעַת חֲבֵרוֹ הַהָפְכִי, אֲבָל לֹא
שֶׁנִּתְבַּטֵּל מִמַּהוּתוֹ לִהְיוֹת בְּמַהוּת הָפְכִי), וְהַיְנוּ מִפְּנֵי
בְּחִינַת אֵימַת גְּדֻלַּת וְרוֹמְמוּת הַמֶּלֶךְ שֶׁמֵּאִיר עֲלֵיהֶם
שֶׁנַּעֲלֶה מֵהֶם הַרְבֵּה, שֶׁעַל יְדֵי זֶה מִתְבַּטְּלִים . . .

וְעַל דֶּרֶךְ זֶה בִּבְחִינַת חֶסֶד וּגְבוּרָה דַּאֲצִילוּת,
מִתְכַּלְּלִים ב' הֲפָכִים מִפְּנֵי הֶאָרַת אוֹר אֵין סוֹף.

The synthesis of the ten *sefirot*—especially those that are opposites, such as *chesed* and *gevurah*—is made possible through the agency of supernal light that transcends the characteristics of the *sefirot*. Upon sensing this supernal light, the *sefirot* experience *bitul*: they relinquish their configuration and synthesize with each other.

Consider the example of two government ministers who hopelessly oppose each other. When they must appear together before the king, they remain who they are, with their preferences, but find themselves working with the opposing viewpoint to reach a required consensus. This is a consequence of their state of *bitul* that results from their overwhelming trepidation and awe of the king's majesty, whose rank by far transcends their own. . . .

Similarly, the opposite forces of *chesed* and *gevurah* in *Atzilut* can synthesize due to the illumination of G-d's infinite light (*or ein sof*).

KEY TERM 3.6

HEBREW TERM	כֶּתֶר
TRANSLITERATION	*keter*
LITERAL MEANING	**crown**
DEFINITION	G-dliness that transcends the *sefirot* and that enables their harmonization

TEXT 8

Bride and Groom

Rabbi Shneur Zalman of Liadi,
Maamarei Admur Hazaken 5567, p. 189

בְּעִנְיַן חָתָן וְכַלָּה, שֶׁהֵמָּה ב' הֲפָכִים מִן הַקָּצֶה, כַּנִּזְכָּר לְעֵיל,
הִנֵּה כְּדֵי שֶׁיִּתְאַחֲדוּ וְיִתְכַּלְלוּ יַחַד צָרִיךְ לִהְיוֹת גַּם כֵּן עַל יְדֵי
בְּחִינַת הָאוֹר שֶׁמֵּאִיר עֲלֵיהֶם מִמָּקוֹם וּמַדְרֵגָה הַיוֹתֵר גָּבוֹהַּ
גַּם מִשְּׁנֵיהֶם יַחַד, עַד שֶׁשָּׁם מִשְׁתַּוִּים יַחַד, כַּמְּבֹאָר לְמַעְלָה.

וְהַיְנוּ עִנְיַן הַחֻפָּה, מַה שֶׁמְּבִיאִים הֶחָתָן וְהַכַּלָּה תַּחַת הַחֻפָּה
שֶׁחוֹפֶפֶת עַל שְׁנֵיהֶם יַחַד, וְעוֹמֶדֶת בְּגֹבַהּ וְרוּם עַל הֶחָתָן
וְהַכַּלָּה כוּ'. וְהָעִנְיָן הוּא, כִּי חֻפָּה זֹאת הוּא בְּחִינַת אוֹר מַקִּיף
הַבָּא מִבְּחִינַת מַקִּיפִים הָעֶלְיוֹנִים, מִבְּחִינַת סוֹבֵב כָּל עָלְמִין.

The bride and groom are opposites. To unite as one, they require an infusion of higher energy that shines from a degree of Divinity that transcends their differences.

This is the significance of leading the bride and groom under a *chupah* that hovers above both of them equally and is positioned at a height above them. It corresponds to the encompassing light of *sovev kol almin*.

Rabbi YY Jacobson
on marriage:
myjli.com/kabbalah

Marriage Circles

The theme of transcendence is reflected in several of the Jewish wedding ceremony rituals, in the form of circles and canopies.

SOURCES:
Maamarei Admur Hazaken 5567, p. 189;
Likutei Torah, Shir Hashirim 47d; Maamarei Admur
Ha'emtza'ei, Bereshit, p. 219; Torat Menachem 3,
p. 294; Maamarei Admur Hazaken 5568:2, p. 423.

❶ *Chupah*

The wedding ceremony is conducted beneath a canopy known as a *chupah*.

❷ Veil

Before the groom is escorted to the *chupah*, he covers the bride's face with a veil. The bride remains veiled for the duration of the wedding ceremony.

❸ Circling

Under the *chupah* but before the actual ceremony begins, it is traditional for the bride to circle the groom seven times.

❹ *Kidushin* ring

The groom places a ring on the bride's finger and declares, "You are hereby consecrated to me with this ring, in accordance with the law of Moses and Israel."

❺ Dancing

After the marriage ceremony has been completed, friends and family break into joyous dancing—traditionally, they dance in a circle.

III. HUMAN DESIRE

The present course has followed a pattern of exploring supernal realms and then identifying their corresponding phenomena within the human microcosm. The human reflection of *sovev kol almin* is a mortal's capacity for will and desire. This explains the power of the human will to influence the mortal mind and all other elements of one's personality.

TEXT 9

The Soul Itself

Rabbi Shneur Zalman of Liadi, *Torah Or* 13c–d

הַנֶּפֶשׁ מִצַּד עַצְמָהּ הִיא אוֹר פָּשׁוּט
בְּלִי הִתְחַלְקוּת שֵׂכֶל וּמִדוֹת.

The soul itself is a simple, undefined light that transcends the division of intellect and emotion.

Can a finite human relate to the infinite G-d? A uniquely engaging presentation:
myjli.com/kabbalah

TEXT 10

Soul Channel

Rabbi Menachem Mendel of Lubavitch, *Or Ha Torah*, *Balak*, p. 972

וְרָצוֹן אוֹתִיּוֹת צִנּוֹר: כְּמוֹ שֶׁהַצִּנּוֹר הוּא הַמְשָׁכָה, כָּךְ הוּא עִנְיַן הָרָצוֹן, שֶׁנִּמְשַׁךְ נַפְשׁוֹ וְכָלְתָה לַדָּבָר הַהוּא.

The Hebrew letters that spell *ratzon* (רָצוֹן), "desire," also spell *tzinor* (צִנּוֹר), "pipeline." Just as a pipeline is employed to channel something, so does the human will channel the soul toward a particular matter.

RABBI MENACHEM MENDEL OF LUBAVITCH (*TZEMACH TZEDEK*) 1789–1866

Chasidic rebbe and noted author. The *Tzemach Tzedek* was the 3rd leader of the Chabad Chasidic movement and a noted authority on Jewish law. His numerous works include Halachic responsa, Chasidic discourses, and kabbalistic writings. Active in the communal affairs of Russian Jewry, he worked to alleviate the plight of the cantonists, Jewish children kidnapped to serve in the czar's army. He passed away in Lubavitch, leaving 7 sons and 2 daughters.

NO IMPRISONMENT FOR THE SOUL
Ariel Fabian Lijtmaer, acrylic and mixed media on canvas, Los Angeles, 2018

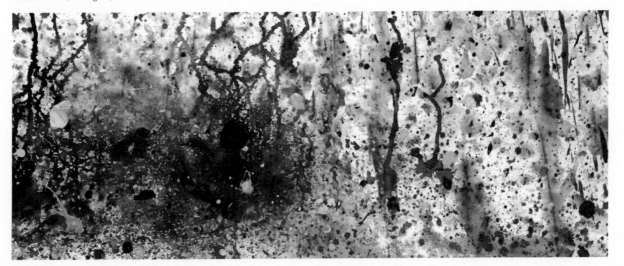

Two Desires

Rabbi Dovber of Lubavitch, *Torat Chayim, Beshalach* 199a–c

אִית רָצוֹן שֶׁנִּקְרָא . . . רָצוֹן הַנּוֹלָד, שֶׁנּוֹלַד לְפִי שָׁעָה.
וְהוּא נִקְרָא רָצוֹן הַתַּחְתּוֹן שֶׁלְּמַטָּה מִן הַדַּעַת.

וְהַיְנוּ כְּמוֹ שֶׁרוֹאִין בְּחוּשׁ שֶׁבִּלְתִּי הַעֲמָקַת הַשֵּׂכֶל וְהַדַּעַת
לְאֵיזֶה דָּבָר מָה, לֹא יוֹלִיד רָצוֹן וְהִתְפַּעֲלוּת הַמִּדּוֹת
אֵלָיו כְּלָל, רַק כְּשֶׁמַּעֲמִיק דַּעְתּוֹ וּמַחֲשַׁבְתּוֹ בְּדָבָר מָה,
כְּמוֹ בִּדְבַר מַאֲכָל, אוֹ לְבוּשׁ וּמָמוֹן, אוֹ רֶוַח גָּדוֹל בְּמַשָּׂא
וּמַתָּן וּכְהַאי גַּוְנָא, אָז יוֹלִיד רָצוֹן וְחֵשֶׁק לְדָבָר זֶה . . .

וְזֶהוּ שֶׁנִּקְרָא מִדָּה, בִּלְשׁוֹן מִדָּה וּגְבוּל מַמָּשׁ, כִּי הֲרֵי
הָרָצוֹן הַזֶּה שֶׁנּוֹלַד מִצַּד הַשֵּׂכֶל וְהַדַּעַת הוּא בָּא בְּמִדָּה
וּגְבוּל בְּאוֹתוֹ דָּבָר שֶׁהוּטַב בְּשִׂכְלוֹ לְפִי אֹפֶן הַטַּעַם שֶׁיֵּשׁ
לוֹ בּוֹ, וְכַאֲשֶׁר בָּטֵל הַטַּעַם - בָּטְלָה הָאַהֲבָה וְהָרָצוֹן הַזֶּה,
שֶׁזֶּהוּ שֶׁנִּקְרָא גְּבוּל, לוֹמַר: עַד פֹּה תָּבֹא וְלֹא יוֹתֵר . . .

אֲבָל אִית רָצוֹן שֶׁנִּקְרָא רָצוֹן הָעֶלְיוֹן . . . שֶׁהֵן בִּלְתִּי
מֻגְבָּלִים בְּשִׁעוּר וּמִדָּה כְּלָל כוּ'. וְהַיְנוּ בְּחִינַת הָרָצוֹן
הַפָּשׁוּט שֶׁלְּמַעְלָה מִן הַשֵּׂכֶל וְהַטַּעַם, שֶׁלֹּא נוֹלַד כְּלָל
מִצַּד הַשֵּׂכֶל בָּרָצוֹן הַנִּזְכָּר לְעֵיל, אֶלָּא הוּא בִּבְחִינַת
עַצְמִיּוּת וְטִבְעִיּוּת . . . כְּמוֹ אַהֲבַת הָאָב אֶל בְּנוֹ שֶׁהוֹלִידוֹ
מֵעַצְמוּתוֹ, וְכֵן הָאֵם שֶׁמְּרַחֶמֶת לְוָלְדָהּ כוּ', שֶׁזֶּהוּ רַק
מִצַּד הַטִּבְעִיּוּת שֶׁלְּמַעְלָה מֵאֵיזֶה שֵׂכֶל וְטַעַם כְּלָל.

RABBI DOVBER OF LUBAVITCH (MITELER REBBE) 1773–1827

Rabbi Dovber was the eldest son of and successor to Rabbi Shneur Zalman of Liadi and greatly expanded upon and developed his father's groundbreaking teachings. He was the 1st Chabad rebbe to live in the village of Lubavitch. Dedicated to the welfare of Russian Jewry, at that time confined to the Pale of Settlement, he established Jewish agricultural colonies. His most notable works on Chasidic thought include *Shaar Hayichud, Torat Chayim,* and *Imrei Binah.*

One type of human desire is referred to as . . . "a born desire" because it is brought into being at a particular time. It is also referred to as the "lower desire" because its position is beneath that of the intellect.

Such a desire takes shape only after we strongly contemplate a particular matter. Without this, we will not experience any desire toward that matter. By contrast, when we think deeply about it—whether it is a specific food, an item of clothing, a financial issue, a lucrative business deal, etc.—then a desire for that thing is born within us. . . .

This type of desire is also called a *midah*, which means measured or limited. For a desire born from intellectual knowledge and contemplation is a measured desire, limited to the specific rationalization that created it. Consequently, when the logical basis for this desire ceases or becomes irrelevant, the desire toward that matter will similarly disappear. . . .

There is, however, a second type of desire, referred to as the "higher desire." . . . This desire is limitless. It is a simple desire that transcends intellect and is not born from it; instead, it is a natural desire that relates to our very selves. . . . For example, a father's love for the offspring that are an extension of his essence, and a mother's compassion for the child that she bore—these are natural desires that entirely transcend intellect and reason.

TEXT 12

A Story of Desire

Talmud, Avodah Zarah 19a

BABYLONIAN TALMUD

A literary work of monumental proportions that draws upon the legal, spiritual, intellectual, ethical, and historical traditions of Judaism. The 37 tractates of the Babylonian Talmud contain the teachings of the Jewish sages from the period after the destruction of the 2nd Temple through the 5th century CE. It has served as the primary vehicle for the transmission of the Oral Law and the education of Jews over the centuries; it is the entry point for all subsequent legal, ethical, and theological Jewish scholarship.

לֵוִי וְרַבִּי שִׁמְעוֹן בְּרַבִּי יָתְבִי קַמֵּיה דְּרַבִּי וְקָא פַּסְקֵי סִדְרָא.
סָלִיק סִפְרָא, לֵוִי אָמַר: לַיְיתוּ לָן מִשְׁלֵי. רַבִּי שִׁמְעוֹן
בְּרַבִּי אָמַר: לַיְיתוּ לָן תִּלִּים. כַּפְיֵה לְלֵוִי וְאַיְיתוּ תִלִּים.

כִּי מָטוּ הָכָא: "כִּי אִם בְּתוֹרַת ה' חֶפְצוֹ" (תְּהִלִּים א, ב), פְּרִישׁ
רַבִּי וְאָמַר: אֵין אָדָם לוֹמֵד תּוֹרָה אֶלָּא מִמָּקוֹם שֶׁלִּבּוֹ חָפֵץ.

אָמַר לֵוִי: רַבִּי, נָתַתָּ לִי רְשׁוּת לַעֲמֹד.

Rabbi Shimon and his colleague Levi were studying the Torah portion with Rabbi Shimon's father, Rabbi Yehudah Hanasi. When they completed it, Levi suggested, "Let them bring us Proverbs to study," whereas Rabbi Shimon suggested, "Let them bring us Psalms to study." Rabbi Shimon prevailed upon Levi to acquiesce, and they brought a book of Psalms.

When they reached the passage, "Praised is the person . . . whose desire is in G-d's Torah" (PSALMS 1:2), Rabbi Yehudah explained, "You can only learn the Torah from a place that your heart desires."

At this point, Levi declared, "My teacher, you have given me permission to leave."

TEXT 13

The Power of Desire

Rabbi Yosef Yitzchak Schneersohn,
Sefer Hamaamarim 5688, p. 31

דְּהָרָצוֹן מוֹשֵׁךְ כָּל הַכֹּחוֹת אֵלָיו וְאַחֲרָיו . . .

וְלָכֵן אָמְרוּ דְּיִלְמֹד אָדָם בְּמָקוֹם שֶׁלִּבּוֹ חָפֵץ, דְּכַאֲשֶׁר לִבּוֹ
חָפֵץ בָּזֶה בְּרָצוֹן וְחֵשֶׁק, הִנֵּה אָז הֲרֵי יַשְׂכִּיל וְיִתְחַכֵּם בְּזֶה.

וּכְמוֹ שֶׁאָנוּ רוֹאִין בְּמוּחָשׁ, דְּהַלּוֹמֵד בְּרָצוֹן
יַשְׂכִּיל יוֹתֵר מִבַּעַל כִּשְׁרוֹנוֹת וְחוּשִׁים נַעֲלִים.
לְפִי שֶׁהָרָצוֹן יַכְרִיחַ הִתְגַּלּוּת הַשֵּׂכֶל.

וְכֵן הוּא בְּכָל הַכֹּחוֹת.

Desire (*ratzon*) compels all of a person's
abilities to be drawn after it. . . .

Therefore, our sages taught us that we should
study specifically a subject that we desire. For
then our minds become more creative and
analytical regarding the object of our desire.

Indeed, we can readily observe that those who
study with desire comprehend the subject better
than intellectually gifted individuals who do
not have a similar desire. For the *ratzon* forces
the intellect to operate on a higher level.

Indeed, it has the same amplifying effect
on all of an individual's abilities.

RABBI YOSEF YITZCHAK
SCHNEERSOHN
(RAYATZ, FRIERDIKER
REBBE, PREVIOUS REBBE)
1880-1950

Chasidic rebbe, prolific
writer, and Jewish
activist. Rabbi Yosef
Yitzchak, the 6th leader
of the Chabad movement,
actively promoted
Jewish religious practice
in Soviet Russia and
was arrested for these
activities. After his
release from prison
and exile, he settled in
Warsaw, Poland, from
where he fled Nazi
occupation and arrived
in New York in 1940.
Settling in Brooklyn,
Rabbi Schneersohn
worked to revitalize
American Jewish life.
His son-in-law Rabbi
Menachem Mendel
Schneerson succeeded
him as the leader of the
Chabad movement.

KEY TERM 3.7

HEBREW TERM	רְצוֹן הַנֶּפֶשׁ
TRANSLITERATION	*ratzon hanefesh*
LITERAL MEANING	**the soul's desire**
DEFINITION	(a) a desire flowing from the soul's innate nature; (b) a desire generated by contemplation

TEXT 14

A Chasid's Struggle

Rabbi Yosef Yitzchak Schneersohn,
Igrot Kodesh 3, pp. 364–368

בָּעִיר לְעֶפְּלִי, גָּר אֶחָד מֵחֲסִידֵי הוֹד כְּבוֹד קְדֻשַּׁת רַבֵּנוּ
הַזָּקֵן, חֶנְוָנִי מוֹכֵר מֶלַח, וְר' יְקוּתִיאֵל שְׁמוֹ. הוּא הָיָה אֶחָד
הָעוֹבְדִים הַיְדוּעִים . . . אֲבָל הַשָּׂגָתוֹ בִּידִיעַת הַתּוֹרָה
בִּכְלָל וְתוֹרַת הַחֲסִידוּת בִּפְרָט הָיְתָה מְצֻמְצָמָה בְּיוֹתֵר.

פַּעַם עָבַר דֶּרֶךְ לְעֶפְּלִי אֶחָד הָאַבְרֵכִים הַמַּשְׁפִּיעִים
וַיִּתְעַכֵּב שָׁם כִּשְׁבוּעַ יָמִים, וּבְכָל יוֹם וָיוֹם הָיָה חוֹזֵר
מַאֲמָר שֶׁל הוֹד כְּבוֹד קְדֻשַּׁת אֲדוֹנִי אָבִי זְקֵנִי מוֹרֵנוּ וְרַבֵּנוּ
אַדְמוֹ"ר הָאֶמְצָעִי בְּעַל פֶּה . . . אָמְנָם הֶחָסִיד ר' יְקוּתִיאֵל
בִּהְיוֹתוֹ בַּעַל שֵׂכֶל לֹא גָדוֹל לֹא הֵבִין אֶת הַמַּאֲמָרִים הָהֵם.
הַדָּבָר נָגַע אֶל לִבּוֹ בִּמְאֹד וְדִכֵּא אֶת רוּחוֹ, וְהָיָה שָׁפֵל
בְּעֵינֵי עַצְמוֹ מִזֶּה . . . בָּכִיתִי בְּכִי רַב בַּאֲמִירַת תְּהִלִּים,
אֲבָל אֵין שׁוּם תּוֹעֶלֶת, וְהָלַכְתִּי לְלִיוּבַּאוִויטְשׁ . . .

כְּשֶׁנִּכְנַסְתִּי בִּיחִידוּת לִכְבוֹד קְדֻשַּׁת אַדְמוֹ"ר
סִפַּרְתִּי מִכָּל הֶעָבַר עָלַי בְּבֵיתִי . . .

כְּבוֹד קְדֻשַּׁת אַדְמוֹ"ר עָנָה:

אֵין לְךָ דָּבָר הָעוֹמֵד בִּפְנֵי הָרָצוֹן . . . דְּהַכֹּחוֹת שֶׁלְּמַטָּה מִן הָרָצוֹן,
כְּמוֹ שֵׂכֶל וּמִדּוֹת, הִנֵּה הָרָצוֹן פּוֹעֵל עֲלֵיהֶם בִּגְזֵרָה וּפְקֻדָּה בְּדֶרֶךְ
כֹּחַ עֶלְיוֹן. וְכַאֲשֶׁר רוֹצִים בֶּאֱמֶת אָז גַּם הַחוּשִׁים מִתְרַחֲבִים.

כַּאֲשֶׁר שָׁמַעְתִּי מִכְּבוֹד קְדֻשַּׁת אַדְמוֹ"ר כִּי אֵין הַדָּבָר תָּלוּי אֶלָּא
בִּרְצוֹנִי, הֶחְלַטְתִּי לְהִשָּׁאֵר בִּלְיוּבַּאוִיטְשׁ עַד אֲשֶׁר אַתְחִיל
לְהָבִין. עִם הָעוֹבְרִים וְשָׁבִים דֶּרֶךְ לִיעֶפְּלִי הוֹדַעְתִּי כִּי אֵיזֶה
זְמַן אֶתְעַכֵּב, וְעַל כֵּן יְנַהֲלוּ אֶת הַחֲנוּת בְּעַצְמָם. כְּאַרְבָּעָה
חֳדָשִׁים יָגַעְתִּי בִּיגִיעָה עֲצוּמָה בִּיגִיעַת נֶפֶשׁ וּבִיגִיעַת בָּשָׂר
לְהַרְגִּיל אֶת עַצְמִי לַחֲשֹׁב עִנְיָן אֶחָד כַּמָּה שָׁעוֹת רְצוּפוֹת,
וּבִיגִיעַת נֶפֶשׁ לַחֲזֹר עַל עִנְיָן אֶחָד כַּמָּה עֲשִׂירִיוֹת פְּעָמִים . . .
בְּחֹדֶשׁ תִּשְׁרֵי הַהוּא הִרְגַּשְׁתִּי עַצְמִי כִּבְרִיָה חֲדָשָׁה . . .

כְּבוֹד קְדֻשַּׁת אֲדוֹנִי אָבִי מוֹרִי וְרַבִּי אָמַר: הֶחָסִיד
ר' יְקוּתִיאֵל לִיעֶפְּלֶער הוּא מוֹפֵת חַי עַל מַאֲמַר
רַבּוֹתֵינוּ זַ"ל: "יָגַעְתָּ וּמָצָאתָ" (מְגִילָּה ו, ב).

In the city of Lepel, there lived a Chasid named Reb
Yekutiel, who worked as a salt merchant. He was
well known for his piety . . . but his comprehension
of Torah and Chasidic teachings was quite limited.

Once, a young teacher of Chasidic philosophy traveled
by way of Lepel and chose to linger in the city for
a week. Each day, he reviewed another Chasidic
discourse that had been delivered by the Miteler
Rebbe, Rabbi Dovber of Lubavitch. . . . However, Reb

Yekutiel found that, due to his limited intelligence, he could not understand these teachings. This bothered him profoundly and he felt utterly broken. . . . He wept bitter tears and recited Psalms but found no solace. He decided to journey to Lubavitch to consult Rabbi Dovber himself. . . .

Reb Yekutiel entered the Rebbe's chambers for a private audience and recounted all that he had experienced at home. . . .

The Rebbe responded:

"Nothing stands in the way of desire. . . . The mind and emotions are positioned beneath desire and are subject to it. The superior power of desire influences the mind and emotions by way of command and directive. If you truly desire something, your abilities will expand accordingly."

Upon hearing this, Reb Yekutiel decided to stay in Lubavitch. He informed those traveling through Lepel to convey to his family that he would be delayed for a while and that they should run the store in his absence. For four months, he toiled with tremendous effort, both physically and mentally. He practiced focusing on a single topic for several hours at a time and reviewed each subject dozens of times. . . . By the time Rosh Hashanah came, he felt like a new man. . . .

Rabbi Menachem Mendel of Lubavitch later stated, "The Chasid Reb Yekutiel of Lepel is a living example of our sages' teaching (TALMUD, MEGILAH 6B), 'If you labor, you will find success.'"

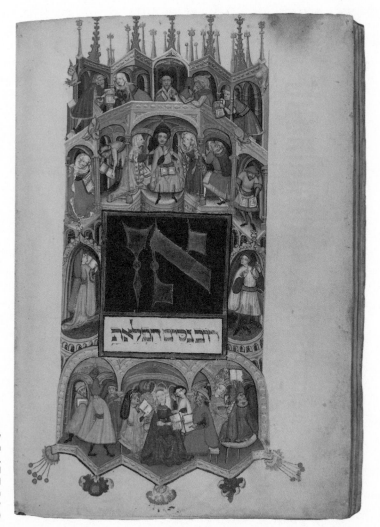

Jews engaged in the study of Torah—a scene from the *Darmstadt Haggadah*, created c. 1430 by Yisrael ben Meir of Heidelberg and illuminated by an unknown artist. (Darmstadt University and State Library, Germany)

TEXT 15

You Can!

The Rebbe, Rabbi Menachem Mendel Schneerson,
Torat Menachem 28, pp. 239–240

פַּעַם אַחַת יָשַׁב הַבַּעַל שֵׁם טוֹב עִם תַּלְמִידָיו בְּבֵית
הַכְּנֶסֶת וּבְבֵית הַמִּדְרָשׁ וְעָסְקוּ בְּתוֹרָה אוֹ בִּתְפִלָּה,
וּבָרְחוֹב הַסָּמוּךְ עָבַר גּוֹי עִם עֲגָלָה, וְכֵיוָן שֶׁבָּרְחוֹב הָיָה
בֹּץ רַב, לֹא הָיְתָה הָעֲגָלָה יְכוֹלָה לְהַמְשִׁיךְ לִנְסֹעַ, וְשָׁקְעָה
בַּבֹּץ. נִגַּשׁ הַגּוֹי לְחַלּוֹן בֵּית הַכְּנֶסֶת שֶׁבּוֹ יָשְׁבוּ הַבַּעַל שֵׁם
טוֹב וְתַלְמִידָיו, הִכְנִיס אֶת רֹאשׁוֹ מִבַּעַד לַחַלּוֹן, וּבִקֵּשׁ
שֶׁיַּעַזְרוּ לוֹ לְהוֹצִיא אֶת הָעֲגָלָה מִן הַבֹּץ. כֵּיוָן שֶׁהָעֲגָלָה
הָיְתָה כְּבֵדָה, וְהַבֹּץ הָיָה גָּדוֹל - הֵשִׁיבוּ הַתַּלְמִידִים
שֶׁאֵין בְּכֹחָם לְהוֹצִיא אֶת הָעֲגָלָה מֵהַבֹּץ הֶעָמֹק.

וְעָנָה לָהֶם הַגּוֹי - בַּשָּׂפָה הָאוּקְרָיְינִית - "מָאזְשֶׁעשׁ דַא
נְיֶע חָאטְשֶׁעשׁ", שֶׁפֵּרוּשׁוֹ: הִנְּךָ יָכוֹל, אַךְ אֵינְךָ רוֹצֶה,
וְכֵיוָן שֶׁאֵינְךָ רוֹצֶה, אֲזַי נִדְמֶה לְךָ שֶׁאֵינְךָ יָכוֹל.

וְאַחַר כָּךְ הִסְבִּיר הַבַּעַל שֵׁם טוֹב לְתַלְמִידָיו, שֶׁהַדְּבָרִים
שֶׁשָּׁמְעוּ מֵהַגּוֹי אֵינָם בְּמִקְרֶה, אֶלָּא יֵשׁ לִלְמֹד מִזֶּה
הוֹרָאָה בַּעֲבוֹדַת ה': כַּאֲשֶׁר מְצַוִּים יֶלֶד יְהוּדִי לִלְמֹד
יוֹתֵר . . . וְעַל דֶּרֶךְ זֶה אֵצֶל מְבֻגָּרִים . . . הִנֵּה לִפְעָמִים
נִדְמֶה לוֹ שֶׁאֵין לוֹ כֹּחַ, כֵּיוָן שֶׁהוּא עָיֵף. הִנֵּה עַל זֶה אוֹמֵר
הַבַּעַל שֵׁם טוֹב, שֶׁצְּרִיכִים לִלְמֹד מִדְּבָרָיו שֶׁל הַגּוֹי,
לְהַבְדִּיל, "מָאזְשֶׁעשׁ דַא נְיֶע חָאטְשֶׁעשׁ", הַיְינוּ, שֶׁהַקָּדוֹשׁ
בָּרוּךְ הוּא נוֹתֵן כֹּחוֹת לַעֲשׂוֹת אֶת כָּל הַדְּבָרִים הַטּוֹבִים,
אֶלָּא כֵּיוָן שֶׁלֹּא רוֹצִים לַעֲשׂוֹת, בִּגְלַל שֶׁמַּקְשִׁיבִים
לַיֵּצֶר הָרַע, אֲזַי נִדְמֶה שֶׁאֵין יְכוֹלִים לַעֲשׂוֹת.

**RABBI MENACHEM
MENDEL SCHNEERSON
1902-1994**

The towering Jewish
leader of the 20th
century, known as "the
Lubavitcher Rebbe," or
simply as "the Rebbe."
Born in southern
Ukraine, the Rebbe
escaped Nazi-occupied
Europe, arriving in
the U.S. in June 1941.
The Rebbe inspired
and guided the revival
of traditional Judaism
after the European
devastation, impacting
virtually every Jewish
community the world
over. The Rebbe often
emphasized that the
performance of just
one additional good
deed could usher in
the era of Mashiach.
The Rebbe's scholarly
talks and writings have
been printed in more
than 200 volumes.

Rabbi Yisrael Baal Shem Tov was once sitting with his students in the synagogue, engaged in Torah study or prayer. In the nearby street, a man was passing with a wagon, and due to the thick mud on the road, the wagon got stuck. The man approached the window of the synagogue where the Baal Shem Tov and his students were sitting and requested their assistance in extracting the wagon from the mud. The students replied that they did not have the strength to assist because the wagon was heavy and the mud was deep.

The man responded in Ukrainian, "*Mozhish! Da nye chotshesh*!" which means, "You *can*, but you don't want!" In other words: you have the ability but not the will—and without the will, you imagine that it is too much for you.

Afterward, the Baal Shem Tov explained to his students that what they heard was not a coincidence but a lesson for serving G-d. When Jewish children set out to study Torah . . . and the same is true of Jewish adults . . . they may feel that they are unable to do so due to fatigue. They need to remember, "*Mozhish! Da nye chotshesh*!": G-d gives us the strength to do all good things. It is just that we sometimes listen to the voice of the negative inclination within us and then lose the desire to act accordingly. At that point, we falsely believe that we are incapable.

IV. GENERATING DESIRE

The above teachings leave us with a practical question: If desire is vital for success, what steps might we be able to take to generate the required desire? The answer lies with the intellectual faculty of *daat* (connection), which can be appreciated through an analytical contrast with the faculties of *chochmah* (wisdom) and *binah* (understanding).

FIGURE 3.1

Three Intellectual Traits

HEBREW NAME		DEFINITION
chochmah	חָכְמָה	spark of intellectual creativity
binah	בִּינָה	logical and analytical breakdown of an idea
daat	דַּעַת	connecting with information in a personal way

Initial word panel to the Book of Genesis in an illuminated Pentateuch thought to have been produced in Germany, c. fourteenth century. (HUC Library, Cincinnati)

KEY TERM 3.8

HEBREW TERM	דַעַת
TRANSLITERATION	*daat*
LITERAL MEANING	**knowledge; connection**
DEFINITION	connecting with something in a personal way

TEXT 16A

Connection

Rabbi Shneur Zalman of Liadi, *Torah Or* 88a

דַעַת הוּא עִנְיַן הַכָּרָה, שֶׁזֶּהוּ בְּחִינַת הִתְקַשְּׁרוּת
הַמֵּבִיא לִידֵי הָרָצוֹן כוּ'. וְכֵן "וְהָאָדָם יָדַע" (בְּרֵאשִׁית
ד, א), לָשׁוֹן הִתְקַשְּׁרוּת וְהִתְחַבְּרוּת.

Daat consists of a familiar connection that triggers desire. Thus, the Torah uses the term *daat* to depict a bond, as in the verse, "Adam knew Eve" (GENESIS 4:1).

Mrs. Rivkah Slonim on enhancing our relationships using the power of *daat*: **myjli.com/kabbalah**

EXERCISE 3.1

Consider a positive quality or behavior that is currently not part of your life. It should be a quality or behavior you are somewhat interested in gaining but don't *strongly* desire.

1.   Consider an occasion when you did not perform well or failed to achieve something important because you *lacked* this quality or behavior.

2.   Consider an instance in which you, or someone you know, performed well or achieved something important due to having this quality or behavior.

3.   Imagine how your life might be enhanced if you gain this quality or behavior.

4.   Imagine how the lives of your loved ones might be enhanced if you gain this quality or behavior.

5.   Identify the most significant challenge(s) to introducing this quality and behavior into your life.

6.   Can you offer a possible solution to mitigate one or some of these challenges?

TEXT 16B

The Trigger

Rabbi Shneur Zalman of Liadi, ibid.

שֶׁהָרָצוֹן הַתַּחְתּוֹן, אַף עַל פִּי שֶׁהוּא לְמַטָּה מִבְּחִינַת רָצוֹן
הָעֶלְיוֹן, אֲבָל עַל כָּל פָּנִים כְּלִי הוּא לְגִלּוּי רְצוֹן הָעֶלְיוֹן.

The lower form of desire, which is inferior to
the higher, innate desire, can nonetheless
trigger the revelation of the higher desire.

**PENETRATING THE
UPPER SPHERES**
Loren Hodes, charcoal on
paper, Johannesburg

KEY TERMS

1. Or ein sof

G-d's infinite self-projection that is intimately connected with G-d's essence and that transcends definition, limitation, and specific attributes

2. Sovev kol almin

G-d as He transcends the emanation of *sefirot* and the creation of *Beriah*, *Yetzirah*, and *Asiyah*

3. Memalei kol almin

G-d as He emanates the *sefirot* and actively creates *Beriah*, *Yetzirah*, and *Asiyah*

4. Seraphim

Angels of *Beriah* who experience a fiery passion to cleave to G-d as He transcends limitation

5. Hitkalelut

The intermingling and harmonization of the G-dly *sefirot*

6. Keter

G-dliness that transcends the *sefirot* and that enables their harmonization

7. Ratzon hanefesh

(a) A desire flowing from the soul's innate nature
(b) A desire generated by contemplation

8. Daat

Connecting with something in a personal way

KEY POINTS

1   The kabbalistic tradition designates the pre-*sefirot* state of Divinity as "the infinite light"—the *or ein sof*. The term "light" implies that it is not G-d's essence, even as it reflects that essence and is indivisibly connected with it.

2   The seraphim who inhabit *Beriah* are dissatisfied with relating to G-d as He projects Himself in a limited fashion; they direct their attention and desire to *or ein sof* with a fiery passion.

3   Each *sefirah* of *Atzilut* perceives the reality that *or ein sof* transcends every form of limitation and definition. This perception fosters Heavenly harmony.

4   Although a husband and wife's souls are rooted in different *sefirot*, they can unify and become soul mates because both souls sense G-d's infinity—much as their root *sefirot* merge before G-d's infinity. For that reason, the concept of infinity is observably present within marriage—in the form of procreation.

5   Divine infinity manifests itself in human desire. Human desire comes in two forms: innate and calculated. Both forms significantly influence an individual's capacity to perform more efficiently, leading to success.

6   *Chochmah* refers to the initial spark of human creativity; *binah* refers to the analysis of a subject matter; *daat* is the personalization of preexisting information.

KEY TAKEAWAYS

1   In many prayers, we acknowledge G-d as the Creator
    and develop a sense of closeness with Him. At the
    same time, our daily prayers include passages
    that emphasize G-d's transcendence, for this
    aspect of G-d similarly deserves our attention.

2   Couples can set aside their differences by learning
    from their souls who were able to become
    soul mates by sensing G-d's infinity. Couples
    can then embrace their personalities and
    experiences and nevertheless find harmony.

3   Success requires strong desire. Therefore, we
    are advised to study those areas of Torah in
    which we already possess an interest.

4   We can generate desire by utilizing our power of *daat*
    (connection) to contemplate the importance of a
    given behavior or quality in a personalized way.

5   Our souls possess an innate desire to cleave to
    G-d. If this desire is concealed, we can awaken
    it by generating a calculated desire for G-d.

4

THE WORLD OF CHAOS

*This lesson studies the primordial spiritual universe
of Tohu ("chaos") and the colossal repercussions that
resulted from its collapse. Understanding its purpose in
the greater scheme for Creation provides eye-opening
insight into the internal human conflict that leaves
us attracted to both noble and ignoble pursuits. We
can harness elements of internal Tohu to accomplish
great good.*

I. TWO SOULS

Jewish mysticism explains that inner human conflict results from the coexistence of two souls within each of us. One is termed the human's "animal soul," and the other is the human's "G-dly soul."

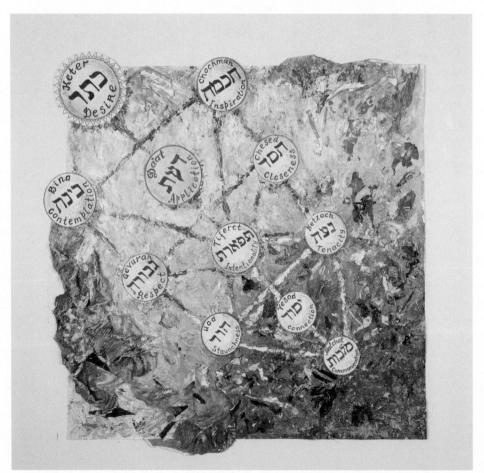

PRE-CREATION
Elena Kalman, from the Jewish History Time Line installation in Chabad of Somerset County, N.J., acrylic and mixed media on paper, 2020–2022

EXERCISE 4.1

As objectively as possible, respond to each of the following self-reflective statements. Consider each question on its merits, without regard for consistency with the other responses.

	YES	NO
I am a selfish person.	○	○
I am not a selfish person.	○	○
At times, I really only care about myself and my well-being.	○	○
Some things are more significant than my existence.	○	○
I would never knowingly do something to hurt another person.	○	○
I know that I've hurt others in pursuit of my goals.	○	○
I sometimes feel glad when someone else fails.	○	○
I do not want to rejoice over someone else's troubles.	○	○
When I want something, I find it very difficult to resist it, even when I recognize that it is harmful to my moral and spiritual well-being.	○	○
I weigh short-term gains against the long-term harm they may invite.	○	○

TEXT 1

Two Souls

Rabbi Shneur Zalman of Liadi, *Tanya*, *Likutei Amarim*, chs. 1–2

נֶפֶשׁ אַחַת מִצַּד הַקְּלִפָּה וְסִטְרָא אַחֲרָא, וְהִיא הַמִּתְלַבֶּשֶׁת
בְּדַם הָאָדָם לְהַחֲיוֹת הַגּוּף . . . וּמִמֶּנָּה בָּאוֹת כָּל הַמִּדוֹת
רָעוֹת . . . וְגַם מִדוֹת טוֹבוֹת שֶׁבְּטֶבַע כָּל יִשְׂרָאֵל בְּתוֹלְדוֹתָם,
כְּמוֹ רַחֲמָנוּת וּגְמִילוּת חֲסָדִים, בָּאוֹת מִמֶּנָּה . . .

וְנֶפֶשׁ הַשֵּׁנִית בְּיִשְׂרָאֵל הִיא חֵלֶק אֱלוֹקַהּ מִמַּעַל מַמָּשׁ.

The first of our souls originates in non-holiness.
This soul resides in our bloodstream to vitalize our
body. . . . It is the source of all our negative character
traits, as well as those positive traits that come
naturally to us, such as compassion and kindness. . . .

A Jew's second soul is an actual part
of the transcendent G-d.

**RABBI SHNEUR
ZALMAN OF LIADI
(ALTER REBBE)
1745–1812**

Chasidic rebbe, Halachic
authority, and founder of
the Chabad movement.
The Alter Rebbe was
born in Liozna, Belarus,
and was among the
principal students of the
Magid of Mezeritch. His
numerous works include
the *Tanya*, an early
classic containing the
fundamentals of Chabad
Chasidism; and *Shulchan
Aruch HaRav*, an
expanded and reworked
code of Jewish law.

KEY TERM 4.1

HEBREW TERM	נֶפֶשׁ הַבַּהֲמִית
TRANSLITERATION	*nefesh habahamit*
LITERAL MEANING	**animal soul**
DEFINITION	the human soul that is self-oriented and can trigger immoral behavior

Rabbi Shais Taub on
the battle between the
two souls:
myjli.com/kabbalah

KEY TERM 4.2

HEBREW TERM	נֶפֶשׁ אֱלֹקִית
TRANSLITERATION	*nefesh Elokit*
LITERAL MEANING	**G-dly soul**
DEFINITION	the human soul that yearns for a closer relationship with G-d and to fulfill its Divine mission

TEXT 2

Power of the Beast

Rabbi Yosef Yitzchak Schneersohn,
Sefer Hasichot 5703, p. 176

"וְרָב תְּבוּאוֹת בְּכֹחַ שׁוֹר" (מִשְׁלֵי יד, ד):
דֶּער כֹּחַ הַמוֹשֵׁךְ פוּן נֶפֶשׁ הַבַּהֲמִית אִיז שְׁטַאְרקֶער
וְוִי דֶּער כֹּחַ הַמוֹשֵׁךְ פוּן נֶפֶשׁ הָאֱלוֹקִית.

"The ox's strength produces abundant crops"
(PROVERBS 14:4). That is to say, the animal soul's
drive is more potent than the G-dly soul's drive.

RABBI YOSEF YITZCHAK SCHNEERSOHN (RAYATZ, FRIERDIKER REBBE, PREVIOUS REBBE) 1880-1950

Chasidic rebbe, prolific writer, and Jewish activist. Rabbi Yosef Yitzchak, the 6th leader of the Chabad movement, actively promoted Jewish religious practice in Soviet Russia and was arrested for these activities. After his release from prison and exile, he settled in Warsaw, Poland, from where he fled Nazi occupation and arrived in New York in 1940. Settling in Brooklyn, Rabbi Schneersohn worked to revitalize American Jewish life. His son-in-law Rabbi Menachem Mendel Schneerson succeeded him as the leader of the Chabad movement.

Initial word panel of the Book of Proverbs in an illuminated manuscript of the fourteenth or fifteenth century. (HUC Library, Cincinnati)

II. LIGHTS AND VESSELS

To appreciate the secret of the animal soul's superior energy, we must first sharpen our understanding of the *sefirot* (explored earlier in Lesson Two). As we will now learn, each *sefirah* consists of two highly dissimilar elements: a Divine "light" that energizes the *sefirah* and a spiritual "vessel" that contains and channels the light.

TEXT 3

Atzilut Unity

Tikunei Zohar 3b

דְּעֶשֶׂר סְפִירוֹת דַּאֲצִילוּת מַלְכָּא בְּהוֹן, אִיהוּ
וְגַרְמֵיהּ חַד בְּהוֹן, אִיהוּ וְחַיּוֹי חַד בְּהוֹן.

The King is present within the ten attributes of *Atzilut*. He and His vessels are one in that world, and He and His lights are one in that world.

TIKUNEI ZOHAR

An appendix to the *Zohar*, the seminal work of kabbalah (Jewish mysticism). *Tikunei Zohar* consists mostly of 70 kabbalistic expositions on the opening verse of the Torah. It was first printed in Mantua in 1558.

HEAVENS GATEWAY
Yoram Raanan, mixed media
collage on canvas, Israel

FIGURE 4.1

Lights and Vessels: Examples

		LIGHT	VESSEL
	BOOK	ideas	words
	MELODY	emotions	musical notes
	BUSINESS	vision	strategy
	RELATIONSHIP	love	action
	RELIGION	beliefs	rituals

Is kabbalah part of the Torah? Find out in "Rabbi Answers 15 Controversial Questions on Judaism": **myjli.com/kabbalah**

TEXT 4A

From Abstract to Defined

Rabbi Shalom Dovber Schneersohn,
Beshaah Shehikdimu 5672:1, p. 582

דְּהָאוֹר מִצַּד עַצְמוֹ הוּא בִּבְחִינַת פְּשִׁיטוּת. וְהַכֵּלִים
עוֹשִׂים תְּמוּנָה בְּהָאוֹר שֶׁהוּא בִּבְחִינַת חָכְמָה וְחֶסֶד כוּ'.

The light itself is in a state of simple
abstractness. The vessel imposes a definition
on the light in the form of particular attributes
of wisdom, kindness, and so forth.

TEXT 4B

Able to Provide

Rabbi Shalom Dovber Schneersohn, ibid., p. 581

דְּהָאוֹר בְּעֶצֶם מַהוּתוֹ הוּא בְּחִינַת אַיִן, וְיֵשׁ בּוֹ טֶבַע
הָעֲלָיָה לִהְיוֹת בִּבְחִינַת אַיִן בְּיוֹתֵר כוּ' . . . שֶׁלְּפְעַל פְּעֻלַּת
הַהִתְהַוּוּת בְּרִיאָה יְצִירָה עֲשִׂיָּה אֵין זֶה בְּעֶרֶךְ הָאוֹר כְּלָל . . .
דְּבִכְדֵי שֶׁיִּהְיֶה הַהִתְהַוּוּת הוּא עַל יְדֵי הַכֵּלִים דַּוְקָא.

The lights of *Atzilut*, by their very nature, are
abstract. They also aspire to return to their
source and to become wholly subsumed within
their sublime origin. . . . Accordingly, they are
far removed from creating the worlds of *Beriah*,
Yetzirah, and *Asiyah*. . . . Rather, the lights must
first install themselves into the vessels of *Atzilut*
in order to energize the Creation of the worlds.

**RABBI SHALOM DOVBER
SCHNEERSOHN
(RASHAB)
1860–1920**

Chasidic rebbe. Rabbi
Shalom Dovber became
the 5th leader of the
Chabad movement
upon the passing
of his father, Rabbi
Shmuel Schneersohn.
He established the
Lubavitch network
of *yeshivot* called
Tomchei Temimim. He
authored many volumes
of Chasidic discourses
and is renowned for
his lucid and thorough
explanations of
kabbalistic concepts.

KEY TERM 4.3

HEBREW TERM	אוֹרוֹת
TRANSLITERATION	*orot*
LITERAL MEANING	**lights**
DEFINITION	abstract Divine energies that are closely tied to their source but are primed to produce Divine attributes

KEY TERM 4.4

HEBREW TERM	כֵּלִים
TRANSLITERATION	*kelim*
LITERAL MEANING	**vessels**
DEFINITION	Divine entities of definition and structure that define the lights and channel their energy to the lower worlds

Opposite Forces

TEXT 4C

Rabbi Shalom Dovber Schneersohn, ibid.

דִּבְעֶצֶם מַהוּתָם הֵם הֲפָכִים זֶה מִזֶּה. דְּהָאוֹר בְּעֶצֶם
מַהוּתוֹ הוּא בְּחִינַת אַיִן, וְיֵשׁ בּוֹ טֶבַע הָעֲלִיָה לִהְיוֹת
בְּחִינַת אַיִן בְּיוֹתֵר כוּ'. וְהַכְּלִי הוּא בִּבְחִינַת יֵשׁ
וּמְצִיאוּת בְּעֶצֶם מַהוּתָה, וְהוּא בְּטֶבַע הַיְרִידָה כוּ'.

Lights and vessels are inherently opposites. The
lights, by their very nature, are abstract. They
also aspire to return to their source and to
become wholly subsumed within their sublime
origin. By contrast, vessels have a defined nature.
They desire to retain their configuration and are
naturally inclined to descend to lower realms.

Loyal to the Source

TEXT 4D

Rabbi Shalom Dovber Schneersohn, ibid., p. 595

וְהוּא הַבִּטוּל אֶל אֲמִתַּת הַכַּוָּנָה הָעֶלְיוֹנָה
דְּלֹא לְתֹהוּ בְּרָאָהּ אֶלָּא לָשֶׁבֶת יְצָרָהּ.

They are entirely submitted to G-d's intent for
Creation, namely, that the universe should become
an orderly habitat and not be left in chaos.

III. THE WORLD OF CHAOS

Appreciating the distinctions between lights and vessels facilitates insight into the mysterious world of *Tohu*.

The Torah begins with a cryptic discussion about a state of chaos, desolation, and darkness. The kabbalists explain that this resulted from a Divine emanation of ten *sefirot* that did not endure. Their lack of endurance was caused by the lights and vessels being unexposed to the ultimate purpose. Consequently, the lights returned to their source, leaving "broken" vessels behind. G-d then generated a second emanation to rectify the failed *sefirot*. However, the remaining vessels of *Tohu* became an integral part of the freshly emanated system.

TEXT 5

Primordial Chaos

Genesis 1:1–3

בְּרֵאשִׁית בָּרָא אֱלֹקִים אֵת הַשָּׁמַיִם וְאֵת הָאָרֶץ. וְהָאָרֶץ הָיְתָה תֹהוּ וָבֹהוּ, וְחֹשֶׁךְ עַל פְּנֵי תְהוֹם, וְרוּחַ אֱלֹקִים מְרַחֶפֶת עַל פְּנֵי הַמָּיִם. וַיֹּאמֶר אֱלֹקִים יְהִי אוֹר וַיְהִי אוֹר.

In the beginning of G-d's Creation of the heavens and the earth, the earth was chaotic and desolate, darkness was on the surface of the deep, and G-d's spirit hovered over the water. G-d said, "Let there be light!"—and there was light.

TEXT 6

The Breaking

Rabbi Chaim Vital, *Likutei Torah*, Genesis 2:2

"וְהָאָרֶץ הָיְתָה תֹהוּ וָבֹהוּ": שֶׁהוּא שְׁבִירַת הַכֵּלִים.

"וְרוּחַ אֱלֹהִים מְרַחֶפֶת עַל פְּנֵי הַמָּיִם": שֶׁהוּא הַחַיּוּת שֶׁלֹּא הָיוּ הַכֵּלִים יְכוֹלִין לְקַבֵּל.

"The earth was chaotic and desolate"—this refers to the breaking of the vessels.

"G-d's spirit hovered over the water"—this refers to the lights that the vessels failed to absorb.

RABBI CHAIM VITAL C. 1542–1620

Lurianic kabbalist. Rabbi Vital was born in Israel, lived in Safed and Jerusalem, and later lived in Damascus. He was authorized by his teacher, Rabbi Yitzchak Luria, the Arizal, to record his teachings. Acting on this mandate, Vital began arranging his master's teachings in written form, and his many works constitute the foundation of the Lurianic school of Jewish mysticism. His most famous work is *Etz Chaim*.

Page from a rare autograph manuscript of Rabbi Chaim Vital's *Etz Hadaat Tov*, c. 1563. Before this manuscript was discovered in a private collection around 2006, only two chapters of the work in the author's own hand were known to have been preserved.

Rabbi Tzvi Freeman on the economics of *Tohu* and *Tikun*: myjli.com/kabbalah

TEXT 7A

Clinging to the Source

Rabbi Shalom Dovber Schneersohn,
Beshaah Shehikdimu 5672:1, pp. 600–601

דְּמָה שֶׁאָנוּ מוֹצְאִים בְּאוֹרוֹת דְּתֹהוּ . . . אוֹרוֹת תַּקִּיפִים וַחֲזָקִים . . .
הַיְנוּ שֶׁהָיָה בָּהֶם בְּחִינַת הַבִּטּוּל בְּתַכְלִית הָאַיִן לִכָּלֵל בִּמְאַצִילָן
בְּתַכְלִית הַהִתְגַּבְּרוּת כוּ'. רַק . . . לֹא הָיָה בָּהֶם בִּכְלָל הֶרְגֵּשׁ
הַכַּוָּנָה הָעֶלְיוֹנָה. וְלָכֵן לֹא הָיָה בָּהֶם הַבִּטּוּל דְּהַנָּחַת עַצְמוּתָן.

The lights of *Tohu* . . . were intense and powerful. . . .
They intensely desired to be nullified and subsumed
within their emanating source. . . . They had no sense
of what their source wanted of them. As a result,
they failed to deviate from their default nature for
the sake of submitting to their greater purpose.

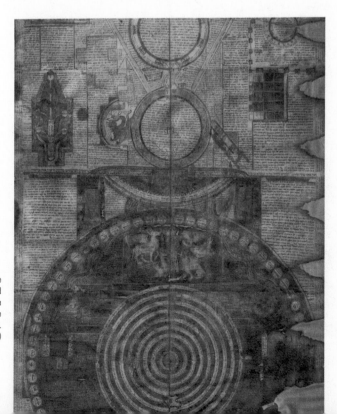

Detail from an intricate
kabbalistic tree created
in the 1500s, possibly in
Italy, featuring extensive
commentary and illumination.
(HUC Library, Cincinnati)

TEXT 7B

Reception Denied

Rabbi Shalom Dovber Schneersohn, ibid.

לֹא הָיָה הַכְּלִי מֵכִיל אֶת הָאוֹר כְּלָל, לִהְיוֹת שֶׁאֵין
בּוֹ בְּחִינַת הַבִּטוּל כָּל כָּךְ לְקַבֵּל גִּלוּי בְּחִינַת אַיִן
כָּל כָּךְ כוּ'. וַהֲרֵי זֶה כִּמְשָׁל הַפְּתִילָה שֶׁאֵינָה
נִשְׂרֶפֶת בָּאֵשׁ, שֶׁהָאֵשׁ מִסְתַּלֵּק מִמֶּנָּה כוּ'.

The vessels could not contain the light
because they were not sufficiently submissive
to pair with the light's intense abstractness.
They acted like a wick resistant to the flame,
resulting in the flame slipping away.

CHAOS AND ORDER
David Friedman, acrylic
on canvas, Israel

KEY TERM 4.5

HEBREW TERM	תֹּהוּ
TRANSLITERATION	*Tohu*
LITERAL MEANING	**chaos**
DEFINITION	a system in which Divine *orot* (lights) and *kelim* (vessels) failed to sense G-d's ultimate purpose for which they had been emanated, resulting in the lights returning to their source and the vessels remaining without the lights

KEY TERM 4.6

HEBREW TERM	שְׁבִירַת הַכֵּלִים
TRANSLITERATION	*shevirat hakelim*
LITERAL MEANING	**breaking of the vessels**
DEFINITION	when the vessels no longer lend definition to the lights but become standalone entities

KEY TERM 4.7

HEBREW TERM	תִּקּוּן
TRANSLITERATION	*Tikun*
LITERAL MEANING	**correction**
DEFINITION	the second emanation of the *sefirot* in which the lights and vessels sense G-d's purpose, causing them to set aside their default natures and allowing them to remain paired with each other

IV. THE PURPOSE OF *TOHU*

G-d orchestrated the breaking of the vessels so that the broken vessels could play a significant role in the chain of devolution. The human's animal soul originates in these broken vessels. And just as *Tikun* rectified *Tohu*, so must the Divine soul—born within *Tikun*—rectify the animal soul, the product of *Tohu*'s collapse.

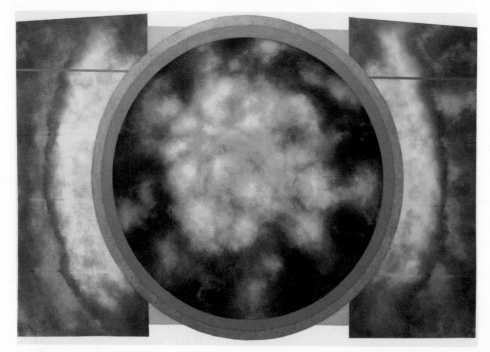

REISHIT (BEGINNING)
Sandy Sokoloff, acrylic on canvas, United States, 2017

TEXT 8

The Chaotic Soul

Rabbi Shneur Zalman of Liadi, *Likutei Torah*, *Matot* 82c–d

הָאָדָם כָּלוּל מִבּ' הַבְּחִינוֹת דְּתֹהוּ וְתִקּוּן.

שֶׁנַּפְשׁוֹ הָאֱלֹקִית נִמְשְׁכָה מִבְּחִינַת שֵׁם מ"ה
דְּתִקּוּן, וְלָכֵן הִיא בְּעֶצֶם בִּבְחִינַת בִּטּוּל.

וְהַנֶּפֶשׁ הַבַּהֲמִית וְהַגּוּף נִמְשְׁכוּ מִשְּׁבִירַת הַכֵּלִים דְּתֹהוּ.

וְאַדְרַבָּה, הַגּוּף וְנֶפֶשׁ הַבַּהֲמִית הֵם בִּבְחִינָה אַחַת לְמַטָּה יוֹתֵר
מִדּוֹמֵם צוֹמֵחַ חַי, כִּי . . . הַבְּהֵמוֹת וְהַחַיּוֹת אֵינָם בִּבְחִינַת נִפְרָד
לְגַמְרֵי, שֶׁהֲרֵי אֵין בָּהֶם עוֹבְרֵי עֲבֵרָה. מַה שֶּׁאֵין כֵּן הָאָדָם מִצַּד גּוּפוֹ
וְנַפְשׁוֹ הַבַּהֲמִית, הוּא בְּחִינַת נִפְרָד יוֹתֵר, שֶׁהֲרֵי יָכוֹל לַעֲבֹר עֲבֵרָה.

We are comprised of both *Tohu* and *Tikun*.

Our G-dly souls are products of *Tikun* and are
therefore inherently subservient to G-d.

Our animal souls and bodies are products
of the broken vessels of *Tohu*.

Although inanimate objects, plants, and animals are also
linked with *Tohu*, the concept of separation from G-d is far
more pronounced in humans. That is because . . . all other
things cannot sin and therefore do not become completely
separated from G-d. Humans, by contrast, on account
of our bodies and animal souls, are capable of sin and,
consequently, of becoming far more separated from G-d.

Rectification

Rabbi Chaim Vital, *Etz Chayim, Shaar Hatzelem* 1:42

כָּל הַמִּצְוֹת אֵינָם אֶלָּא לְצָרֵף וּלְבָרֵר הַצֶּלֶם וְהַחוֹמֶר.

אַךְ הַצּוּרָה אֵינָהּ צְרִיכָה תִּיקּוּן כְּלָל. וְלֹא הוּצְרְכָה לְהִתְלַבֵּשׁ בְּצֶלֶם וְחוֹמֶר, רַק לְהַמְשִׁיךְ בָּהֶם אוֹר לְתַקְּנָם.

וְהָבֵן זֶה מְאֹד. כִּי זֶה טַעַם יְרִידַת הַנְּשָׁמָה בָּעוֹלָם הַזֶּה לְתַקֵּן וּלְבָרֵר.

All of the *mitzvot* are designed exclusively to purify the animal soul and mortal body.

By contrast, the Divine soul does not require rectification. It has no intrinsic need to become installed within an animal soul and mortal body; the sole purpose for doing so is for it to illuminate and rectify them.

Understand this well: the reason the soul descends to this world is to rectify and purify.

TEXT 10

Translation

Rabbi Yosef Yitzchak Schneersohn, *Sefer Hasichot* 5701, p. 54

ר' גֶּרְשׁוֹן בֶּער אִיז גֶעוֶוען אַ טִיפֶער עַמְקָן אִין חֲסִידוּת,
אָבֶּער אַ מְקַצֵּר בְּדִבּוּרוֹ. עֶר פְלֶעגְט פַארְטַייטְשְׁן אַלְץ אוֹיף
אִידִישׁ. אִיךְ הָאבּ אִים גֶעהֶערְט צֵיילְן סְפִירָה, "הַיּוֹם יוֹם אֶחָד
לָעֹמֶר", פְלֶעגְט עֶר זָאגְן: "הַיּוֹם הַיְינְט, הַיְינְט אִיז אֵיין טָאג
לָעֹמֶר". וּכְמוֹ כֵן בִּשְׁאַר הַיָמִים, דְמִצְוָה לִמְנֵי יוֹמֵי וּמִצְוָה
לִמְנֵי שָׁבְעֵי, פְלֶעגְט עֶר אַלְץ פַארְטַייטְשְׁן אִין אִידִישׁ.

עֶר הָאט אַמָאל גֶעפְרֶעגְט בַּא הֶחָסִיד ר' פֶּרֶץ, רַב פוּן
נֶעוֶועל אוּן דֶערְנָאךְ אִין טְשֶׁעֶרְנִיגָאוו, אוֹיבּ עֶר מֶעג
פַארְטַייטְשְׁן דֶעם דַאוְונֶען אוֹיף בְּמָקוֹם שֶׁאָסוּר לְהַפְסִיק.

הָאט אִים הֶחָסִיד ר' פֶּרֶץ גֶעזָאגְט:
צוּלִיב וָואס דַארְפְסטוּ דָאס?

הָאט עֶר אִים גֶעעֶנְטפֶערְט: מַיין נֶפֶשׁ הַבַּהֲמִית
פַארְשְׁטֵייט בֶּעסֶער אוֹיף אִידִישׁ.

Rabbi Gershon Ber of Pahar deeply understood
Chasidic philosophy and was a man of few
words. Nevertheless, he had a habit of translating
everything into Yiddish. I heard him counting
the *omer* on the first night, translating each
Hebrew word into Yiddish as he did so. He
did the same on each subsequent night of the
omer—translating everything into Yiddish.

He once asked Rabbi Peretz, the rabbi of Nevel
and later of Chernigov, whether it was permissible
to translate every prayer into Yiddish—including
portions of the prayers during which one
is forbidden to make an interruption.

Rabbi Peretz asked, "Why would
you want to do that?"

He responded, "My animal soul
understands Yiddish better!"

TEXT 11

In All Ways

Rabbi Menachem Nachum Twersky,
Me'or Einayim, Likutim, Devarim 13:5

וְאָמְנָם אַל יַחְשׁוֹב הָאָדָם שֶׁבִּהְיוֹתוֹ עָסוּק בְּתוֹרָה
וּתְפִלָּה וּמִצְוֹת אָז הוּא קָרוֹב אֶל הַבּוֹרֵא, וְעַל יְדֵי זֶה
יוּכַל לְהַשִּׂיג, וּכְשֶׁעוֹסֵק בִּדְבָרִים אַרְצִיִּים בַּאֲכִילָה
וּשְׁתִיָּה וּשְׁאָר צָרְכֵי הָאָדָם, הוּא פּוֹנֶה מֵאֵת ה'.

כִּי לֹא כֵן הוּא בֶּאֱמֶת. כְּדִכְתִיב (מִשְׁלֵי ג, ו)
"בְּכָל דְּרָכֶיךָ דָעֵהוּ" - כִּי בְּכָל הַדְּבָרִים
מִתְקַשֵּׁר אֶל חַיּוּת הַבּוֹרֵא יִתְבָּרֵךְ שְׁמוֹ.

Do not assume that the only time we are close to
G-d is while we are engaged in Torah study, prayer,
and the performance of a mitzvah, and that we have

**RABBI MENACHEM NACHUM
TWERSKY OF CHERNOBYL
1730-1797**

Born in Garinsk, Ukraine;
Chasidic rebbe, founder
of the Chernobyl dynasty;
student of the Baal Shem
Tov and of the Magid of
Mezeritch. Orphaned
as a child, he was raised
by his uncle Nachum,
who educated him in
the style of the great
Lithuanian *yeshivot*. His
book, *Me'or Einayim*,
comprised of insights on
the weekly Torah portion,
is a Chasidic classic. He
was succeeded by his son,
Rabbi Mordechai Twersky.

turned away from G-d while engaged in earthly endeavors such as eating, drinking, and other needs.

This is not the case, for we are instructed, "Know G-d in all of your ways" (PROVERBS 3:6). We can connect with G-d through every endeavor.

TEXT 12

Great Passion

Rabbi Shneur Zalman of Liadi, *Likutei Torah*, *Devarim*, p. 75c

מֵחֲמַת רֹב הַכֹּחַ שֶׁל הַנֶּפֶשׁ הַבַּהֲמִית, שֶׁשָּׁרְשָׁהּ מְאֹד לְמַעְלָה וְנִשְׁפְּלָה לְמַטָּה, שֶׁלָּכֵן יֵשׁ בָּהּ הַכֹּחַ לִהְיוֹת בִּבְחִינַת רַעַשׁ גָּדוֹל יוֹתֵר מִבְּנֶפֶשׁ אֱלֹקִית מִצַּד עַצְמָהּ.

The animal soul is tremendously powerful due to its lofty source. Consequently, although it has fallen far below, it continues to generate far greater passion than the G-dly soul can produce on its own.

Jacob and Esau—
Tohu and *Tikun*

The sibling rivalry between Jacob and Esau
is one of the book of Genesis's prominent
narratives. The kabbalists discuss the cosmic
roots of this conflict; they identify Jacob
with the orderly world of *Tikun* and Esau
with the chaotic sphere of *Tohu*.
The following are selections
of the biblical account of
the Jacob/Esau rivalry
with commentary culled
from the kabbalistic
perspective.

GENESIS   25:20–27

²⁰ Isaac was forty years old when he married Rebecca, the daughter of Bethuel the Aramean from Padan Aram, and the sister of Laban the Aramean. ²¹ Isaac stood opposite his wife and prayed to G-d because she was barren. G-d accepted Isaac's prayer, and his wife Rebecca conceived. ²² The babies struggled within her, and she said, "If it is so painful, why should I want to be pregnant?" She went to [a prophet to] seek Divine advice. ²³ The response was, "There are two nations in your womb, and two kingdoms will separate from within you. One kingdom will become mightier than the other, and the elder will serve the younger. ❶

²⁴ When the time came for Rebecca to give birth, there were twins in her womb. ²⁵ The first one to emerge was ruddy, and his whole body was like a hairy garment. They named him Esau. ²⁶ Then his brother emerged, with his hand grasping Esau's heel. He was named Jacob. Isaac was sixty years old when Rebecca gave birth to them. ❷ ²⁷ The boys grew up, and Esau became a skilled hunter, a man of the field. Jacob, by contrast, was a wholesome man, who dwelled in tents of study. ❸

KABBALISTIC COMMENTARY

❶ The children Rebecca was carrying, Jacob and Esau, represented two "kingdoms" struggling for dominion; these were *Tikun* (Jacob) and *Tohu* (Esau). Jacob tangled with Esau because he wished to reclaim the powerful lights of *Tohu* that Esau possessed.

❷ If Jacob was destined to become the "firstborn" and the "master," why was he not born first? The answer is that Jacob

and Esau mirrored the cosmic sequence of Creation: the powerful and chaotic world of Tohu emerged first and was followed by the "younger," more harmonious world of *Tikun*.

❸ The wild, untamed Esau personified the *Tohu* world of powerful passions and few constraints. Jacob, the wholesome and studious man, personified the orderly and disciplined world of *Tikun*.

GENESIS   27:1–40

1 When Isaac was old and his eyesight was dimmed, he called for Esau his elder son and he said to him, "My son." "Here I am," Esau answered. 2 Isaac said, "I have grown old now, and I don't know the day of my death. 3 Go now, sharpen your equipment, your sword and your bow, and go out to the field and hunt some game for me." . . .

6 Rebecca told Jacob, "I overheard your father saying to your brother Esau, 7 'Bring me game and prepare me tasty food to eat. I will then bless you, G-d willing, before I die.' 8 Now my son, listen to me carefully and do what I instruct you: 9 Go out now to the flock and bring me two choice young goats, and I will prepare tasty food for your father, as he likes. 10 You will then bring the food to your father to eat, so that he may bless you before he dies." . . .

18 Jacob went to his father and said, "My father!" "Here I am," said Isaac. "Who are you, my son?" 19 Jacob said to his father, "I am Esau your firstborn. I have done as you have told me. Please sit up and eat some of my game, so that you may give me your blessing." . . .

KABBALISTIC COMMENTARY

4 Why did Isaac initially wish to give his blessings to Esau, the wild hunter?

The kabbalists explain that Isaac had intended to split his blessings. He would first provide material blessings to Esau, and then equip Jacob with spiritual blessings.

Isaac viewed Esau's materialism and raw, animalistic passions—the fact that he was a "man of the field" and a "skilled hunter"—in light of their ultimate purpose: these strong passions and plentiful resources should be directed toward powerfully positive and G-dly aims.

Isaac also recognized the nature of his younger son, Jacob. He knew that Jacob embodied the structure and focus of *Tikun*: the vision provided by spirituality, and the selflessness of the G-dly soul.

Consequently, Isaac planned to provide each of the brothers the resources required to fulfill their respective roles: Esau, who embodies the "elder," more powerful *Tohu* world, would receive political power and blessings that unleash material abundance. Jacob, possessing the unique strengths of spirituality and *Tikun*, would receive the spiritual blessings and powers to fulfill his side of this "twinship of worlds."

Isaac believed that *Tohu* and *Tikun* could coexist side by side, each blessed with resources to fully develop their realm in accordance with the Divine plan for creation.

Rebecca realized that this is indeed a beautiful, utopian vision—in a perfect world. Isaac's vision could have played out in a world that is free of evil, or at the very least, in a world in which the

²⁷ Jacob drew near to his father. Isaac kissed Jacob, smelled the fragrance of his garments, and blessed him: "Behold, the fragrance of my son is like the fragrance of a field that G-d has blessed!   ²⁸ May G-d give you of the dew of the heavens, the fatness of the earth, and an abundance of grain and wine.   ²⁹ Nations shall serve you and kingdoms shall bow down to you. You shall be a master over your brothers, and your mother's sons shall bow down to you. Those who curse you shall be cursed, and those who bless you shall be blessed." . . .

³⁴ When Esau heard his father's words, he burst out with a loud and bitter cry and he said to his father, "Bless me too, my father!" . . .

³⁷ Isaac answered Esau, "I have made him a master over you, I gave him all his brothers as servants, and I have sustained him with grain and wine. So, what can I do for you now?"   ³⁸ Esau said to his father, "Do you only have one blessing, my father? Bless me too, my father!" Esau raised his voice and wept.   ³⁹ His father Isaac answered him, "Your dwelling place shall be the fat places of the earth and of the dew of the heaven from above.   ⁴⁰ You shall live by your sword, and you shall serve your brother." ④

KABBALISTIC COMMENTARY

boundaries between good and evil are clearly delineated. However, in our world as it is, this plan could not work.

A material world ruled by materialists will never rise to its true purpose, but will instead descend into unbridled corruption. For unbridled passions (Esau) do not build a G-dly world of holiness and goodness, but a corrupt world of selfishness and violence.

Rebecca saw this sad truth reflected in her own son Esau's personal life. Esau, as the master of his own realm, was descending into a life of evil, murder, rape, and thievery.

Isaac, however, was viewing his sons in terms of their primordial origins, the cosmic "Jacob" and "Esau." He was therefore convinced that Esau

could yet be redeemed through Isaac showering him with blessings directly from his supernal origins (*Tohu*). By contrast, Rebecca better understood the reality on the ground—these blessings would simply empower Esau's corrupt behavior.

Therefore, Rebecca contrived to have Jacob obtain mastery of the material world. She dressed Jacob in Esau's clothes and supplied him with delicious food of the material world—demonstrating that the spiritual Jacob was capable of playing that role. Rebecca understood that the powerful resources of Esau (*Tohu*) can be redeemed only when Jacob (*Tikun*) is made their master.

The two brothers can indeed join forces, but only when "the elder will serve the younger"—when the leadership role is firmly in the hands of Jacob.

SOURCES: Rabbi Shneur Zalman of Liadi; *Torah Or*, Toldot, pp. 20b–25b; Ibid., Vayishlach, 24a–25a.

The Fallen Sparks

When the powerful Divine lights of *Tohu* caused their inadequate vessels to shatter, the shards of those vessels fell down the cosmic system all the way to our material world. Clinging to these shards were 288 sparks of light—the residue of *Tohu*'s powerful Divinity—and these sparks subsequently became embedded within the physical substance of our world. We were entrusted with the mission of elevating these sparks and restoring them to their original sacred source. The following texts chart the history of these fallen sparks and our efforts to elevate them.

Multitude at the Exodus

Rabbi Shneur Zalman of Liadi, *Torah Or*, *Bo* 60c

When the Torah describes the Exodus of the Jewish people from Egypt, it adds that "a great mixed multitude ascended [from Egypt] together with the Children of Israel. . . . All of G-d's legions left the land of Egypt" (Exodus 12:38–41). The Hebrew term for multitude is *rav* (רב), the letters of which are numerically equivalent to 202. The deeper significance of this passage is that when the Jewish people left their first exile, they brought along with them a bounty of 202 fallen sparks from among the total of 288 sparks. Consequently, subsequent to the Exodus, the Jews have been left with only 86 sparks to rectify.

Fallen Sparks at Creation

Rabbi Shneur Zalman of Liadi, *Torah Or*, *Vayeshev* 27c-d

The Torah informs us that at the beginning of Creation, "[The earth was *Tohu* . . .] and G-d's spirit hovered over the surface of the water" (Genesis 1:2). The kabbalists reveal that the Hebrew letters that spell *merachefet* (מרחפת), "hovered," also spell *rapach met* (רפח מת), "288 dead."

This alludes to the shattering of the spiritual vessels of the world of *Tohu*, as a result of the overly powerful Divine light that radiated into that world. 288 shards of the shattered vessels fell ("died") and landed in our world of *Tikun*. They brought along with them residual sparks of the powerful light that they once contained.

The initial number of sparks created by the shattering of *Tohu*'s vessels, at the point they descended into the world of *Atzilut*, stood at 288. However, the sparks did not stop there. They continued their descent through the chain of spiritual worlds until arriving in our physical world of *Asiyah*, by which point they had subdivided into countless smaller sparks. Therefore, when we mention 288 sparks, we refer only to the source sparks. By contrast, the sparks as they exist in our world are divided into an innumerable quantity.

This explains the incredible length of our current exile, the goal of which is the rectification of the 288 sparks; when that is accomplished, our Redemption will arrive. However, we do not have to contend with a mere 288 sparks, for that number refers only to the original sparks. Rather, we are tasked with the rectification of the myriads of subdivided sparks, and it is thus understandable why it is taking us many hundreds of years to complete such an extensive rectification effort.

The Temple's Light and Exile's Fight

Rabbi Shneur Zalman of Liadi, *Likutei Torah*, *Bamidbar* 3d–4a

Fallen sparks may be repaired in one of two ways. To explain these methods, we can lean on the example of mortal kingdoms that seek to establish their dominance. One method of establishing dominance is for a kingdom to build itself up as a superpower, thereby encouraging lesser kingdoms to voluntarily subject themselves to its rule and protection. A second method is to wage war to force other kingdoms to submit to its authority.

The same is true of our spiritual efforts to rectify the fallen sparks. One method is to project significant spiritual light, thereby attracting the fallen sparks to return of their own accord and subsume themselves in the great light we have generated. The advantage of this method is that we do not require direct engagement with the sparks while they are trapped in their fallen state; rather, the sparks are attracted to us on their own. A second method is to wage war, through direct and deep engagement with the material world in which the sparks are trapped. We can battle the temptations it throws at us and eventually conquer the sparks with the strength of spirituality.

During the Temple Era, there was a tremendous revelation of the Divine presence. The Temple that stood in Jerusalem served as a giant magnet to attract fallen sparks. Following the Temple's destruction, the Divine light no longer shines overtly, and in order to rectify the sparks we are required to descend and engage with the sparks and their material trappings on their own level. Throughout the era of exile, the Jewish people have been scattered all over the world, and the deeper purpose of this dispersion is to actively conquer the Divine sparks located in each location.

Mitzvah Rectification

Rabbi Shneur Zalman of Liadi, *Likutei Torah*, *Shelach* 37b–c

The goal of the Torah and its *mitzvot* is to discern between the positive and negative elements in our material world and to actively elevate the positive—the sparks of Divine light that became embedded in materiality as a result of the primordial shattering of the vessels of *Tohu*. Practical *mitzvot* are the ultimate tools for achieving this aim, for they require direct engagement with physical entities.

The *mitzvot* actually come in two forms: prohibitions and active requirements. The prohibitions protect us from engaging in specific acts, and their observance enables us to establish a distinction between the positive and negative elements of the material world. The positive, active *mitzvot* require us to obtain a physical item and use it in the service of G-d—such as wool for *tzitzit*, animal hides for *tefilin*, and the like; we thereby actively rectify the buried sparks and elevate them to their sacred source.

KEY TERMS

1. Nefesh habahamit

The human soul that is self-oriented and can trigger immoral behavior

2. Nefesh Elokit

The human soul that yearns for a closer relationship with G-d and to fulfill its Divine mission

3. Orot

Abstract Divine energies that are closely tied to their source but are primed to produce Divine attributes

4. Kelim

Divine entities of definition and structure that define the lights and channel their energy to the lower worlds

5. Tohu

A system in which Divine *orot* (lights) and *kelim* (vessels) failed to sense G-d's ultimate purpose for which they had been emanated, resulting in the lights returning to their source and the vessels remaining without the lights

6. Shevirat hakelim

When the vessels no longer lend definition to
lights but become standalone entities

7. Tikun

The second emanation of the *sefirot* in which the lights and vessels
sense G-d's purpose, causing them to set aside their default
natures and allowing them to remain paired with each other

KEY POINTS

1   The *sefirot* are composed of two elements—*orot* (lights) and *kelim* (vessels)—that are very dissimilar. The *orot* and *kelim* must operate contrary to their respective natures to merge into the entities known as *sefirot*. They can accomplish this only when they sense G-d's desire that there be a formation of the *sefirot*.

2   The emanation of *Atzilut* was preceded by a prior emanation of ten *sefirot* that resulted in intentional chaos and desolation. The Divine *orot* and *kelim* were made to not sense their purpose, and as a result, they were unwilling to connect with each other. Consequently, the *orot* departed and the *kelim* broke.

3   G-d then emanated a rectified version of the *sefirot* in which the *orot* and *kelim* did sense their purpose. This world was created against the backdrop of the broken vessels of *Tohu*.

4   Subsequently, when worlds that sense themselves to be independent emerged, the surviving vessels of *Tohu* became a force for negativity, devolving into entities that are apathetic and often contrary to G-d.

5   The most dramatic example is the human's animal soul. It is driven by the remnants of the powerful world of *Tohu*, and it, therefore, generates more passion for its selfish interests than the G-dly soul can generate for G-dly pursuits.

6   The Divine soul is born from within the world of *Tikun*—the rectified *sefirot* of *Atzilut*—and, therefore, it excels in its submission to G-d's desire. The ultimate goal for which the entire setup was orchestrated is for our Divine soul to redirect our animal soul's passion to holy and noble pursuits. When we succeed, a broken vessel from *Tohu* is restored and becomes a harmonious vessel for G-dliness.

KEY TAKEAWAYS

1   There is no reason to be overly impressed or intimidated by the strong desires of the animal soul. The fact that it shouts louder does not make it more genuinely you. It's more forceful simply because of its chaotic *Tohu* origin.

2   The performance of a mitzvah and immersive prayer transform the animal soul into a receptacle for G-d's light. Additionally, we can infuse spirituality into those areas of life within the domain of the animal soul. This turns the animal soul into a vessel for a higher purpose, which is an act of *tikun*.

3   If we ignore the G-dly soul, we remain unfulfilled. If we grant it what it desires without linking it to the animal soul, we remain fragmented. Only when we allow the G-dly soul to influence the animal soul and to infuse it with direction do we introduce harmony to our lives.

THE GREAT CONCEALMENT

This lesson analyzes the seemingly impossible transition from absolute Divine infinity to the generation of finite realities with a sense of independence. It tackles the spiritually sensitive topic of tzimtzum—G-d concealing His infinity and identity—and translates this esoteric topic into empowering guidance for exploiting life's dark moments for positive growth through personal replication of the tzimtzum process.

I. THE *TZIMTZUM*

This class delves into the enigmatic concept of *tzimtzum* as discussed in kabbalistic literature. While the Hebrew term is often rendered as "constriction" or "contraction," its true meaning lies in its function as a profound *concealment* of the Divine presence.

To illustrate why *tzimtzum* is indispensable to existence, how it operates, and how it fails to contradict the principle that there is nothing outside of G-dliness, Chasidic philosophy draws upon a parable of a gifted teacher attempting to elucidate a complex topic to a simple student. This pedagogic metaphor serves as an analog to understanding *tzimtzum*.

GENESIS 1:1
Abel Pann (Pfeffermann), pastel on cardboard, Jerusalem, 1957

Before vs. After

Rabbi Chaim Vital, *Etz Chayim, Derush Igulim Veyosher* 1:2

טֶרֶם שֶׁנֶּאֶצְלוּ הַנֶּאֱצָלִים וְנִבְרְאוּ הַנִּבְרָאִים, הָיָה אוֹר
עֶלְיוֹן פָּשׁוּט מְמַלֵּא כָּל הַמְּצִיאוּת . . . וְלֹא הָיָה לוֹ בְּחִינַת
רֹאשׁ וְלֹא בְּחִינַת סוֹף . . . וְהוּא הַנִּקְרָא "אוֹר אֵין סוֹף".

וְכַאֲשֶׁר עָלָה בִּרְצוֹנוֹ הַפָּשׁוּט לִבְרֹא הָעוֹלָמוֹת
וּלְהַאֲצִיל הַנֶּאֱצָלִים . . . הִנֵּה אָז צִמְצֵם עַצְמוֹ
הָאֵין סוֹף . . . וְאָז נִשְׁאַר מָקוֹם פָּנוּי . . .

וְאָז הִמְשִׁיךְ הָאֵין סוֹף קַו אֶחָד יָשָׁר מִן הָאוֹר
הֶעָגֹל שֶׁלּוֹ מִלְמַעְלָה לְמַטָּה וּמִשְׁתַּלְשֵׁל וְיוֹרֵד
תּוֹךְ הֶחָלָל הַהוּא . . . וּבִמְקוֹם הֶחָלָל הַהוּא,
הֶאֱצִיל וּבָרָא וְיָצַר וְעָשָׂה כָּל הָעוֹלָמוֹת כֻּלָּם.

Before *Atzilut* was emanated, and before the creations were created, a simple Divine light filled all of reality. . . . It had no aspect of beginning or end. . . . It is called *or ein sof*, the infinite light.

When it arose in His will to create the worlds and to emanate *Atzilut* . . . He contracted His infinite light . . . and an empty space emerged. . . .

He then projected downward a single straight line from His circular light, devolving into this empty space. . . . Within this empty space, He emanated, created, fashioned, and made all worlds.

RABBI CHAIM VITAL
C. 1542-1620

Lurianic kabbalist. Rabbi Vital was born in Israel, lived in Safed and Jerusalem, and later lived in Damascus. He was authorized by his teacher, Rabbi Yitzchak Luria, the Arizal, to record his teachings. Acting on this mandate, Vital began arranging his master's teachings in written form, and his many works constitute the foundation of the Lurianic school of Jewish mysticism. His most famous work is *Etz Chayim*.

KEY TERM 5.1

HEBREW TERM	צִמְצוּם הָרִאשׁוֹן
TRANSLITERATION	*tzimtzum harishon*
LITERAL MEANING	**the first contraction**
DEFINITION	the first act of concealment, enabling the transition from Divine infinity to the Divine *sefirot*

KEY TERM 5.2

HEBREW TERM	קַו
TRANSLITERATION	*kav*
LITERAL MEANING	**line**
DEFINITION	G-d's manifestation of limited light, from which the *sefirot* arise

DIE WEISSAGUNG DES JESAIA (THE PROPHECY OF ISAIAH)
Ephraim Moses Lilien, engraving, illustration for *Juda: Gesange*, by Börries, Freiherrn von Münchhausen (Berlin: Egon Fleischel & Co., 1900) (Gross Family Collection, Tel Aviv)

TEXT 2A

The First Error

Rabbi Yosef Irgas, *Shomer Emunim* 2:35–40

כָּל הָרוֹצֶה לְהָבִין עִנְיַן הַצִּמְצוּם כִּפְשׁוּטוֹ מַמָּשׁ, הֲרֵי הוּא נוֹפֵל בְּכַמָּה שִׁבּוּשִׁים וּסְתִירוֹת שֶׁל רוֹב עִיקְרֵי הָאֱמוּנָה. וְאַצִּיגֵם לְפָנֶיךָ אֶחָד לְאֶחָד: הָאֶחָד, הִנֵּה כָּתוּב הָדָר הוּא: "וְאֶל מִי תְּדַמְיוּן קֵל, וּמַה דְּמוּת תַּעַרְכוּ לוֹ" (יְשַׁעְיָה מ, יח) . . . וְאִם אַתָּה אוֹמֵר שֶׁהַצִּמְצוּם הוּא כִּפְשׁוּטוֹ, הֲרֵי יֵשׁ בּוֹ דְּיוֹקְנָא וְצִיּוּר, דְּהַיְנוּ צוּרַת עָגוּל סָבִיב, וּמָקוֹם פָּנוּי בְּאֶמְצָעִיתוֹ, וְקַו יָשָׁר בְּתוֹכוֹ.

Those who wish to understand the *tzimtzum* in a literal manner will be led to beliefs that contradict most of the fundamentals of our faith. First of all, we were explicitly taught, "To whom do you compare G-d, and what likeness can you arrange for Him?" (ISAIAH 40:18). . . . If, however, you take the *tzimtzum* literally, you are indeed imposing an image on G-d: an encompassing circle, an empty space, and a straight channel within that space.

RABBI YOSEF IRGAS
1685–1730

Italian kabbalist. Rabbi Irgas was born in Livorno. He established a yeshiva in Pisa and later became the rabbi of Livorno. He authored several works, including *Shomer Emunim,* which is considered an important work of kabbalah.

Rabbi David Aaron on the transformative potential of *tzimtzum* for strengthening families: myjli.com/kabbalah

TEXT 2B

The Second Error

Rabbi Yosef Irgas, ibid.

אִיתָא בְּזֹהַר חָדָשׁ דַּף נ"ה ג' וּבְכַמָּה מְקוֹמוֹת מֵהַזֹּהַר
וְהַתִּקּוּנִים, "דְּלֵית אֲתַר דְּלָאו אִיהוּ תַּמָּן לְעֵלָּא עַד אֵין
סוֹף, וּלְתַתָּא עַד אֵין תַּכְלִית, וּלְכָל סִטְרָא". וְאִם הַצִּמְצוּם
הוּא כִּפְשׁוּטוֹ הֲרֵי יֵשׁ מָקוֹם דְּלָאו אִיהוּ תַּמָּן, שֶׁהֲרֵי
בְּכָל הַמָּקוֹם פָּנוּי לֹא יָרַד רַק קַו אֶחָד דַּק כְּחוּט.

Additionally, the *Zohar* states numerous times (E.G., *ZOHAR CHADASH* 55C) that "there is no place where He is not—from the highest of levels to the lowest of levels and in every direction." If you suggest that the *tzimtzum* is literal, you are insinuating that there is a place devoid of Him, for in this empty space, only a narrow channel descended.

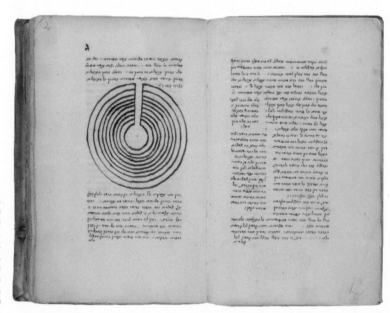

Kabbalistic diagram in a manuscript containing two kabbalistic treatises by Rabbi Yitzchak Luria, produced c. 1715. The manuscript is part of the collection at Ets Haim, the oldest functioning Jewish library in the world, founded in 1616. (Ets Haim Library/Livraria Montezinos, Amsterdam)

TEXT 3

Revelation vs. Concealment

Rabbi Shneur Zalman of Liadi, *Likutei Torah,*
Vayikra, Hosafot 52c

כִּי צִמְצוּם זֶה אֵינוֹ כִּפְשׁוּטוֹ שֶׁנִּסְתַּלֵּק הָאוֹר חַס וְשָׁלוֹם.
כִּי בֶּאֱמֶת "לֵית אֲתַר פָּנוּי מִינֵיהּ" (תִּקּוּנֵי זֹהַר נז). וּכְמוֹ
שֶׁכָּתוּב בְּמִדְרָשׁ רַבָּה (שְׁמוֹת, פָּרָשָׁה ב): לָמָה מִתּוֹךְ
סְנֶה? לְלַמֵּד שֶׁאֵין מָקוֹם פָּנוּי בְּלֹא שְׁכִינָה, אֲפִלּוּ סְנֶה.

אֶלָּא הַפֵּרוּשׁ שֶׁהִסְתַּלְּקוּת זוֹ הַיְנוּ מִבְּחִינַת
הַגִּלּוּי לִהְיוֹת בִּבְחִינַת הֶעְלֵם.

**RABBI SHNEUR
ZALMAN OF LIADI
(ALTER REBBE)
1745–1812**

Chasidic rebbe, Halachic
authority, and founder of
the Chabad movement.
The Alter Rebbe was
born in Liozna, Belarus,
and was among the
principal students of the
Magid of Mezeritch. His
numerous works include
the *Tanya,* an early
classic containing the
fundamentals of Chabad
Chasidism; and *Shulchan
Aruch HaRav,* an
expanded and reworked
code of Jewish law.

The *tzimtzum* does not mean that G-d's infinite
light departed (G-d forbid), for in truth, "there
is no place devoid of Him" (*TIKUNEI ZOHAR*
57). This principle is also expressed in the
Midrash (*SHEMOT RABAH* 2:5): "Why did G-d
choose to reveal Himself to Moses from within
a thornbush? To teach that there is no place
devoid of G-d's presence, even a thornbush."

Instead, in this context, the meaning of *tzimtzum* is
that *or ein sof* went from a state of revelation to one
of concealment without actually departing at all.

KEY TERM 5.3

HEBREW TERM	גִּלּוּי
TRANSLITERATION	*giluy*
LITERAL MEANING	**revelation**
DEFINITION	a reality (usually G-dliness) that is apparent

KEY TERM 5.4

HEBREW TERM	הֶעְלֵם
TRANSLITERATION	*helem*
LITERAL MEANING	**concealment**
DEFINITION	a reality (usually G-dliness) that is present but not apparent

PRECIOUS RAY OF HEAVENLY LIGHT
Loren Hodes, charcoal on archival paper, Johannesburg

TEXT 4A

Teacher and Student

Rabbi Shalom Dovber Schneersohn, *Sefer Hamaamarim* 5670, p. 48

וְיָדוּעַ הַמָּשָׁל בָּזֶה מֵהַשְׁפָּעַת הָרַב לַתַּלְמִיד,
דְּכַאֲשֶׁר הָרַב מַשְׂכִּיל אֶת הַשֵּׂכֶל לְעַצְמוֹ, הֲרֵי
אֵין הַשֵּׂכֶל בְּעֶרֶךְ שֵׂכֶל הַמְקַבֵּל כְּלָל.

וַהֲגַם שֶׁיֵּשׁ בּוֹ מָה שֶׁשַּׁיָּךְ אֶל הַמְקַבֵּל, וְהוּא בְּחִינַת חִיצוֹנִיּוּת
הַשֵּׂכֶל כו', אָמְנָם, גַּם בְּחִיצוֹנִיּוּת הַשֵּׂכֶל מֵאִיר אוֹר רַב, שֶׁגַּם
זֶה אֵינוֹ בְּעֶרֶךְ כְּלָל אֶל הַמְקַבֵּל. וְהָעִקָּר הוּא שֶׁאֵינוֹ נִכָּר
חִיצוֹנִיּוּת הַשֵּׂכֶל מִן הַפְּנִימִיּוּת. וְכַאֲשֶׁר יִרְצֶה הָרַב לְהַשְׁפִּיעַ
הַשֵּׂכֶל אֶל הַתַּלְמִיד, יַשְׁפִּיעַ מִמֵּילָא בְּחִינַת פְּנִימִיּוּת
הַשֵּׂכֶל, לְפִי שֶׁאֵין הַבְדָּלָה בֵּינֵיהֶם בְּעֶצֶם הַמַּשְׁפִּיעַ כו'.

כִּי אִם, כַּאֲשֶׁר הָרַב מְצַמְצֵם וּמַעֲלִים אוֹר שִׂכְלוֹ, אָז
נִבְדָּל אֵצֶל הַמַּשְׁפִּיעַ בְּחִינַת חִיצוֹנִיּוּת אוֹר הַשֵּׂכֶל
הַשַּׁיָּךְ אֶל הַמְקַבֵּל, וְנַעֲשָׂה נִכָּר בִּפְנֵי עַצְמוֹ. וְגַם
נִתְעַלֵּם מִמֶּנּוּ הָאוֹר הָרַב, שֶׁאֵינוֹ מֵאִיר בּוֹ כָּל כָּךְ.

RABBI SHALOM DOVBER
SCHNEERSOHN
(RASHAB)
1860–1920

Chasidic rebbe. Rabbi
Shalom Dovber became
the 5th leader of the
Chabad movement
upon the passing
of his father, Rabbi
Shmuel Schneersohn.
He established the
Lubavitch network
of *yeshivot* called
Tomchei Temimim. He
authored many volumes
of Chasidic discourses
and is renowned for
his lucid and thorough
explanations of
kabbalistic concepts.

Consider the example of a teacher imparting
information to students: the profound concept
the teacher understands is incompatible
with the students' mental abilities.

True, the profound concept contains less significant
elements that *are* compatible with the students'
minds. Nevertheless, in the teacher's mind, these
elements are filled with the profundity of the overall
concept, and they, therefore, remain too deep to

deliver to the students. The main obstacle here is that there is no distinction in the teacher's mind between the core of the concept and its less significant elements. Consequently, if the teacher proceeds to transmit this knowledge to the students, the teacher will deliver the full profundity along with the less significant components. The students will understand none of it.

The solution is for the teacher to conceal the entire concept, mentally pushing the whole idea aside to approach it anew. The teacher can now distinguish between the idea's core and the more superficial elements. The teacher can then deliver the transmittable details without flooding these elements with the overwhelming complexity of the core concept.

A teacher instructs three seated pupils in an initial word panel of the *Sassoon Haggadah*, a manuscript of the fourteenth century created in Spain or Southern France, containing various illustrations on the text of the Haggadah and the holiday customs. (Israel Museum, Jerusalem)

FIGURE 5.1

The Parable of Teacher and Student

PARABLE	ANALOG
The genius has an abstract and complex idea whose core is not relatable to ordinary students.	A simple Divine light filled all of reality. It was infinite, leaving no room for a finite expression.
This abstract idea contains a minor implication that is relatable to ordinary students.	G-d's infinity includes the power to be finite.
By default, this minor implication is part of the core idea and remains too difficult for ordinary students.	By default, this power to be finite is indistinguishable within the larger context of the revealed Divine infinity.
The abstract idea is removed from the genius's conscious thinking.	G-d concealed His infinite light.
The minor implication becomes discoverable and can be shared with the students.	G-d projected His finite power into this space of concealment.

TEXT 4B

The Analog

Rabbi Shalom Dovber Schneersohn, ibid.

וְהַדְּגְמָא מִזֶּה יוּבַן לְמַעְלָה:

דְּקוֹדֶם הַצִּמְצוּם הָיָה בִּבְחִינַת חִיצוֹנִיּוּת הָאוֹר גַּם כֵּן גִּלּוּי אוֹר רַב בִּבְחִינַת בְּלִי גְבוּל מַמָּשׁ כוּ', לְפִי שֶׁכְּלָלוּת הָאוֹר הוּא בִּבְחִינַת גִּלּוּי הָעֶצֶם וּמֵעֵין הָעֶצֶם דְּאֵין סוֹף עַצְמוֹ יִתְבָּרֵךְ . . .

וְעַל יְדֵי הַצִּמְצוּם נַעֲשָׂה הַהַבְדָּלָה בֵּינֵיהֶם.

The above parable allows us to appreciate
the concept of *tzimtzum*:

Before the *tzimtzum*, G-d's ability to express finite
Divinity was part and parcel of His prevailing
infinity, because the entire theme of *or ein sof*
before the *tzimtzum* is to reflect the infinite
capacity of G-d's essence and to resemble it. . . .

The *tzimtzum* enabled the separation
of these two powers of expression.

II. THE CONCEALING CURTAIN

The above-described concealment sets the stage for several subsequent transitions, including from *Atzilut*, a state whereby Divinity is manifested through ten *sefirot*, to the emergence of egocentric identity. This latter transformation is produced through a phenomenon that kabbalah labels a "dividing curtain."

TEXT 5

Two Illustrations

Rabbi Menachem Mendel of Lubavitch, *Derech Mitzvotecha, Shoresh Mitzvat Hatefilah*, ch. 24

שֶׁכָּתוּב בְּעֵץ חַיִּים שֶׁבֵּין אֲצִילוּת לַבְּרִיאָה יֵשׁ מָסָךְ
וּפַרְגּוֹד. כִּי הַמָּסָךְ הוּא הַלְּבוּשׁ הַמַּעֲלִים וּמַסְתִּיר כְּדֵי
שֶׁעַל יְדֵי זֶה יִהְיֶה בְּחִינַת יֵשׁ וְדָבָר נִפְרָד . . . וְהוּא
כִּמְשָׁל הַמָּסָךְ גַּשְׁמִי שֶׁמַּסְתִּיר הָאוֹר, וְאַף עַל פִּי
שֶׁהָאוֹר בּוֹקֵעַ הַמָּסָךְ, הוּא רַק אוֹר שֶׁל תּוֹלָדָה . . .

וּבִמְקוֹם אַחֵר מְבֹאָר גַּם כֵּן עִנְיַן הַפַּרְסָא . . . כִּמְשָׁל
אוֹתִיּוֹת הַמָּשָׁל שֶׁמַּסְתִּירִים וּמַעֲלִימִים לְגַמְרֵי עֹמֶק
הַנִּמְשָׁל. וּכְעִנְיָן מִשְׁלֵי שְׁלֹמֹה, שֶׁהִלְבִּישׁ רָזִין עִלָּאִין
בִּמְשָׁלִים מֵעִנְיָנִים גַּשְׁמִיִּים, הֲרֵי אוֹתִיּוֹת אֵלּוּ מַעֲלִימִים
וּמַסְתִּירִים אוֹר הַשֵּׂכֶל, וּמַה שֶּׁמַּשִּׂיג מִזֶּה אֵיזוֹ
הֶאָרָה, אֵין עֶרֹךְ כְּלָל לְגַבֵּי עֶצֶם הָרָזִין עִלָּאִין.

In his *Etz Chayim*, Rabbi Chaim Vital discusses a "dividing curtain" between *Atzilut* and *Beriah*. This curtain is the concealing garment that

RABBI MENACHEM MENDEL OF LUBAVITCH (*TZEMACH TZEDEK*) 1789–1866

Chasidic rebbe and noted author. The *Tzemach Tzedek* was the 3rd leader of the Chabad Chasidic movement and a noted authority on Jewish law. His numerous works include Halachic responsa, Chasidic discourses, and kabbalistic writings. Active in the communal affairs of Russian Jewry, he worked to alleviate the plight of the cantonists, Jewish children kidnapped to serve in the czar's army. He passed away in Lubavitch, leaving 7 sons and 2 daughters.

enables the creation of entities with a sense of independence. . . . It is comparable to a physical screen that conceals light: although some light succeeds in piercing the barrier, that light is merely a secondary product of the original light. . . .

Other sources explain further that this *parsa* (curtain) . . . is akin to a parable's words, which entirely conceal the profound message of the analog. For example, consider the parables cited by King Solomon: he vested supernal secrets in mundane ideas that hide the mystical truths. One who reads these parables gains a mere glimmer that is incomparable to the core supernal secrets.

KEY TERM 5.5

HEBREW TERM	פַּרְסָא
TRANSLITERATION	*parsa*
LITERAL MEANING	**curtain**
DEFINITION	the concealment after the world of *Atzilut* that enables a sense of independence within the lower worlds of *Beriah*, *Yetzirah*, and *Asiyah*

III. MAKING PLACE FOR OTHERS

The concept of *tzimtzum* bears significant practical implications for our lives. One such implication, as explored in Chasidic philosophy, is that it is essential to harness our power for *tzimtzum* to create space for others and G-d.

TEXT 6A

Narcissism

Rabbi Yosef Yitzchak Schneersohn,
Sefer Hamaamarim Kuntresim 1, p. 19a

דְּמִי שֶׁהוּא אוֹהֵב אֶת עַצְמוֹ וְיָקָר בְּעֵינֵי עַצְמוֹ, הֲרֵי תָּמִיד
טָרוּד רַק בְּעַצְמוֹ, עֶר אִיז פַאַרְנוּמֶען מִיט זִיךְ וּבְתַאֲוֹותָיו
וּרְצוֹנוֹתָיו, וְעַל הָאֱלֹוקוּת הוּא שׁוֹכֵחַ לְגַמְרֵי, חַס וְשָׁלוֹם.

וְכֵן כַּאֲשֶׁר הוּא אוֹהֵב אֶת עַצְמוֹ, אָז אֵין לוֹ מָקוֹם
לְאַהֲבַת זוּלָתוֹ, וְאַדְרַבָּה, הָאַהֲבַת עַצְמוֹ גּוֹרֵם פֵּרוּד
לְבָבוֹת, דְּאֵינוֹ יָכוֹל לִסְבֹּל אֶת זוּלָתוֹ, וְחוֹשֵׁב דְּכָל מָה
שֶׁהַזּוּלַת אוֹמֵר אוֹ עוֹשֶׂה הוּא בִּשְׁבִיל לְנֶגֶד אֵלָיו.

וְכַיָּדוּעַ בְּאֶחָד שֶׁבָּא לִכְבוֹד קְדֻשַּׁת אֲדוֹנִי אָבִי זְקֵנִי
מוֹרִי וְרַבִּי, הָרַב הַקָּדוֹשׁ אַדְמוֹ"ר צֶמַח צֶדֶק נִשְׁמָתוֹ
עֵדֶן עַל יְחִידוּת, (בַּר דַּעַת גָּדוֹל בְּהַשְׂכָּלָה) וְאָמַר לוֹ:

רַבִּי, מִי טְרַעט אוֹיף מִיר אִין בֵּית מִדְרָשׁ. וָואס אִיךְ
זָאג גִיפֶעלְט זֵיי נִיט, אוּן זֵיי פִירִין זֶער נִיט כָּרָאוּי
לְהִתְנַהֵג עִמִּי, וְעוֹשִׂים כִּמְעַט לְהֵפֶךְ מִדַּעְתִּי.

RABBI YOSEF YITZCHAK SCHNEERSOHN (RAYATZ, FRIERDIKER REBBE, PREVIOUS REBBE) 1880–1950

Chasidic rebbe, prolific writer, and Jewish activist. Rabbi Yosef Yitzchak, the 6th leader of the Chabad movement, actively promoted Jewish religious practice in Soviet Russia and was arrested for these activities. After his release from prison and exile, he settled in Warsaw, Poland, from where he fled Nazi occupation and arrived in New York in 1940. Settling in Brooklyn, Rabbi Schneersohn worked to revitalize American Jewish life. His son-in-law Rabbi Menachem Mendel Schneerson succeeded him as the leader of the Chabad movement.

Rabbi Manis Friedman
on what it means to
be a *mensch*:
myjli.com/kabbalah

וְהֵשִׁיב לוֹ כְּבוֹד קְדֻשַּׁת אֲדוֹנִי אָבִי זְקֵנִי מוֹרִי וְרַבִּי:
דּוּ בִּיסְט זֶער מִתְפַּשֵּׁט אִיבֶּער דֶעם גַאנְצִין בֵּית
מִדְרָשׁ, אִיז וְואוּ יֶעוֶער טְרֶעט אִיז אַלְץ אוֹיף דִיר.

Those who are self-obsessed and narcissistic become engrossed in their desires and wishes and completely forget about G-d.

Similarly, their self-obsession precludes loving others. Their self-love generates divisiveness because it doesn't allow them to tolerate others. They think that whatever someone else says or does is directed against them.

There was an incident that well illustrates this point: A fellow who happened to be a tremendous scholar and well versed in Torah once had a private audience (*yechidut*) with my great-grandfather, Rabbi Menachem Mendel of Lubavitch.

"Rebbe!" he complained, "The others are stepping all over me in the study hall! They do not appreciate what I have to say, they do not behave properly toward me, and they do almost the exact opposite of my opinion!"

The holy Rebbe replied, "Your ego expands throughout the entire study hall—wherever anyone steps, it's bound to be on you!"

TEXT 6B

Instructive Detail

The Rebbe, Rabbi Menachem Mendel Schneerson,
Torat Menachem: Sefer Hamaamarim Melukat 2, p. 6

וְיֵשׁ לוֹמַר, דְּזֶה שֶׁמֵּבִיא בְּהַמַאֲמָר שֶׁהַטַּעֲנָה שֶׁלּוֹ הָיְתָה
שֶׁדּוֹרְסִים עָלָיו **בְּבֵית מִדְרָשׁ**, דְּהַגַּם שֶׁבֵּית מִדְרָשׁ הוּא
מִקְדָּשׁ מְעַט, דְּהַשְׁרָאַת הַשְׁכִינָה שֶׁבְּמִקְדָּשׁ מְעַט
הִיא מֵעֵין הַשְׁרָאַת הַשְׁכִינָה שֶׁבְּבֵית הַמִּקְדָּשׁ, מִכָּל
מָקוֹם, גַּם שָׁם הָיְתָה הִתְפַּשְׁטוּת הַיֵּשׁוּת שֶׁלּוֹ . . .

וְלָכֵן מֵבִיא בְּהַמַאֲמָר פְּרָטִים הַנִּזְכָּרִים לְעֵיל דְּהַסִפּוּר,
בִּכְדֵי לְהַדְגִּישׁ שֶׁעַל יְדֵי הַשְׁפָּלָה לְבַד בְּלִי עֲבוֹדָה
אֶפְשָׁר לִהְיוֹת הִתְפַּשְׁטוּת הַיֵּשׁוּת גַּם בְּמִקְדָּשׁ
מְעַט . . . דְּמִזֶּה מוּבָן הַהֶכְרַח בְּעִנְיַן הָעֲבוֹדָה.

You will notice that the above story mentions that
the individual felt like people were stepping all over
him in *the study hall*. This is a highly instructive
detail because a hall designated for Torah study is
considered a miniature Holy Temple. Divinity is
more acutely present and perceptible in a place
filled with Torah study, similar to the presence
of Divinity within the Holy Temple. Despite
that, this individual succeeded in maintaining
a bloated ego even in this holy place. . . .

This detail of the story was included to underscore
that knowledge alone, without working on

**RABBI MENACHEM
MENDEL SCHNEERSON
1902-1994**

The towering Jewish
leader of the 20th
century, known as "the
Lubavitcher Rebbe," or
simply as "the Rebbe."
Born in southern
Ukraine, the Rebbe
escaped Nazi-occupied
Europe, arriving in
the U.S. in June 1941.
The Rebbe inspired
and guided the revival
of traditional Judaism
after the European
devastation, impacting
virtually every Jewish
community the world
over. The Rebbe often
emphasized that the
performance of just
one additional good
deed could usher in
the era of Mashiach.
The Rebbe's scholarly
talks and writings have
been printed in more
than 200 volumes.

self-refinement, is woefully insufficient—so much so that one's ego will infiltrate even a miniature sanctuary. . . . This proves the indispensability of *avodah*—the internal work of character refinement.

KEY TERM 5.6

HEBREW TERM	עֲבוֹדָה
TRANSLITERATION	*avodah*
LITERAL MEANING	**toil**
DEFINITION	working to enhance one's character and to become more aware of G-d, often facilitated by immersive prayer

REBBE IN FOREST (DETAIL)
Zalman Kleinman

TEXT 7

Reciprocation

Rabbi Shneur Zalman of Liadi, *Tanya*, *Likutei Amarim*, ch. 48

וְהִנֵּה כַּמַּיִם הַפָּנִים לַפָּנִים.

כְּמוֹ שֶׁהַקָּדוֹשׁ בָּרוּךְ הוּא כִּבְיָכוֹל הִנִּיחַ וְסִלֵּק לְצַד
אֶחָד, דֶּרֶךְ מָשָׁל, אֶת אוֹרוֹ הַגָּדוֹל הַבִּלְתִּי תַּכְלִית, וּגְנָזוֹ
וְהִסְתִּירוֹ . . . וְהַכֹּל בִּשְׁבִיל אַהֲבַת הָאָדָם הַתַּחְתּוֹן,
לְהַעֲלוֹתוֹ לַה', כִּי אַהֲבָה דּוֹחֶקֶת הַבָּשָׂר . . .

כַּאֲשֶׁר יָשִׂים הַמַּשְׂכִּיל אֵלֶּה הַדְּבָרִים אֶל עִמְקָא דְלִבָּא
וּמֹחָא, אֲזַי מִמֵּילָא כַּמַּיִם הַפָּנִים לַפָּנִים תִּתְלַהֵט
נַפְשׁוֹ וְתִתְלַבֵּשׁ בְּרוּחַ נְדִיבָה, לְהִתְנַדֵּב לְהַנִּיחַ וְלַעֲזֹב
כֹּל אֲשֶׁר לוֹ מִנֶּגֶד, וְרַק לְדָבְקָה בּוֹ יִתְבָּרֵךְ.

Reciprocation is a natural response.

G-d set aside, figuratively speaking, His great
infinite light and concealed it. . . . He did this due
to His love for us, to raise us up to Him, for love
induces one to restrict oneself for another. . . .

When we reflect on this deeply, our
souls will spontaneously be ignited to
reciprocate. We will feel motivated to forsake
everything in order to cleave to Him.

IV. LET THERE BE LIGHT!

A further valuable lesson imparted by the concept of *tzimtzum* can be derived from the pattern of darkness preceding light. This sequence corresponds with the Halachic day, wherein night precedes day to constitute one whole day. This pattern embodies a significant truth for life: the key to success frequently hides behind hardships and setbacks.

TEXT 8A

Root of the Matter

Rabbi Dovber of Lubavitch, *Imrei Binah, Pesach Hashaar*, ch. 9

"וַיְהִי עֶרֶב וַיְהִי בֹקֶר יוֹם אֶחָד" (בְּרֵאשִׁית א, ה): הֲרֵי אֵין יוֹם אִם לֹא שֶׁקָּדַם הָעֶרֶב לַבֹּקֶר דַּוְקָא. וְיֵשׁ לְהָבִין לָמָה לֹא נִקְרָא יוֹם רַק כְּשֶׁכָּלוּל מֵעֶרֶב וּבֹקֶר, וְלֹא כְּשֶׁכֻּלּוֹ יוֹם אוֹ כֻּלּוֹ לַיְלָה, וְדַוְקָא לַיְלָה קֹדֶם לְיוֹם? ...

שֹׁרֶשׁ הָעִנְיָן הוּא כַּיָּדוּעַ שֶׁבְּשֹׁרֶשׁ וּמְקוֹר הַבְּרִיאָה מֵאַיִן לְיֵשׁ הָיָה גַּם כֵּן עַל יְדֵי עֶרֶב וָבֹקֶר - חֹשֶׁךְ קוֹדֵם לְאוֹר ... צִמְצוּם וְדִין תְּחִלָּה וְקוֹדֵם לְחֶסֶד זֶה ... שֶׁאָז נִמְשַׁךְ בְּחִינַת חִבּוּר שְׁתֵּי אֵלֶּה בְּכָל הָעוֹלָמוֹת עַד עוֹלָם הַזֶּה הַשָּׁפֵל ... שֶׁהַלַּיְלָה קוֹדֵם לְיוֹם בָּעוֹלָם הַזֶּה הַגַּשְׁמִי.

"There was evening and there was morning—one day" (GENESIS 1:5). This verse informs us that there is no day without a night that precedes it. Why must it be so? Why does a day not exclusively consist of daylight hours—or perhaps just the night hours? Why must it include both evening and morning? And why must night precede the day? ...

RABBI DOVBER OF LUBAVITCH (MITELER REBBE) 1773-1827

Rabbi Dovber was the eldest son of and successor to Rabbi Shneur Zalman of Liadi and greatly expanded upon and developed his father's groundbreaking teachings. He was the 1st Chabad rebbe to live in the village of Lubavitch. Dedicated to the welfare of Russian Jewry, at that time confined to the Pale of Settlement, he established Jewish agricultural colonies. His most notable works on Chasidic thought include *Shaar Hayichud, Torat Chayim,* and *Imrei Binah.*

The root of the matter is that at the source of Creation, there was evening before morning— that is, darkness preceded light.... For the *tzimtzum* preceded the sharing of G-d's kindness.... This darkness-light combination extends to all the worlds . . . including our world, where night precedes day.

TEXT 8B

In Everyday Life

Rabbi Dovber of Lubavitch, ibid., ch. 10

וְאָנוּ רוֹאִים דָּבָר זֶה גַּם בְּמִלֵּי דְעָלְמָא, שֶׁלֹּא יָבֹא אָדָם לְאֵיזֶה עֲלִיָּה - אִם בְּמָמוֹן, אוֹ בִּגְדֻלָּה, אוֹ בְּבָנִים, אוֹ שְׁאַר הַצְלָחַת דְּבַר מָה, כְּמוֹ גַם בְּחָכְמָה בְּלִמּוּדוֹ וּכְהַאי גַּוְנָא - בִּלְתִּי שֶׁיִּקְדַּם לוֹ תְּחִלָּה הַפּוּכוֹ דַּוְקָא, שֶׁהוּא הַשִּׁפְלוּת וְהַצַּעַר וְהַנֶּזֶק וּכְהַאי גַּוְנָא . . . כִּי גַם הָעוֹסֵק בְּלִמּוּדוֹ לֹא בְּנָקֵל יָבֹא לִשְׁלֵמוּת לִמּוּדוֹ כִּי אִם אַחֲרֵי הַיְגִיעָה הָרַבָּה וְהַצַּעַר בְּנַפְשׁוֹ, עַד הֱיוֹתוֹ מְרֻחָק כְּמוֹ יֵאוּשׁ בְּנַפְשׁוֹ לַעֲמֹד עַל דְּבַר הַחָכְמָה . . . וְאֵין אָדָם עוֹמֵד עַל דְּבַר הֲלָכָה אֶלָּא אִם כֵּן נִכְשַׁל בָּהּ תְּחִלָּה (גִּטִּין מג, א) כוּ' . . .

וּכְמוֹ שֶׁאָנוּ רוֹאִים גַּם בְּעֵסֶק פַּרְנָסָה, שֶׁלֹּא יַצְלִיחַ שׁוּם אָדָם בְּלִי יְגִיעַת הַנֶּפֶשׁ וְצַעַר רַב בַּתְּחִלָּה עַד שֶׁיֹּאמַר נוֹאָשׁ בְּנַפְשׁוֹ כוּ', אָז יִמְצָא רֶוַח וּבְרָכָה רַבָּה . . . וְכָךְ הוּא בְּגוּף הָעֵסֶק, שֶׁצָּרִיךְ לְהוֹצִיא הוֹצָאוֹת וּלְהַפְקִיר מָמוֹן רַב, וְגַם וַדַּאי יִהְיוּ כַּמָּה מוֹנְעִים וּמַפְסִידִים מֵהָעֵסֶק עַד שֶׁבַּסּוֹף יִמְצָא הָרֶוַח . . .

Mrs. Chavi Epstein on the purpose behind inner struggles: **myjli.com/kabbalah**

וְכָל זֶה מִפְּנֵי שֶׁכָּךְ הִיא הַמִּדָּה בְּכָל שֶׁפַע וְאוֹר הַנִּמְשָׁךְ בָּעוֹלָמוֹת
הָעֶלְיוֹנִים עַד גַּם לְמַטָּה מַטָּה . . . דְּאֵין אוֹר בְּלֹא חֹשֶׁךְ הַפּוּכוֹ
שֶׁקָּדַם לוֹ . . . שֶׁ"לְפוּם צַעֲרָא אַגְרָא" (אָבוֹת ה, כא).

We observe the same pattern reflected in the affairs
of the world, whereby individuals do not achieve
growth—in wealth, leadership, building a family,
study, or any other accomplishment—without
first experiencing humiliation, pain, loss, and the
like. . . . For example, individuals engaged in study
will not arrive at a complete understanding of the
subject without much toil and stress, feeling distant
from understanding and tempted to despair from
mastering the subject. . . . Indeed, the Talmud states
(GITIN 43A), "One does not understand statements
of Torah without first being mistaken." . . .

We observe the same in earning a livelihood, whereby
we succeed only after putting forth great effort and
enduring much pain, even feeling despair. Only
thereafter do we find profit and great blessing. . . .

This is the way that G-d's blessings flow in the
upper worlds and travel down to the lowest
realm. . . . There is no light without the darkness
that precedes it. . . . As it is stated, "According
to the pain is the reward" (AVOT 5:21).

TEXT 9

No Deal!

Rabbi Yosef Yitzchak Schneersohn,
cited in *Sefer Hatoldot* 3, p. 236

אִם מִי שֶׁהוּא יַצִּיעַ לִמְכֹּר לִי בְּמִילְיַרְד רֶגַע
אֶחָד שֶׁל יִסּוּרִים בֶּעָתִיד - לֹא אֶקְנֶה.

וְאִם מִי שֶׁהוּא יִרְצֶה לִקְנוֹת אֶצְלוֹ עֲבוּר
מִילְיַארְד רֶגַע מִיִסּוּרַי בֶּעָבָר - לֹא אֶמְכֹּר.

If someone would offer to sell me a single
moment of additional suffering for a
billion dollars, I would not buy.

If someone would offer to purchase a
single moment of my past suffering for
a billion dollars, I would not sell.

At the Beginning

The *Zohar* opens with a cryptic description of the process of Divine revelation. We present here the terse, original text of the *Zohar*, followed by two further texts that explain foundational kabbalistic concepts before we return to review the *Zohar's* teaching in a new light.

Zohar 1:15a

At the beginning of the manifestation of the King's will, the lamp of darkness engraved engravings in the supernal purity.

It emanated from the most concealed of all concealed things, from the secret of endlessness.

A formless vapor was inserted into a circle that was neither white nor black nor red nor green, nor any color at all.

When He began its measurements, He created bright colors to shine forth. From within the center of the lamp a fountain spouted, from which the colors down below were painted.

◄

The excerpted passage as it appears in the first edition of the *Zohar*, Mantua, 1558. (National Library of Israel)

Revelation of Concealment

Rabbi Shalom Dovber Schneersohn,
Sefer Hamaamarim 5657, pp. 48–51

The act of *tzimtzum* is simultaneously an act of concealment and revelation.

To appreciate this phenomenon, consider the case of a teacher and a student. The teacher wishes to impart a truly profound concept to the student, but the student's intellectual capacities are insufficiently developed to be able to grasp the concept in its entirety. Revealing the full depth and breadth of the concept to the student would simply cause confusion, and the student would understand nothing.

In order to effectively communicate the concept, the teacher must conceal the full depth and breadth of their own understanding of the concept. The teacher must reveal to the student only an external glimmer of the idea in a concentrated form that is appropriate for the student's level.

Moreover, even the point that the teacher reveals must be communicated in a concealed form, through the use of an analogy. The analogy is distinct from the analogue—it actually conceals the analogue. At the same time, the analogy serves as a medium that allows the student to grasp and comprehend the analogue.

This process cannot be considered true concealment. After all, it is specifically as a result of this process of *tzimtzum* that the student will be able to grasp the profound idea. In fact, if intellectual *tzimtzum* is not employed in this case, nothing at all will be revealed to the student.

Moreover, the highly condensed teaching that the teacher successfully communicates to the student actually contains the full depth and breadth of the teacher's own understanding of the concept, albeit in a concealed manner. As time passes and the student's intellectual capacity develops further, the teacher will unveil more and more of the profundity contained in the condensed teaching. Eventually, the student will achieve the same full understanding of the concept that the teacher personally enjoyed.

In this way, the process of *tzimtzum* used by the teacher does not truly really conceal. On the contrary, its entire objective is to reveal. Through the *tzimtzum*, the teacher communicates the full depth and breadth of their wisdom to a lower level. This process allows the teacher's light to shine and be revealed to an intellectual platform that on its own cannot obtain the revelation of such profound concepts.

The same is true of G-d's *tzimtzum* of His Infinite Light: It is not merely an act of concealment because, ultimately, it is an act of revelation.

Colorless Colors

Rabbi Moshe Cordovero, *Pardes Rimonim* 4:4

At the very beginning, G-d emanated ten *sefirot*. . . . We can provide an appropriate analogy that will allow the mind of the wise thinker to comprehend this matter:

The analogy is of water that is distributed between several containers. These containers are of different colors: one is white, another is red, another is green, and so on with the rest of them. The water that is channeled into these containers is colorless. Nevertheless, when the water is viewed through the walls of these colored containers, the water will appear in the color of the respective vessels—as if it has somehow changed and adopted the containers' coloring. In truth, the water did not acquire any new color. Rather, the colored vessels have imposed their colors on the water—and even this imposition is only true from the perspective of those who view it externally through the containers. For the water itself is unchanged.

So it is with the *sefirot*. The containers in the analogy correspond to the Divine attributes that we refer to as *chesed* (kindness), *gevurah* (strength), *tiferet* (beauty), and so on. Each of these is colored by a particular function, so that it is—so to speak—white, red, or green, and so on. However, the essence of the ten Divine energies that flows into the ten *sefirot* is the light of the Emanator, and that light is like the colorless water—it transcends all variations and specific functions. In other words, the variations of each of the ten *sefirot*'s influence on the world is the result of distinctions in the functioning of their containers.

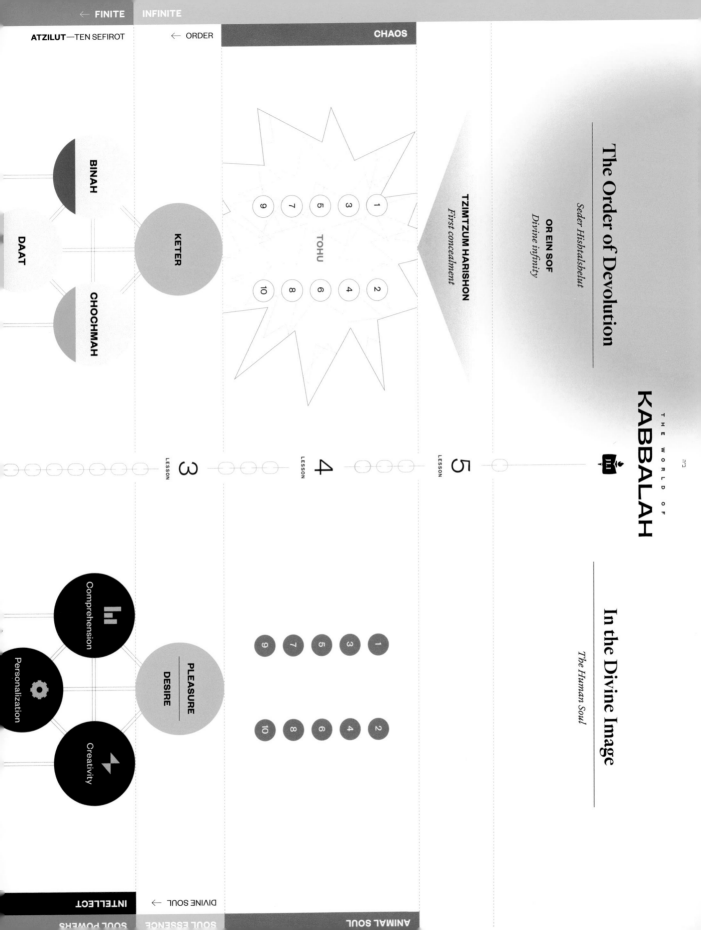

The Order of Devolution

Seder Hishtalshelut

OR EIN SOF
Divine infinity

TZIMTZUM HARISHON
First concealment

FINITE | INFINITE

ATZILUT—TEN SEFIROT | ← ORDER | CHAOS

BINAH

DAAT

CHOCHMAH

KETER

TOHU

1 3 5 7 9

2 4 6 8 10

LESSON 3

LESSON 4

LESSON 5

In the Divine Image

The Human Soul

Comprehension

Personalization

Creativity

PLEASURE
DESIRE

1 3 5 7 9

2 4 6 8 10

INTELLECT | ← DIVINE SOUL | SOUL POWERS

ANIMAL SOUL

SOUL ESSENCE

LESSON 4

4.1 נפש הבהמית
- *nefesh habahamit*
- **animal soul**
- the human soul that is self-oriented and can trigger immoral behavior

4.2 נפש אלקית
- *nefesh Elokit*
- **G-dly soul**
- the human soul that yearns for a closer relationship with G-d and to fulfill its Divine mission

4.3 אורות
- *orot*
- **lights**
- abstract Divine energies that are closely tied to their source but are primed to produce Divine attributes

4.4 כלים
- *kelim*
- **vessels**
- Divine entities of definition and structure that define the lights and channel their energy to the lower worlds

4.5 תהו
- *Tohu*
- **chaos**
- a system in which Divine *orot* (lights) and *kelim* (vessels) failed to sense G-d's ultimate purpose for which they had been emanated, resulting in the lights returning to their source and the vessels remaining without the lights

4.6 שבירת הכלים
- *shevirat hakelim*
- **breaking of the vessels**
- when the vessels no longer lend definition to the lights but become standalone entities

4.7 תיקון
- *Tikun*
- **correction**
- the second emanation of the *sefirot* in which the lights and vessels sense G-d's purpose, causing them to set aside their default natures and allowing them to remain paired with each other

LESSON 5

5.1 צמצום הראשון
- *tzimtzum harishon*
- **the first contraction**
- the first act of concealment, enabling the transition from Divine infinity to the Divine *sefirot*

5.2 קו
- *kav*
- **line**
- G-d's manifestation of limited light, from which the *sefirot* arise

5.3 גילוי
- *giluy*
- **revelation**
- a reality (usually G-dliness) that is apparent

5.4 העלם
- *helem*
- **concealment**
- a reality (usually G-dliness) that is present but not apparent

5.5 פרסא
- *parsa*
- **curtain**
- the concealment after the world of *Atzilut* that enables a sense of independence within the lower worlds of *Beriah*, *Yetzirah*, and *Asiyah*

5.6 עבודה
- *avodah*
- **toil**
- working to enhance one's character and to become more aware of G-d, often facilitated by immersive prayer

LESSON 6

6.1 עצמות
- *Atzmut*
- **essence**
- the essence of G-d from which all else emerges

6.2 נמנע הנמנעות
- *nimna hanimna'ot*
- **the impossibility of the impossible**
- it is impossible to ascribe an impossibility to *Atzmut*

6.3 בחירה חפשית
- *bechirah chafshit*
- **free choice**
- a choice that originates completely from within the chooser and is not "compelled" even in the slightest by any external consideration

6.4 יחידה
- *yechidah*
- **the united one**
- the essence of the soul that is inexorably united with G-d

6.5 יש מאין
- *yesh me'ayin*
- **something from nothing**
- the creation of an entity that does not intuitively sense and respect its source

6.6 דירה בתחתונים
- *dirah betachtonim*
- **a home in the lowly**
- G-d's desire to have a home in this world, fashioned by our doing *mitzvot*

Key Terms

LESSON 1

סֵדֶר הִשְׁתַּלְשְׁלוּת   1.1

- *seder hishtalshelut*
- **system of devolution**

the many degrees of systematic descent that stretch between G-d's desire to create the universe and the tangible result of that goal

בִּי"ע   1.2

- *BiYA*
- **created, shaped, made**

acronym for the grouping of the three spiritual words, **B**eriah, **Y**etzirah, and **A**siyah

יֵשׁוּת   1.3

- *yeshut*
- **existence**

existence with a sense of self-awareness and independence

בִּטוּל   1.4

- *bitul*
- **surrender, suspension, nullification**

a subdued sense of self due to being absorbed by something overwhelmingly impressive, and the desire to become one with it

לְבוּשֵׁי הַנֶּפֶשׁ   1.5

- *levushei hanefesh*
- **the soul's garments**

Thought, speech, and action—the soul's behaviors, which are external to the soul itself

LESSON 2

כּוֹחוֹת הַנֶּפֶשׁ   2.1

- *kochot hanefesh*
- **the soul's powers**

the soul's ten attributes that are broadly divided into two categories: intellect (*sechel*) and emotion (*midot*)

פְּשִׁיטוּת   2.2

- *peshitut*
- **simplicity**

a state of abstractness in the sense of transcending definable qualities and specific attributes

סְפִירוֹת   2.3

- *sefirot*
- **numbered entities**

ten specific, definable attributes that G-d manifested from His infinite Self

אֲצִילוּת   2.4

- *Atzilut*
- **emanation; togetherness**

G-d's emanation of the ten *sefirot*, attributes of Divine but finite expression

אֱלוֹקוּת   2.5

- *Elokut*
- **G-dliness**

an expression of G-d that is not G-d's essential self

חֶסֶד   2.6

- *chesed*
- **kindness**

the disposition to give and share, irrespective of the recipient's state

גְּבוּרָה   2.7

- *gevurah*
- **strength**

the disposition to restrain giving and sharing in order to provide only in proportion to what the recipient deserves

תִּפְאֶרֶת   2.8

- *tiferet*
- **beauty**

the harmonization of opposites, such as *chesed* and *gevurah*, yielding a beautiful balance

שֹׁרֶשׁ הַנְּשָׁמָה   2.9

- *shoresh haneshamah*
- **the soul's root**

the specific *sefirah* in *Atzilut* from which a particular soul derives

LESSON 3

אוֹר אֵין סוֹף   3.1

- *or ein sof*
- **infinite light**

G-d's infinite self-projection that is intimately connected with G-d's essence and that transcends definition, limitation, and specific attributes

סוֹבֵב כָּל עָלְמִין   3.2

- *sovev kol almin*
- **encompasses all worlds**

G-d as He transcends the emanation of *sefirot* and the creation of *Beriah*, *Yetzirah*, and *Asiyah*

מְמַלֵּא כָּל עָלְמִין   3.3

- *memalei kol almin*
- **fills all worlds**

G-d as He emanates the *sefirot* and actively creates *Beriah*, *Yetzirah*, and *Asiyah*

שְׂרָפִים   3.4

- *seraphim*
- **burning beings**

angels of *Beriah* who experience a fiery passion to cleave to G-d as He transcends limitation

הִתְכַּלְלוּת   3.5

- *hitkalelut*
- **incorporation**

the intermingling and harmonization of the G-dly *sefirot*

כֶּתֶר

- *kete...*
- **crow...**

G-dlines...
transce...
and tha...
harmo...

הַנֶּפֶשׁ

- *ratz...*
- **the s...**

(a) a des...
the sou...
(b) a de...
contem...

דַּעַת

- *daa...*
- **kno...**
- **conr...**

connec...
someth...
persona...

MATERIAL | SPIRITUAL →

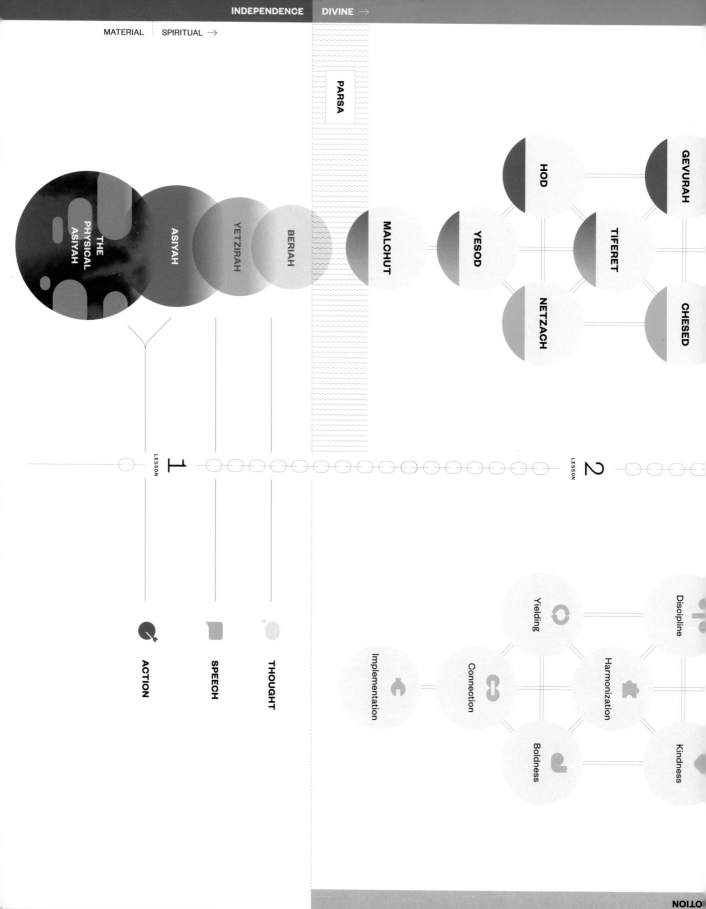

PARSA

THE PHYSICAL ASIYAH

ASIYAH

YETZIRAH

BERIAH

MALCHUT

YESOD

HOD

NETZACH

TIFERET

GEVURAH

CHESED

LESSON 1

LESSON 2

ACTION

SPEECH

THOUGHT

Yielding

Discipline

Implementation

Connection

Harmonization

Boldness

Kindness

OTION

Zohar 1:15a, Reprised

At the beginning of the manifestation of the King's will, *when G-d desired to create a universe, there was an "obstacle" to be overcome: Divine infinity. The infinite light of G-dliness precluded the existence of finite creations.*

Therefore, G-d established the lamp of darkness, *the* tzimtzum. *With* tzimtzum, *G-d concealed His infinite light, generating space for finite existence. This concealment is "darkness," but it also served as a lamp, allowing for the revelation of something new:* engraved engravings in the supernal purity.

The "engraved engravings" are the ten sefirot *through which G-d expresses Himself and relates with us. These* sefirot *were hewn from the "supernal purity" of G-d's infinite Divine light—*it emanated from the most concealed of all concealed things, from the secret of endlessness.

The Divine light contained within the sefirot *is a formless vapor, a Divine energy that transcends any variation and particular role,* inserted into a circle that was neither white nor black nor red nor green, nor any color at all.

However, when He began its measurements, He created bright colors to shine forth. From within the center of the lamp a fountain spouted, from which the colors down below were painted, *and which allowed each of the* sefirot *to gain a specific function.*

Autograph manuscript of *Or Yakar,* Rabbi Moshe Cordovero's commentary on the *Zohar.* (Library of Agudas Chasidei Chabad)

G-d Is Everywhere

The belief that G-d is present everywhere—in every entity, phenomenon, and individual—is a basic principle of *Chasidut*. The following texts are culled from the teachings of Rabbi Yisrael Baal Shem Tov, the founder of the Chasidic movement, and demonstrate how this principle of Divine omnipresence animates many of *Chasidut's* foundational teachings that define its approach to life and Divine service.

Joyful Faith

Rabbi Yisrael Baal Shem Tov, *Tzavaat Harivash*, no. 137

Contemplate the reality that the Creator is present everywhere, and consequently, G-d is always with you. He is the Master of the entire universe and can do with it as He pleases. Therefore, you should place your trust in Him exclusively.

Be joyful always, and believe with complete faith that G-d is with you and actively protecting you. You are connected to G-d, and G-d is connected to you. You are gazing at G-d's presence, and He is gazing at you. Everything that happens in this world—positive and negative developments alike—comes from G-d. Therefore, you should trust G-d exclusively and experience trepidation concerning no one besides Him.

Rabbi Yisrael Baal Shem Tov, ibid., nos. 44–45

A basic principle of Divine service is to distance ourselves from sadness to the greatest possible extent.

Crying is terribly detrimental, because we need to serve G-d with joy. Needless to say, if we are weeping tears of sheer joy, such tears are very good indeed.

In the Mundane Pursuits

Rabbi Yisrael Baal Shem Tov, *Tzavaat Harivash*, no. 109

When you dress yourself in a particular set of clothing, eat a specific choice of food, or use a certain tool, you are benefiting from the Divine energy present with that item. Each item indeed hosts a particular Divine energy, for without it, the entity would simply not exist.

The inner reason for your natural attraction to a particular item is because that item contains Divine sparks that are linked to your soul specifically. Therefore, when you use the garment, food, or tool to satisfy your physical or material needs you rectify the specific Divine sparks they contain. For with the energy, protection, and convenience that these material items provided, you will subsequently be empowered to serve G-d.

Rabbi Yisrael Baal Shem Tov, cited in *Likutei Yekarim* (Jerusalem, 1974), no. 120

If you are forced to travel and therefore cannot pray or study Torah to the extent you are accustomed, do not feel dismayed. G-d desires that we serve Him in a variety of ways: sometimes through prayer, sometimes through study, and at other times, in altogether different ways. This is the deeper significance of the opportunity or necessity that prompted you to travel, or to meet certain individuals, or to engage in a particular conversation, and the like. These are all Divinely orchestrated opportunities to serve G-d in alternative ways.

Working with the Body

Rabbi Yisrael Baal Shem Tov, cited by Rabbi Yosef Yitzchak Schneersohn, *Igrot Kodesh* 3, p. 325

If you carefully ponder your body's state of corporeality . . . you may experience disdain toward it. You may be moved to refrain from helping your body fulfill the mission for which it was created. You may wish to afflict it, to break its crass corporeality. That, however, would be antithetical to the Torah's approach. Rather, you must aid it—purify your body, bring it a measure of spiritual

Prayer

Rabbi Yisrael Baal Shem Tov,
Tzavaat Harivash, **no. 137**

You may be engrossed in prayer and suddenly find yourself distracted by someone carrying on a conversation nearby. Ask yourself: Why has G-d brought this individual here right now, causing him to converse while you are in the middle of praying? After all, everything that occurs is by Divine Providence—so what might be G-d's purpose for orchestrating this disturbance?

The truth is that G-d's intimate presence has chosen to act through the agency of this individual's mouth, deliberately disturbing you for the sake of propelling you to invest a far more powerful degree of concentration into your Divine service.

Imagine that! G-d has invested Himself into someone's idle chatter—and the individual may well be significantly distanced from G-d or even from intelligent conversation—all for the sake of spurring you to focus more on your prayers! This thought should move you to mightily strengthen your concentration and dedication to G-d's service.

Title page of one of the first editions of *Tzavaat Harivash,* printed in 1793.

Rabbi Yisrael Baal Shem Tov, cited by Rabbi Yaakov Yosef of Polnoye, *Toldot Yaakov Yosef, Vayigash* 1

"The prayer of a pauper who is pained and pours out his speech before G-d" (Psalms 102:1). The deeper significance of this verse can be appreciated by way of a parable:

There was once a king who proclaimed on the day of his personal rejoicing that all requests submitted to him on that day would be granted. Many approached to request high office and honors, others asked for wealth, and the king duly granted each wish.

However, one wise individual approached with an altogether different kind of request. He asked that the king permit him to approach and address the king three times each day.

The king was most pleased with this request, far more so than with any other, for it demonstrated that this particular subject valued a conversation with the king more than riches and honors. The king granted the request, allowing the individual entry to the king's chamber. However, once the individual arrived, the king went further and lay the royal treasury open before him, with permission to benefit freely from wealth and thereby acquire honor as well.

This, then, is the deeper meaning of our opening passage. It is a prayer that G-d grant the beseecher the ability to "pour out his speech before G-d"—to converse with the King of the universe.

Title page of the first print of *Toldot Yaakov Yosef*, printed in Koretz, 1780. *Toldot Yaakov Yosef* includes many teachings of Rabbi Yisrael Baal Shem Tov, and was one of the first Chasidic texts to be published.

KEY TERMS

1. *Tzimtzum harishon*

The first act of concealment, enabling the transition
from Divine infinity to the Divine *sefirot*

2. *Kav*

G-d's manifestation of limited light, from which the *sefirot* arise

3. *Giluy*

A reality (usually G-dliness) that is apparent

4. *Helem*

A reality (usually G-dliness) that is present but not apparent

5. *Parsa*

The concealment after the world of *Atzilut* that enables a sense of
independence within the lower worlds of *Beriah*, *Yetzirah*, and *Asiyah*

6. *Avodah*

Working to enhance one's character and to become more
aware of G-d, often facilitated by immersive prayer

KEY POINTS

1   The process of *tzimtzum* is essential in enabling the emanation of the Divine *sefirot*.

2   Interpreting *tzimtzum* literally can lead to serious errors in important Jewish beliefs. In reality, G-d's infinite light always remains omnipresent.

3   The *tzimtzum* represents a shift between the states of revelation and concealment. Through the *tzimtzum*, G-d's infinite light transitions from a state of revelation to concealment, while the power for finite expression shifts from concealment to revelation.

4   The *sefirot* recognize that they are a part of G-d and His powers. The *parsa* serves as a barrier that conceals Divinity from *Beriah*, *Yetzirah*, and *Asiyah*, giving them the impression that they are independent entities.

5   At the outset of Creation, concealment preceded revelation. This fundamental pattern of concealment and revelation is evident throughout the entire *seder hishtalshelut*. This pattern is also reflected in the sequence of night and day, where night precedes the day, forming an inseparable unit.

KEY TAKEAWAYS

1   The human tendency for self-absorption leads one
to deny others the space to express themselves. It is
essential to utilize the power of personal *tzimtzum*
to not needlessly impose ourselves upon the rightful
domain of others. This is primarily accomplished
through *avodah*, the work of enhancing one's character.

2   Pondering the extent to which G-d exercised
tzimtzum out of His love for us can inspire us to
intentionally create space for G-d in our daily lives.

3   The path to success is frequently obscured by hardship.
To achieve our aspirations, it is essential to realize
that the drawbacks are steps toward success.

LADDER OF CONNECTION
Yoram Raanan, acrylic on
canvas, Israel, 2020

LESSON 6

THE ESSENCE OF EVERYTHING

*This lesson takes a daring dive into the reality
that precedes everything: the essence of the Divine
Self. It finds a surprising association with the
material universe that sits at the bottom rung of
existence. This fascinating study provides a glimpse
into the essence of all existence, facilitates insight
into the essence of the human self, and applies
this wisdom to the ability to repair wrongs.*

I. OF THE ESSENCE

Welcome to the sixth and final lesson of *The World of Kabbalah*.

Until this point in the course, we've explored G-d's light—i.e., the energy that emerges from Him—and His creations. In this lesson, we shift the conversation and we will discuss G-d Himself.

It should not surprise us that the essence of G-d, known as *Atzmut*, is a discussion completely unto itself and is qualitatively removed from all that is sourced in Him.

TEXT 1

Beginningless vs. Endless

Rabbi Shneur Zalman of Liadi,
Maamarei Admur Hazaken 5562:1, pp. 279–280

מַה שֶׁנִּקְרָא בִּלְשׁוֹן "אֵין סוֹף" וְלֹא נִקְרָא בִּלְשׁוֹן
"אֵין לוֹ תְּחִלָּה" - וְלָמָּה יִשְׁתַּנֶּה הַסּוֹף מִן הַתְּחִלָּה?
מֵאַחַר שֶׁהֵן שָׁוִין בִּבְחִינַת הָעַצְמוּת, שֶׁכָּל דָּבָר
שֶׁאֵין לוֹ תְּחִלָּה אֵין לוֹ סוֹף, כַּיָּדוּעַ.

אַךְ הָעִנְיָן הוּא, דְּאִם הָיָה הַכַּוָּנָה עַל מַהוּתוֹ יִתְבָּרֵךְ בֶּאֱמֶת,
הָיָה רָאוּי לְקָרוֹתוֹ בְּשֵׁם אֵין לוֹ תְּחִלָּה כוּ'. אֲבָל הַכַּוָּנָה
הוּא עַל אוֹרוֹ וְזִיווֹ לְבַד, וְהוּא הַנִּקְרָא אֵין סוֹף דַּוְקָא.

וּכְמוֹ שֶׁנִּתְבָּאֵר בְּמָקוֹם אַחֵר שֶׁפֵּרוּשׁ "אוֹר אֵין סוֹף"
הַנִּזְכָּר בְּסִפְרֵי הַמְּקֻבָּלִים, הַכַּוָּנָה לוֹמַר שֶׁהָאוֹר
הוּא אֵין סוֹף, וְלֹא שֶׁהוּא אוֹרוֹ שֶׁל אֵין סוֹף - כִּי
בְּמַהוּתוֹ יִתְבָּרֵךְ לֹא יִתָּכֵן לוֹמַר לְשׁוֹן "אֵין סוֹף".

RABBI SHNEUR ZALMAN OF LIADI (ALTER REBBE) 1745–1812

Chasidic rebbe, Halachic authority, and founder of the Chabad movement. The Alter Rebbe was born in Liozna, Belarus, and was among the principal students of the Magid of Mezeritch. His numerous works include the *Tanya*, an early classic containing the fundamentals of Chabad Chasidism; and *Shulchan Aruch HaRav*, an expanded and reworked code of Jewish law.

We refer to G-d's light as *ein sof,* "without end,"
instead of *ein lo techilah*, "without a beginning."
This preference appears puzzling, because
essentially there is no difference—anything that
has no beginning also has no end, as is known.

The truth is that if we intend to refer to G-d's very
essence, it would indeed be appropriate to use
the phrase *ein lo techilah,* "without a beginning."
However, what we describe as *ein sof* is in fact
G-d's light and radiance, and not G-d Himself.

To clarify: When the kabbalists speak of
the *or ein sof* their intention is "the endless
light [of G-d]," not "the light of the endless
One." They are not attempting to describe
the origin of the light as endless, for we
cannot describe G-d Himself as endless.

KEY TERM 6.1

HEBREW TERM	עַצְמוּת
TRANSLITERATION	*Atzmut*
LITERAL MEANING	**Essence**
DEFINITION	the essence of G-d from which all else emerges

TEXT 2

When Words Fail

Rabbi Shalom Dovber Schneersohn,
Sefer Hamaamarim 5668, pp. 187–188

שֶׁיְדִיעָתֵנוּ בִּבְחִינַת הָעַצְמוּת הוּא רַק בְּמָה שֶׁהוּא
בּוֹרֵא . . . וְלָכֵן אֵין אָנוּ יְכוֹלִים לְכַנּוֹת אוֹתוֹ יִתְבָּרֵךְ בְּשׁוּם
כִּנּוּי, כִּי אִם מָה שֶׁהוּא בּוֹרֵא. כִּי כָּל כִּנּוּי הוּא תֹאַר דָּבָר
מָה שֶׁמְתָאֵר אֶת הַדָּבָר הַנִּקְרָא בְּהַשֵּׁם הַהוּא, וְאִם כֵּן
בְּהֶכְרֵחַ שֶׁהַמְתֹאָר הוּא בְּאֵיזֶה מְצִיאוּת דָּבָר בְּעַצְמוֹ
שֶׁשַּׁיָּךְ בּוֹ הַתְּפִיסָא וְהַהַגְבָּלָה בְּאֵיזֶה דָּבָר, דְּמִשּׁוּם זֶה
אֶפְשָׁר לְתָאֲרוֹ, מָה שֶׁבְּעַצְמוּת אֵינוֹ שַׁיָּךְ כָּל זֶה כוּ'.
וְלָכֵן אֵין לְתָאֵר אוֹתוֹ יִתְבָּרֵךְ בְּשׁוּם שֵׁם וְכִנּוּי כְּלָל.

Every title is a description, an attempt to describe something about a particular entity. It follows that the recipient of the title is an entity with a degree of definition or limitation that lends itself to description. Now, none of this is true of G-d's essence, and we are left without any form of name or title by which to refer to Him.

Our knowledge of *Atzmut* is limited to the fact that He creates. . . . Consequently, we have no way to refer to *Atzmut* other than to describe Him as Creator.

RABBI SHALOM DOVBER SCHNEERSOHN (RASHAB) 1860–1920

Chasidic rebbe. Rabbi Shalom Dovber became the 5th leader of the Chabad movement upon the passing of his father, Rabbi Shmuel Schneersohn. He established the Lubavitch network of *yeshivot* called Tomchei Temimim. He authored many volumes of Chasidic discourses and is renowned for his lucid and thorough explanations of kabbalistic concepts.

"What Is G-d?" A lecture by
Rabbi Manis Friedman:
myjli.com/kabbalah

FIGURE 6.1

Atzmut . . .

1. Has no definition whatsoever.

FIGURE 6.2

Atzmut . . .

1. Has no definition whatsoever.
2. Is the only entity that *necessarily* exists.

UNDEFINED
Acrylic on canvas,
Tel Aviv, Israel, 2020

Revelation Below

The following collection of texts demonstrates, in a range of areas, how the desire of *Atzmut* is realized specifically in the lower realms.

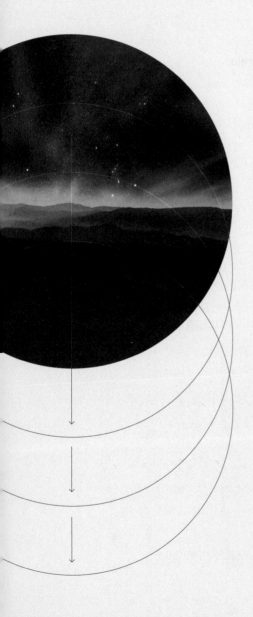

The Lowly World

Rabbi Shneur Zalman of Liadi, *Tanya, Likutei Amarim*, ch. 36

There is a known statement of our sages that G-d created this world to enable the fulfillment of His desire for an abode in this lowest realm.

Now, there is no higher and lower in G-d's presence, because He fills every realm of existence equally. Rather, the description of our world as the lowest realm can be understood by first appreciating that, before the Creation of the universe, all that existed was G-d Himself. The very space that the universe now occupies was entirely filled with G-d's presence. In fact, that remains the reality even now, from the truth of G-d's perspective. The change caused by Creation is only in the perspective of the recipients of G-d's vivifying energy—because they receive this by way of multiple screens that dim and conceal G-d's light, from their perspective. . . .

This concealing process is referred to as the *hishtalshelut* of the worlds, meaning: their devolution from each other via interlinked, progressively dimmer realities, by way of countless steps of concealment of the Divine light and energy. This continues all the way until the Creation of this physical, corporeal, tangible world of ours—the bottom of the entire chain. There is no lower realm in terms of the concealment of G-d's light. It is a world of incredible darkness, to the extent that it is filled with *kelipot* that oppose G-d in actuality and claim that nothing exists beyond their immediate reality.

The goal of the entire chain of interlinked realms of spiritual existence, and the purpose of their progressively steeper descents in terms of Divine concealment, is not for any of those spiritual worlds. . . . Rather, the purpose is to arrive at this lowly, tangible world. For it was G-d's original desire to derive pleasure from mortal efforts to suppress the forces of evil and to transform the darkness into light, until G-d's infinite light shines openly through the entirety of this world—the very habitat of ultimate darkness and the forces that oppose sanctity!

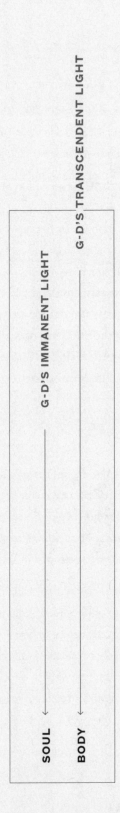

G-D'S TRANSCENDENT LIGHT

G-D'S IMMANENT LIGHT

SOUL

BODY

The Lowly Body
Rabbi Shmuel Schneersohn, *Likutei Torah: Torat Shmuel* 5637:2, pp. 621–625

In our physical world, the degree to which we can experience G-dliness is exceedingly limited due to the physical nature of our bodies. By contrast, after a person's passing, their soul is released from the shackles of the body and rises to Paradise, where it basks in the glory of G-d's presence. That, however, is not the end of the road. In the messianic era, G-d will resurrect the departed, and every soul in Heaven will return to this world to live a physical life in a corporeal body. At first glance, for a soul to be reinstated in a corporeal body seems to be a tragic descent—why would G-d force it to endure this experience in the messianic era?

The truth, however, is that the root of the physical body is higher than that of the soul. For the soul is rooted in G-d's immanent light, whereas the body is rooted in G-d's transcendent light. Now, in its present form, our world is incapable of experiencing G-d's transcendent light in a revealed way. For that reason, the body is far beneath the soul in its spiritual standing, and it is incapable of self-sustenance: it requires the consumption of physical food to sustain it.

That will all change in the future messianic era. At that time, G-d's transcendent light will be revealed, and the true superiority of the physical body will then be realized. No longer will the body require physical food to sustain it, for it will then be sustained by the spiritual, transcendent light of G-d. Consequently, the body will attain a more advanced Divine standing than the soul, and the soul will draw its spiritual sustenance from the body!

The Lowly Form of Life
Rabbi Shneur Zalman of Liadi, *Torah Or*, *Vayigash*, 43c–d

Our physical world is divided into four categories: inanimate, vegetation, animal, and human. Inanimate material is considered the lowest form of existence, while vegetation is considered one step higher, and so on. This raises a question: If the inanimate soil [minerals, water, etc.] is the source of life for vegetation, while vegetation itself sustains animal life, and humans are sustained by both vegetation and animals, then the lowest form of earthly existence—the inanimate earth—is actually the greatest, for it is the foundation of life through which all else is sustained!

A parallel question can be posed regarding the dissimilar sacred structures of (a) the Mishkan, the temporary sanctuary that served the Jewish people in the Sinai Desert, and (b) the Holy Temple, the permanent sanctuary in Jerusalem. The Mishkan appears to have been constructed in a logical fashion: its floor was earth (inanimate); its walls, one step higher, were wooden (vegetation); and higher still, its roof was fashioned from animal hides. Now, the Holy Temple in Jerusalem was spiritually superior to the Mishkan—nevertheless, it was constructed exclusively from the lowest material: inanimate stone!

This paradox is resolved through perceiving the deeper reality: in our tangible world, inanimate objects are the lowest form of existence, but in the Divine source of all things, inanimate material is the highest. For G-d established a rule within His Creation of the cosmos whereby "that which exists in the initial stages of the Divine plan are the final steps to be developed in actual practice."

The Mishkan was but a temporary home for G-d, and therefore, its structure followed the order that prevails within our tangible world: inanimate, vegetation, and animal. By contrast, the Holy Temple was designed to be a permanent home for G-d, where the Divine presence can be fully revealed. In this home, the Divine plan takes primacy over material perception and the spiritual root of each matter is revealed. Consequently, the inanimate is superior to all other forms of existence.

The original Divine reality reflected in the structure of the Holy Temple will be revealed to the fullest extent in the future era of the Redemption. At that time, the lofty origins of the lowly earth will become apparent to all.

The Lowly Actions
Rabbi Shneur Zalman of Liadi, *Tanya, Likutei Amarim*, ch. 35

A few unique individuals may successfully develop such a complete passion and love for G-d that they permanently and perfectly subdue their animalistic soul and selfish desires. The vast majority of us, however, face an endless internal struggle against impulses and desires. Our animalistic soul will always be there, and we will forever need to contend with it. This leaves us with a question: What is the purpose of a perpetual struggle in which we cannot possibly prevail?

However, we must first appreciate that while not everyone is suited to the intellectual comprehension or emotional experience of G-d's Infinite Light, the observance of the practical *mitzvot* is available to all people equally. Moreover, practical observance is the greatest form of connection with G-d. That is because our soul, as tremendous as it may be in spiritual terms, nevertheless exists in this world as an entity that is separate from G-d's Infinite Light. By contrast, the practical *mitzvot* are expressions of G-d's desire and wisdom—they are G-d's deepest and most original desire—and are therefore completely united with G-d. Consequently, G-d cannot be grasped by the soul's faculties of deep understanding of Him and passionate love for Him, but only by investing ourselves in His wisdom and desire.

Some *mitzvot* are strictly intellectual, such as Torah study. When we engage in the study of Torah, our soul's faculties of thought and speech are fully invested in the Divine Infinite Light, but this envelops our spiritual faculties alone. In order to bring the Divine into our soul's power for action, we must observe the practical *mitzvot* with our physical limbs. Therefore, when we perform a practical mitzvah such as wearing *tefilin* or lighting Shabbat candles, our soul's physical side—the body and its corporeal energies enabled by the soul—is properly invested in G-d's Infinite Light.

In this way, the pinnacle of human connection with the Divine, and the actualization of G-d's ultimate purpose for creation, is readily available to all of us.

II. THE EXCEPTION TO EVERY RULE

The essence of G-d is not bound to or governed by any rules whatsoever. He created all of them, which makes Him necessarily above and beyond them all. This holds true regarding the rules of nature and physics, and even about the rules of morality and right and wrong. Hence, utterly *free* choice is His domain alone.

While *Atzmut* may not be bound by any rules, He is bound to the *yechidah*, the essence of the Jewish soul.

TEXT 3

Beyond Infinity

The Rebbe, Rabbi Menachem Mendel Schneerson,
Torat Menachem 5724:2, p. 371

בֶּאֱמֶת גַּם בְּחִינַת הַבְּלִי גְבוּל אֵינוֹ מְגַלֶּה אֶת
הָעַצְמוּת, כִּי הָעַצְמוּת אֵינוֹ גְבוּל וְאֵינוֹ בְּלִי גְבוּל,
שֶׁשְּׁנֵיהֶם הֵם בִּבְחִינַת הַגִּלּוּיִים בִּלְבַד.

In truth, even infinity does not express *Atzmut*; rather, G-d's essence is neither finite nor infinite. The qualities of infinity and finitude apply exclusively to Divine revelation.

RABBI MENACHEM MENDEL SCHNEERSON 1902–1994

The towering Jewish leader of the 20th century, known as "the Lubavitcher Rebbe," or simply as "the Rebbe." Born in southern Ukraine, the Rebbe escaped Nazi-occupied Europe, arriving in the U.S. in June 1941. The Rebbe inspired and guided the revival of traditional Judaism after the European devastation, impacting virtually every Jewish community the world over. The Rebbe often emphasized that the performance of just one additional good deed could usher in the era of Mashiach. The Rebbe's scholarly talks and writings have been printed in more than 200 volumes.

KEY TERM 6.2

HEBREW TERM	נִמְנָע הַנִמְנָעוֹת
TRANSLITERATION	*nimna hanimna'ot*
LITERAL MEANING	**the impossibility of the impossible**
DEFINITION	it is impossible to ascribe an impossibility to *Atzmut*

FIGURE 6.3

Atzmut . . .

1. Has no definition whatsoever.
2. Is the only entity that *necessarily* exists.
3. **Follows no rules whatsoever—it is the source of all rules.**

QUANTUM UNCERTAINTY
David Friedman, Israel

Will It Be Wickedness or Righteousness?

Midrash, *Bereshit Rabah* 2:5

מִתְּחִלַת בְּרִיָּתוֹ שֶׁל עוֹלָם צָפָה הַקָּדוֹשׁ בָּרוּךְ הוּא
בְּמַעֲשֵׂיהֶן שֶׁל צַדִּיקִים וּמַעֲשֵׂיהֶן שֶׁל רְשָׁעִים. הֲדָא הוּא
דִכְתִיב (תְּהִלִּים א, ו): "כִּי יוֹדֵעַ ה' דֶּרֶךְ צַדִּיקִים וְגוֹ'".

"וְהָאָרֶץ הָיְתָה תֹהוּ וָבֹהוּ" (בְּרֵאשִׁית א,
ב) - אֵלוּ מַעֲשֵׂיהֶן שֶׁל רְשָׁעִים.

"וַיֹּאמֶר אֱלֹקִים יְהִי אוֹר" (שָׁם, ג) -
אֵלוּ מַעֲשֵׂיהֶן שֶׁל צַדִּיקִים.

אֲבָל אֵינִי יוֹדֵעַ בְּאֵיזֶה מֵהֶם חָפֵץ, אִם בְּמַעֲשֵׂה
אֵלוּ וְאִם בְּמַעֲשֵׂה אֵלוּ? כֵּיוָן דִכְתִיב "וַיַּרְא אֱלֹקִים
אֶת הָאוֹר כִּי טוֹב" (שָׁם, ד), הֱוֵי - בְּמַעֲשֵׂיהֶן שֶׁל
צַדִּיקִים חָפֵץ, וְאֵינוֹ חָפֵץ בְּמַעֲשֵׂיהֶן שֶׁל רְשָׁעִים.

From the start of the universe's creation, G-d foresaw the deeds of the righteous and the deeds of the wicked, as it is stated, "G-d knows the way of the righteous [and the way of the wicked that is doomed]" (PSALMS 1:6).

[This was represented at the start of Creation as follows:]

"The earth was chaotic and desolate" (GENESIS 1:2). This refers to the deeds of the wicked.

BERESHIT RABAH

An early rabbinic commentary on the Book of Genesis. This Midrash bears the name of Rabbi Oshiya Rabah (Rabbi Oshiya "the Great"), whose teaching opens this work. This Midrash provides textual exegeses and stories, expounds upon the biblical narrative, and develops and illustrates moral principles. Produced by the sages of the Talmud in the Land of Israel, its use of Aramaic closely resembles that of the Jerusalem Talmud. It was first printed in Constantinople in 1512 together with 4 other Midrashic works on the other 4 books of the Pentateuch.

"G-d said, 'Let there be light!'" (IBID., 1:3).
This refers to the deeds of the righteous.

However, the narrative has yet to clarify the
genre of deeds that G-d desires; is it these or
those? This is clarified in the following verse:

"G-d saw that the light was good" (IBID., 1:4)—
clearly, G-d desires the deeds of the righteous
and does not desire the deeds of the wicked.

KEY TERM 6.3

HEBREW TERM	בְּחִירָה חָפְשִׁית
TRANSLITERATION	*bechirah chafshit*
LITERAL MEANING	**free choice**
DEFINITION	a choice that originates completely from within the chooser and is not "compelled" even in the slightest by any external consideration

FIGURE 6.4

Atzmut . . .

1. Has no definition whatsoever.
2. Is the only entity that *necessarily* exists.
3. Follows no rules whatsoever—it is the source of all rules.
4. **Is the only entity that has absolute free choice.**

TEXT 5

The Absolute Power of Repentance

Maimonides, *Mishneh Torah*, Laws of *Teshuvah* 3:14

אֵין לְךָ דָּבָר שֶׁעוֹמֵד בִּפְנֵי הַתְּשׁוּבָה. אֲפִלּוּ כָּפַר בָּעִקָּר כָּל יָמָיו וּבָאַחֲרוֹנָה שָׁב, יֵשׁ לוֹ חֵלֶק לָעוֹלָם הַבָּא.

Nothing stands in the way of *teshuvah* (repentance). Even if one denied G-d's existence throughout their life and then repented in their final moments— they merit a portion in the World to Come.

RABBI MOSHE BEN MAIMON (MAIMONIDES, RAMBAM) 1135–1204

Halachist, philosopher, author, and physician. Maimonides was born in Córdoba, Spain. After the conquest of Córdoba by the Almohads, he fled Spain and eventually settled in Cairo, Egypt. There, he became the leader of the Jewish community and served as court physician to the vizier of Egypt. He is most noted for authoring the *Mishneh Torah*, an encyclopedic arrangement of Jewish law; and for his philosophical work, *Guide for the Perplexed*. His rulings on Jewish law are integral to the formation of Halachic consensus.

TEXT 6

The Ultimate Boss

The Rebbe, Rabbi Menachem Mendel Schneerson, *Reshimot* #164

אַף שֶׁהַפְּגָם נִרְגָּשׁ בְּיוֹתֵר, בַּעַל הָרָצוֹן שֶׁלְּמַעְלָה מֵרָצוֹן,
אֲבָל לְאִידָךְ גִּיסָא - "מִי יֹאמַר לוֹ מַה תַּעֲשֶׂה כוּ'"
(קֹהֶלֶת ח, ד). וְעַל יְדֵי תְּשׁוּבָה שֶׁגְּבוֹהַּ מִכָּל הַמִּצְוֹת
וּמַגַּעַת בְּעֹמֶק הָרָצוֹן - מִתְכַּפֵּר לוֹ עַל יְדֵי זֶה.

Violations of the Divine will are felt most keenly
by the Divine Author who scripted that will. On
the other hand, G-d transcends His own will
[and is not compelled to react to violations in a
particular way, for] "Who can tell Him: What are
You doing?" (ECCLESIASTES 8:4). Consequently,
through *teshuvah*—which is loftier than all of the
mitzvot, and which touches the innermost depth
of G-d's desire—one can obtain atonement.

YOM HAKIPURIM HAZEH
Saul Raskin, gouache
and pencil on paper,
United States, 1958

FIGURE 6.5

Atzmut . . .

1. Has no definition whatsoever.
2. Is the only entity that *necessarily* exists.
3. Follows no rules whatsoever—it is the source of all rules.
4. Is the only entity that has absolute free choice.
5. **Is the source of the atonement granted when we do *teshuvah*.**

KEY TERM 6.4

HEBREW TERM	יְחִידָה
TRANSLITERATION	*yechidah*
LITERAL MEANING	**the united one**
DEFINITION	the essence of the soul that is inexorably united with G-d

TEXT 7

Essential Bond

The Rebbe, Rabbi Menachem Mendel Schneerson,
Likutei Sichot 3, p. 928

אִידְן מִיטְן אוֹיבֶּערְשְׁטְן צוּזַאמֶען זַיינֶען כִּבְיָכוֹל אֵיין
גַאנְצֶע זַאך, אוּן דָאס אִיז דּוּרְך דֶעם פַארְבּוּנְד פוּן
עֶצֶם הַנְּשָׁמָה מִיט עַצְמוּת. אִין דֶעם פַארְבּוּנְד פוּן דִי
כֹּחוֹת הַגְּלוּיִים מִיט אֱלֹקוּת קֶען אַמָאל זַיין אַ פְּגָם,

אָבֶּער עֶצֶם הַנְּשָׁמָה אִיז אַלֶע מָאל בַּאהֶעפְט
אוּן פַארְאֵיינִצִיקְט מִיט דֶעם אוֹיבֶּערְשְׁטְן,
"חֲבוּקָה וּדְבוּקָה בָּךְ, יְחִידָה לְיַחֶדָךְ".

Together, the Jewish people and G-d form one
complete entity, so to speak. This is due to the
bond between the very essence of the soul and
G-d's essence. (By contrast, while the souls' various
expressions and powers also enjoy a relationship
with G-d, the relationship is susceptible to damage
[as a consequence of the person's choices].)

The soul's essence is always intimately bound and
united with G-d, [in a unity that our sages depict
as] "merged and bonded with You in a oneness, to
be one with You" (LITURGY, HOSHAANOT).

FIGURE 6.6

Atzmut . . .

1. Has no definition whatsoever.

2. Is the only entity that *necessarily* exists.

3. Follows no rules whatsoever—it is the source of all rules.

4. Is the only entity that has absolute free choice.

5. Is the source of the atonement granted when we do *teshuvah*.

6. **Is connected to the essence of our souls, the *yechidah*.**

The North French Hebrew Miscellany is an elaborate collection of eighty-four different Hebrew texts produced during the last quarter of the thirteenth century. The manuscript's pages are decorated with fine art and feature several full-page miniatures like this one depicting the Tree of Life. (British Library, London)

III. TYING THE ENDS TOGETHER

On the surface, it would seem that all this discussion about *Atzmut*—while fascinating—is not terribly relevant to us here in this lowly physical world. The mystics, however, teach us that *Atzmut* is actually most relevant to us—because we here are the most relevant to *Atzmut*.

TEXT 8

A Feeling of Independence

The Rebbe, Rabbi Menachem Mendel Schneerson,
Torat Menachem: Sefer Hamaamarim Melukat 1, p. 267

הַהֶפְרֵשׁ בֵּין עוֹלָמוֹת הָעֶלְיוֹנִים לְעוֹלָם הַזֶּה:
דְּבָעוֹלָם הַזֶּה נִרְגָּשׁ שֶׁמְּצִיאוּתוֹ מֵעַצְמוּתוֹ.

(וְכַמְבֹאָר . . . הַהֶפְרֵשׁ בֵּין נִבְרָא וְאוֹר, דְּאוֹר הוּא רְאָיָה
עַל הַמָּאוֹר - דִּכְשֶׁאָנוּ רוֹאִים אוֹר, הָאוֹר עַצְמוֹ מַרְאֶה
וּמְגַלֶּה שֶׁיֵּשׁ מָאוֹר. מַה שֶּׁאֵין כֵּן יֵשׁ הַנִּבְרָא, הִנֵּה לֹא
זוּ בִּלְבַד שֶׁאֵינוֹ מְגַלֶּה בּוֹרֵא, אֶלָּא עוֹד זֹאת שֶׁהוּא
מַעֲלִים וּמַסְתִּיר עַל זֶה. וְאַדְּרַבָּה, נִרְגָּשׁ שֶׁמְּצִיאוּתוֹ
מֵעַצְמוּתוֹ (אֶלָּא שֶׁמִּצַּד הַשֵּׂכֶל מֻכְרָח שֶׁאֵינוֹ כֵּן)).

וְאַף שֶׁזֶּהוּ רַק בְּהַרְגָּשָׁתוֹ, מִכָּל מָקוֹם הִנֵּה זֶה גּוּפָא
שֶׁיִּהְיֶה נִדְמֶה עַל כָּל פָּנִים שֶׁמְּצִיאוּתוֹ מֵעַצְמוּתוֹ, זֶהוּ
מִפְּנֵי שֶׁשָּׁרְשׁוֹ מֵהָעַצְמוּת שֶׁמְּצִיאוּת מֵעַצְמוּתוֹ.

The difference between the upper, spiritual worlds and this material world of ours is that only the inhabitants of our material world experience their existence as entirely independent of any source.

What makes Jewish mysticism different? **Mrs. Shimona Tzukernik** answers: **myjli.com/kabbalah**

This is the difference between light and a created being: Light points to a source; when we see light, its existence informs us that there must be a source of light. By contrast, a material creature does not indicate the existence of the Creator; in fact, it actively conceals G-d's existence by projecting itself as an utterly independent existence. (Only logic demonstrates the incorrectness of this natural perception.)

In truth, our existence is entirely dependent on G-d, and it is only our perception that generates a sense of independence. Nevertheless, the very fact that we imagine ourselves to be self-generated is because our source is *Atzmut*, the absolutely independent existence.

KEY TERM 6.5

HEBREW TERM	יֵשׁ מֵאַיִן
TRANSLITERATION	*yesh me'ayin*
LITERAL MEANING	**something from nothing**
DEFINITION	the creation of an entity that does not intuitively sense and respect its source

TEXT 9

A Matter of Differing Perspectives

Rabbi Shneur Zalman of Liadi, *Tanya, Igeret Hakodesh*, ch. 20

וַהֲגַם שֶׁהַיֵּשׁ הַנִּבְרָא הוּא גַּם כֵּן כְּלֹא חָשִׁיב קַמֵּיהּ,
דְּהַיְנוּ שֶׁבָּטֵל בִּמְצִיאוּת . . . הַיְנוּ קַמֵּיהּ דַּוְקָא,
שֶׁהִיא יְדִיעָתוֹ יִתְבָּרַךְ מִלְמַעְלָה לְמַטָּה.

אֲבָל בִּידִיעָה שֶׁמִּמַּטָּה לְמַעְלָה, הַיֵּשׁ הַנִּבְרָא הוּא דָּבָר
נִפְרָד לְגַמְרֵי בִּידִיעָה וְהַשָּׂגָה זוֹ שֶׁמִּמַּטָּה. כִּי הַכֹּחַ הַשּׁוֹפֵעַ
בּוֹ אֵינוֹ מָשָּׂג כְּלָל וּכְלָל . . . וְלָכֵן נִקְרָא יֵשׁ מֵאַיִן דַּוְקָא.

The created entity is "considered like nothing before Him," meaning that it has no independent existence and is therefore utterly nullified before G-d. . . . Nevertheless, that is only "before Him," in G-d's perception, as viewed with the truth that is available exclusively Above.

However, the perception from below, i.e., the created being's perception, is that it is an entirely independent creation. This is because the energy that flows into a created entity is not understood or experienced by the entity at all. . . . This is why we refer to creation as "something from nothing."

TEXT 10

Independence Breeds Independence

Rabbi Shneur Zalman of Liadi, ibid.

מַהוּתוֹ וְעַצְמוּתוֹ שֶׁל הַמַּאֲצִיל בָּרוּךְ הוּא, שֶׁמְּצִיאוּתוֹ הוּא
מֵעַצְמוּתוֹ וְאֵינוֹ עָלוּל מֵאֵיזֶה עִלָּה שֶׁקְּדָמָה לוֹ חַס וְשָׁלוֹם,
וְלָכֵן הוּא לְבַדּוֹ בְּכֹחוֹ וִיכָלְתּוֹ לִבְרֹא יֵשׁ מֵאַיִן וְאֶפֶס הַמֻּחְלָט
מַמָּשׁ, בְּלִי שׁוּם עִלָּה וְסִבָּה אַחֶרֶת קוֹדֶמֶת לַיֵּשׁ הַזֶּה.

The very essence of the Creator, the ultimate
independent existence that has no antecedent or
cause at all, He alone has the exclusive power and
ability to create an entity from absolute and total
nothingness, to the extent that the created entity
[senses that it] has no cause or antecedent at all.

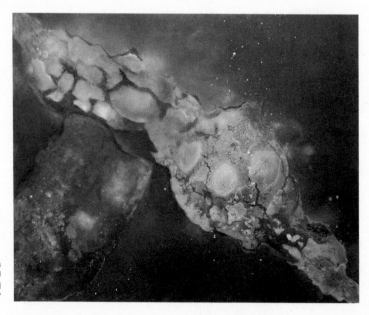

FIGURE 6.7

Atzmut . . .

1. Has no definition whatsoever.

2. Is the only entity that *necessarily* exists.

3. Follows no rules whatsoever—it is the source of all rules.

4. Is the only Entity that has absolute free choice.

5. Is the source of the atonement granted when we do *teshuvah*.

6. Is connected to the essence of our souls, the *yechidah*.

7. **Solely possesses the power to create entities that feel independent from their Divine origin.**

Opening page of the Book of Genesis in the *Wrocław Bible*, a fourteenth-century Hebrew manuscript of Germanic origin, featuring many detailed illuminations. (Ossolineum Pawlikowski Collection, Wrocław, Poland)

At the Source

The Rebbe, Rabbi Menachem Mendel Schneerson,
Torat Menachem: Sefer Hamaamarim Melukat 2, p. 282

הַנְּשָׁמָה הִתְהַוּוּתָהּ מֵהָאוֹרוֹת, דְּכִלְלוּת הָאוֹרוֹת הוּא
גְלוּיִים. וְהַגּוּף, הִתְהַוּוּתוֹ מֵעַצְמוּת, שֶׁמְּצִיאוּתוֹ הוּא
מֵעַצְמוּתוֹ וְאֵין שׁוּם עִלָּה וְסִבָּה קוֹדֶמֶת לוֹ חַס וְשָׁלוֹם.

וְהַנְּשָׁמָה שֶׁהִיא מַכִּירָה אֶת מַעֲלַת הַגּוּף בָּזֶה, וִויל
בַּאקוּמֶען עַצְמִי, וּמִשּׁוּם זֶה הִיא רוֹצָה לְהִתְחַבֵּר עִם
הַגּוּף וְנֶפֶשׁ הַבַּהֲמִית אוּן אִיבֶּעראַרבֶּעטְן אִיהם.

The soul is a product of Divine light, which is
itself merely an expression of Divinity. Conversely,
the body is created directly by G-d's essence,
whose existence is absolutely independent and
has no preceding cause or antecedent at all.

The soul recognizes that the body contains the
above superiority. Because it longs to gain a
similar advantage, it desires to bond with the
body and its animalistic soul and to guide them
through a positive spiritual transformation.

TEXT 12

With the End In Mind

Sefer Yetzirah 1:7

נָעוּץ סוֹפָן בִּתְחִלָּתָן וּתְחִלָּתָן בְּסוֹפָן.

The end is wedged in the beginning
and the beginning in the end.

SEFER YETZIRAH

Kabbalistic work. *Sefer Yetzirah* is an ancient Jewish mystical text, commonly attributed to Abraham, the forefather of the Jewish people. This work describes how G-d created the world, using ten *sefirot* (Divine attributes) and the 22 letters of the Hebrew alphabet. The cryptic style of the *Sefer Yetzirah* has spawned many commentaries, which interpret the text in different forms.

TEXT 13

A Home for *Atzmut*

Rabbi Shneur Zalman of Liadi, *Tanya, Likutei Amarim*, ch. 36

מוּדַעַת זֹאת מַאֲמַר רַבּוֹתֵינוּ ז״ל, שֶׁתַּכְלִית בְּרִיאַת עוֹלָם הַזֶּה הוּא שֶׁנִּתְאַוָּה הַקָּדוֹשׁ בָּרוּךְ הוּא לִהְיוֹת לוֹ דִירָה בַּתַּחְתּוֹנִים.

וְהִנֵּה לֹא שַׁיָּךְ לְפָנָיו יִתְבָּרֵךְ בְּחִינַת מַעֲלָה וּמַטָּה, כִּי הוּא יִתְבָּרֵךְ מְמַלֵּא כָּל עָלְמִין בְּשָׁוֶה.

אֶלָּא בֵּאוּר הָעִנְיָן, כִּי קֹדֶם שֶׁנִּבְרָא הָעוֹלָם הָיָה הוּא לְבַדּוֹ יִתְבָּרֵךְ יָחִיד וּמְיֻחָד, וּמְמַלֵּא כָּל הַמָּקוֹם הַזֶּה שֶׁבָּרָא בּוֹ הָעוֹלָם. וְגַם עַתָּה כֵּן הוּא לְפָנָיו יִתְבָּרֵךְ. רַק שֶׁהַשִּׁנּוּי הוּא אֶל הַמְקַבְּלִים חַיּוּתוֹ וְאוֹרוֹ יִתְבָּרֵךְ, שֶׁמְּקַבְּלִים עַל יְדֵי לְבוּשִׁים רַבִּים הַמְכַסִּים וּמַסְתִּירִים אוֹרוֹ יִתְבָּרֵךְ . . .

וְזֶהוּ עִנְיַן הִשְׁתַּלְשְׁלוּת הָעוֹלָמוֹת וִירִידָתָם מִמַּדְרֵגָה לְמַדְרֵגָה עַל יְדֵי רִבּוּי הַלְּבוּשִׁים הַמַּסְתִּירִים הָאוֹר וְהַחַיּוּת שֶׁמִּמֶּנּוּ יִתְבָּרֵךְ, עַד שֶׁנִּבְרָא עוֹלָם הַזֶּה הַגַּשְׁמִי וְהַחָמְרִי מַמָּשׁ. וְהוּא הַתַּחְתּוֹן בַּמַּדְרֵגָה, שֶׁאֵין תַּחְתּוֹן לְמַטָּה מִמֶּנּוּ בְּעִנְיַן הֶסְתֵּר

"But Where Is G-d?"
Elliot Lasky shares his transforming encounter with the Rebbe:
myjli.com/kabbalah

אוֹרוֹ יִתְבָּרֵךְ, וְחֹשֶׁךְ כָּפוּל וּמְכֻפָּל, עַד שֶׁהוּא מָלֵא קְלִפּוֹת
וְסִטְרָא אַחֲרָא שֶׁהֵן נֶגֶד ה' מַמָּשׁ, לוֹמַר אֲנִי וְאַפְסִי עוֹד.

וְהִנֵּה תַּכְלִית הִשְׁתַּלְשְׁלוּת הָעוֹלָמוֹת וִירִידָתָם מִמַּדְרֵגָה
לְמַדְרֵגָה אֵינוֹ בִּשְׁבִיל עוֹלָמוֹת הָעֶלְיוֹנִים . . . אֶלָּא הַתַּכְלִית
הוּא עוֹלָם הַזֶּה הַתַּחְתּוֹן. שֶׁכָּךְ עָלָה בִּרְצוֹנוֹ יִתְבָּרֵךְ,
לִהְיוֹת נַחַת רוּחַ לְפָנָיו יִתְבָּרֵךְ כַּד אִתְכַּפְיָא סִטְרָא אַחֲרָא
וְאִתְהַפֵּךְ חֲשׁוֹכָא לִנְהוֹרָא, שֶׁיָּאִיר אוֹר ה' אֵין סוֹף בָּרוּךְ הוּא
בִּמְקוֹם הַחֹשֶׁךְ וְהַסִּטְרָא אַחֲרָא שֶׁל כָּל עוֹלָם הַזֶּה כֻּלּוֹ.

There is a known statement of our sages that G-d created this world to enable the fulfillment of His desire for an abode in this lowest realm.

Now, there is no higher and lower in G-d's presence, because He fills every realm of existence equally. Rather, the description of our world as the lowest realm can be understood by first appreciating that, before the Creation of the universe, all that existed was G-d Himself. The very space that the universe now occupies was entirely filled with G-d's presence. In fact, that remains the reality even now, from the truth of G-d's perspective. The change caused by Creation is only in the perspective of the recipients of G-d's vivifying energy—because they receive this by way of multiple screens that dim and conceal G-d's light, from their perspective. . . .

This concealing process is referred to as the *hishtalshelut* of the worlds, meaning: their devolution from each other via interlinked, progressively dimmer realities, by way of countless steps of concealment of the Divine light and energy. This continues all the way until the Creation of this physical, corporeal, tangible world of ours—the bottom of the entire chain. There is no lower realm in terms of the concealment of G-d's light. It is a world of incredible darkness, to the extent that it is filled with *kelipot* that oppose G-d in actuality and claim that nothing exists beyond their immediate reality.

The goal of the entire chain of interlinked realms of spiritual existence, and the purpose of their progressively steeper descents in terms of Divine concealment, is not for any of those spiritual worlds. . . . Rather, the purpose is to arrive at this lowly, tangible world. For it was G-d's original desire to derive pleasure from mortal efforts to suppress the forces of evil and to transform the darkness into light, until G-d's infinite light shines openly through the entirety of this world—the very habitat of ultimate darkness and the forces that oppose sanctity!

Addressing the Divine

The Torah employs a variety of names to refer to G-d, and this diversity is reflected in our traditional prayers. Each Divine name represents a specific aspect of G-d—a specific and nuanced manner of Divine interaction with His creations.

In addition to the set of formal Divine names, the Torah and our liturgy occasionally refer to G-d by way of informal reference. These references are intended to address G-d directly, meaning, G-d's most simple and sublime Self. Naturally, the Self—*Atzmut*—transcends any formal names and cannot be distilled into any specific descriptor.

G-d's Names		
NAME	יְ־הֹ־וָ־ה	אֵ־ל	אֱ־לֹהִים
TRANSLITERATION	Y-H-V-H	E-l	E-lohim
MEANING	The unfathomable G-d	Mighty One	Lord, judge, powerful, omnipotent
ASSOCIATED SEFIRAH	*Tiferet*	*Chesed*	*Gevurah*
FURTHER EXPLANATION	Y-H-V-H, also known as the Tetragrammaton, is considered G-d's primary name (*shem hameforash*). This name is treated with unequalled reverence in that it is never pronounced as written, even in the course of prayer. Instead, the name is pronounced Ado-nai during prayers; it is commonly pronounced Havayah outside of prayer. This name carries several connotations at once, including G-d's perpetual creation, His compassion, and His absolute infinity and timelessness.	The name E-l, pronounced as Kel outside of prayer, denotes G-d's abundant kindness and revelation.	The name E-lohim, pronounced as Elokim outside of prayer, refers to G-d as He generates and invests Himself within nature. Accordingly, the numerical value of the Hebrew letters that spell E-lohim equals the value (86) of the term *hateva*—nature. This name signifies G-d's concealment, His moderation, and His attribute of justice.

	Divine References			
TERM	אָנֹכִי	אַתָּה	הַשֵּׁם	לְפָנֶיךָ
TRANSLITERATION	Anochi	Atah	Hashem	Lefanecha
MEANING	I	You	The Name	"To You" (literally: before You)
FURTHER EXPLANATION	The less common pronoun Anochi is used by G-d to refer to Himself in the first person. It simply means "I," but implies, "I am Who I am." When used by G-d, it refers to G-d on His own terms, as He exists within His exclusive Self, beyond any title or descriptor. At the Giving of the Torah on Mount Sinai, G-d prefaced His delivery of the Ten Commandments by introducing Himself as Anochi—"I am G-d Your L-rd Who extracted you from Egypt."	The standard formulation of our blessings begins with the common pronoun Atah, "You," a most direct and personal reference to G-d: "Blessed are You (Atah), G-d (Y-H-V-H) our L-rd (E-loheinu), King of the universe...." Before we mention specific Divine names that refer to specific features of G-d's interactions with the universe we address Him directly and completely, simply as "You."	Our profound reverence for G-d prevents us from uttering His sacred name outside the context of prayer. Therefore, it is common practice to refer to G-d simply as Hashem, meaning, "the Name." Unlike the spectrum of actual Divine names that describe particular aspects of G-d, the title, "The Name," is deliberately generic to capture the essence of G-d that transcends all titles.	Immediately upon awakening in the morning, we offer a brief prayer that begins with the words *modeh ani lefanecha*, "I give thanks to You"—expressing our gratitude to G-d for lending us another day of life. Unlike most of our liturgy, this prayer omits any of the Divine names, because it is considered inappropriate to utter a sacred name prior to ritually purifying our hands after sleep. Consequently, we simply state Lefanecha, "to You." From a deeper perspective, however, "before You" refers to G-d's transcendent essence—*Atzmut*—which is beyond the entire concept of impurity.

KEY TERM 6.6

HEBREW TERM	דִּירָה בְּתַחְתּוֹנִים
TRANSLITERATION	*dirah betachtonim*
LITERAL MEANING	**a home in the lowly**
DEFINITION	G-d's desire to have a home in this world, fashioned by our doing *mitzvot*

FIGURE 6.8

Atzmut . . .

1. Has no definition whatsoever.

2. Is the only entity that *necessarily* exists.

3. Follows no rules whatsoever—it is the source of all rules.

4. Is the only Entity that has absolute free choice.

5. Is the source of the atonement granted when we do *teshuvah*.

6. Is connected to the essence of our souls, the *yechidah*.

7. Solely possesses the power to create entities that feel independent from their Divine origin.

8. **Desires a home in this physical world.**

TEXT 14

Only You!

Rabbi Menachem Mendel of Lubavitch, *Derech Mitzvotecha*,
Shoresh Mitzvat Hatefilah, ch. 40

שֹׁרֶשׁ עִנְיַן אַהֲבָה דִּבְחִינַת "[מִי לִי בַּשָּׁמַיִם] וְעִמְּךָ
לֹא חָפַצְתִּי [בָאָרֶץ]" (תְּהִלִּים עג, כה), שֶׁלֹּא לַחְפֹּץ
שׁוּם דָּבָר זוּלָתוֹ יִתְבָּרֵךְ, וְלֹא אֲפִלּוּ שָׁמַיִם וָאָרֶץ, שֶׁהֵם
גַּן עֵדֶן עֶלְיוֹן וְתַחְתּוֹן . . . אֶלָּא תִּהְיֶה הָאַהֲבָה רַק לוֹ
יִתְבָּרֵךְ לְבַד, דְּהַיְנוּ לְמַהוּתוֹ וְעַצְמוּתוֹ יִתְבָּרֵךְ מַמָּשׁ.

וְכָךְ הָיָה נִשְׁמָע הַלָּשׁוֹן מִמּוֹרֵינוּ וְרַבֵּנוּ נִשְׁמָתוֹ
עֵדֶן בִּדְבֵיקוּתוֹ, שֶׁהָיָה אוֹמֵר בָּזֶה הַלָּשׁוֹן:

"אִיךְ וִויל זֶע גָאר נִישְׁט. אִיךְ וִויל נִיט דַאיִין גַּן עֵדֶן, אִיךְ וִויל
נִיט דַאיִין עוֹלָם הַבָּא כוּ'. אִיךְ וִויל מֶער נִיט אַז דִיר אַלֵיין".

"[Whom do I have in Heaven!] I desire nothing
with You [on Earth]!" (PSALMS 73:25).

The love of G-d expressed in the verse is to
crave nothing at all other than G-d alone, not
even "the Heavens or the earth," metaphors
for the higher and lower levels of Paradise. . . .
Instead, all one's love is reserved for G-d's very
essence and Self, to the exclusion of all else.

When our master and teacher [Rabbi Shneur
Zalman of Liadi] would enter a state of rapturous
bonding with G-d, he was often heard to exclaim:

**RABBI MENACHEM
MENDEL OF LUBAVITCH
(*TZEMACH TZEDEK*)
1789-1866**

Chasidic rebbe and noted
author. The *Tzemach
Tzedek* was the 3rd
leader of the Chabad
Chasidic movement
and a noted authority
on Jewish law. His
numerous works include
Halachic responsa,
Chasidic discourses, and
kabbalistic writings.
Active in the communal
affairs of Russian
Jewry, he worked to
alleviate the plight of
the cantonists, Jewish
children kidnapped
to serve in the czar's
army. He passed away
in Lubavitch, leaving 7
sons and 2 daughters.

"I want nothing at all! I don't want Your Garden of Eden! I don't want Your World to Come! . . . All I want is You!"

Initial word panel to Psalm 73 in the *Parma Psalter*, a majestically decorated Italian manuscript, c. 1280. (Palatina Library, Parma, Italy)

KEY TERMS

1. Atzmut

The essence of G-d from which all else emerges

2. Nimna hanimna'ot

It is impossible to ascribe an impossibility to *Atzmut*

3. Bechirah chafshit

A choice that originates completely from within the chooser and is not "compelled" even in the slightest by any external consideration

4. Yechidah

The essence of the soul that is inexorably united with G-d

5. Yesh me'ayin

The creation of an entity that does not intuitively sense and respect its source

6. Dirah betachtonim

G-d's desire to have a home in this world, fashioned by our doing *mitzvot*

KEY POINTS

1   *Atzmut*, G-d's very essence, is the source of the *or ein sof* and all else. Unlike all that emanates from G-d and all that He created, *Atzmut* itself defies all descriptions and is qualitatively different and infinitely removed from all else.

2   *Atzmut* has no cause and *necessarily* exists. By contrast, the existence of everything else is contingent upon *Atzmut* and does not have to exist at all.

3   *Atzmut* is bound by no rules whatsoever—because He creates all rules and definitions.

4   *Atzmut* is also not essentially bound by the rules of morality or right and wrong. *Atzmut freely chose* to embrace goodness and spurn evil and is free to dispense with such rules. Thus, it is from *Atzmut* that we receive the ability for *teshuvah* and to thereby erase our sins.

5   The parallel to *Atzmut* in our selves is the essence of our souls, the *yechidah,* which is intimately and inexorably connected to *Atzmut.*

6   *Atzmut* is completely independent of any source, and we feel the same way about ourselves. Only *Atzmut* has the ability to create an entity that feels independent of its source, and therefore, the power of *Atzmut* is most revealed in our physical world.

7   *Atzmut* desires a home in this physical world. All the infinite spiritual states and worlds exist to further the fulfillment of G-d's desire to have a home in *this* world.

KEY TAKEAWAYS

1   Everything that exists in the infinite spiritual states
    and worlds—from the *or ein sof*, to *Tohu* and *Tikun*,
    to *Keter*, to *Atzilut* and *BiYA*—exists for one purpose:
    the fulfillment of G-d's desire to have a home in
    this world, where *Atzmut* will be revealed. This
    home for G-d is fashioned by our doing *mitzvot*.

2   Despite the loftiness of the various worlds and levels
    of *seder hishtalshelut,* we ought not be distracted or
    tempted by any of them; we should desire *Atzmut* alone.

COURSE CONCLUSION

CONCLUDING EXERCISE A

Match each of the following human features with its corresponding layer of existence within the mystical system of devolution:

Ten attributes (*kochot hanefesh*)

Thought (*machshavah*)

Speech (*dibur*)

Action (*maaseh*)

Desire (*ratzon*)

Soul essence (*yechidah*)

Animal soul (*nefesh habahamit*)

Atzmut

Or ein sof

Tohu

Sefirot (Atzilut)

Beriah

Yetzirah

Asiyah

**CONCLUDING
EXERCISE B**

1. This course introduced forty-one key terms
    from the literature of kabbalah and *Chasidut*.
    Which term (concept) did you find to be most
    interesting? Why?

2. This course offered nineteen key takeaways
    from the profound ideas of Jewish mysticism.
    Which takeaway do you connect with the most?

Acknowledgments

We are grateful to the following individuals for their contributions to this course:

Flagship Director
RABBI SHMULY KARP

Curriculum Coordinator
RIVKI MOCKIN

Flagship Administrator
NAOMI HEBER

Author
RABBI MORDECHAI DINERMAN

Curriculum Development Team
RABBI LAZER GURKOW
RABBI NAFTALI SILBERBERG
RABBI SHMUEL SUPER

Instructors Advisory Board
RABBI MENACHEM FELDMAN
RABBI DOVID FLINKENSTEIN
RABBI LEVI GREENBERG
RABBI DOVID LABKOWSKI
RABBI SHALOM M. PALTIEL

Course Consultants
RABBI SHOLOM CHARITONOW
RABBI YOSEF KLYNE

Research
RABBI YAKOV GERSHON

Copywriters
RABBI YONI BROWN
RABBI YAAKOV PALEY

Proofreading
RACHEL MUSICANTE
YA'AKOVAH WEBER

Hebrew Punctuation
RABBI MOSHE WOLFF

Instructor Support
RABBI ISAAC ABELSKY

Design and Layout Administrator
SARA OSDOBA

Textbook and Marketing Design
CHAYA MUSHKA KANNER
ESTIE RAVNOY
RABBI LEVI WEINGARTEN

Textbook Layout
RABBI MOTTI KLEIN

Imagery
SARA ROSENBLUM

Permissions
SHULAMIS NADLER

Publication and Distribution
RABBI LEVI GOLDSHMID
RABBI MENDEL SIROTA

PowerPoint Presentations
ESTY GEISINSKY
CHANIE SHEMTOV

Course Videos
GETZY RASKIN
MOSHE RASKIN

Key Points Videos
RABBI MOTTI KLEIN

We are immensely grateful for the encouragement of JLI's visionary chairman, and vice-chairman of *Merkos L'Inyonei Chinuch*—Lubavitch World Headquarters, **Rabbi Moshe Kotlarsky**. Rabbi Kotlarsky has been highly instrumental in building the infrastructure for the expansion of Chabad's international network and is also the architect of scores of initiatives and services to help Chabad representatives across the globe succeed in their mission. We are blessed to have the unwavering support of JLI's principal benefactor, **Mr. George Rohr**, who is fully invested in our work, continues to be instrumental in JLI's monumental growth and expansion, and is largely responsible for the Jewish renaissance that is being spearheaded by JLI and its affiliates across the globe.

The commitment and sage direction of JLI's dedicated Executive Board—**Rabbis Chaim Block**, **Hesh Epstein**, **Ronnie Fine**, **Yosef Gansburg**, **Shmuel Kaplan**, **Yisrael Rice**, and **Avrohom Sternberg**—and the countless hours they devote to the development of JLI are what drive the vision, growth, and tremendous success of the organization.

Finally, JLI represents an incredible partnership of more than 1,600 *shluchim* and *shluchot* in more than 1,000 locations across the globe, who contribute their time and talent to furthering Jewish adult education. We thank them for generously sharing feedback and making suggestions that steer JLI's development and growth. They are our most valuable critics and our most cherished contributors.

Inspired by the call of the **Lubavitcher Rebbe**, of righteous memory, it is the mandate of the Rohr JLI to provide a community of learning for all Jews throughout the world where they can participate in their precious heritage of Torah learning and experience its rewards. May this course succeed in fulfilling this sacred charge!

On behalf of the Rohr Jewish Learning Institute,

RABBI EFRAIM MINTZ
Executive Director

RABBI YISRAEL RICE
Chairman, Editorial Board

20 Av, 5783

The Rohr Jewish Learning Institute

CURRICULUM DEVELOPMENT

Rabbi Mordechai Dinerman
Rabbi Naftali Silberberg
EDITORS IN CHIEF

Rabbi Shmuel Klatzkin, PhD
ACADEMIC CONSULTANT

Rabbi Yanki Tauber
SENIOR EDITOR

Rabbi Eli Block
Rabbi Yoni Brown
Rabbi Eliezer Gurkow
Rabbi Berel Polityko
Rabbi Yochanan Rivkin
Rabbi Shmuel Super
CURRICULUM AUTHORS

Rabbi Ahrele Loschak
EDITOR, TORAH STUDIES

Rabbi Yaakov Paley
Rabbi Boruch Werdiger
WRITERS

Rabbi Mendel Glazman
Rabbi Moshe Wolff
EDITORIAL SUPPORT

Rabbi Yakov Gershon
RESEARCH

Rabbi Michoel Lipskier
Rabbi Mendel Rubin
EXPERIENTIAL LEARNING

Mrs. Rivki Mockin
CONTENT COORDINATOR

MARKETING AND BRANDING

Mr. David Kaplan
CHIEF MARKETING OFFICER

Rabbi Mendel Backman
Risa Bursk
Lazer Cohen
Tova Farro
Yosef Feigelstock
Tzivi Gorowitz
Menachem Klein
Basya Stevenson
Baila Vogel
MARKETING AND SOCIAL MEDIA

Ms. Sara Osdoba
DESIGN ADMINISTRATOR

Mrs. Chaya Mushka Kanner
Ms. Chaya Mintz
Ms. Estie Ravnoy
Mrs. Shifra Tauber
Rabbi Levi Weingarten
GRAPHIC DESIGN

Mrs. Rivky Fieldsteel
Rabbi Motti Klein
Rabbi Zalman Korf
Rabbi Moshe Wolff
PUBLICATION DESIGN

Rabbi Yaakov Paley
COPYWRITER

Rabbi Yossi Grossbaum
Rabbi Mendel Lifshitz
Rabbi Shraga Sherman
Rabbi Ari Sollish
Rabbi Mendel Teldon
MARKETING COMMITTEE

MARKETING CONSULTANTS

Alan Rosenspan
ALAN ROSENSPAN & ASSOCIATES
Sharon, MA

Gary Wexler
PASSION MARKETING
Los Angeles, CA

JLI CENTRAL

Rabbi Isaac Abelsky
Ms. Chanie Chesney
Rabbi Levi Goldshmid
Ms. Mushka Majeski
Ms. Mimi Rabinowitz
Rabbi Avremi Rapoport
Mrs. Aliza Scheinfeld
Ms. Mushka Silberstein
Mrs. Orah Smith
Rabbi Menashe Treitel
Rabbi Yosef Vogel
ADMINISTRATION

Ms. Liba Leah Gutnick
Rabbi Motti Klein
Mrs. Sara Rosenblum
Rabbi Shlomie Tenenbaum
PROJECT MANAGERS

Mrs. Mindy Wallach
AFFILIATE ORIENTATION

Ms. Tova Farro
Mrs. Esty Geisinsky
Rabbi Motti Klein
Getzy Raskin
Moshe Raskin
Mrs. Chanie Shemtov
MULTIMEDIA DEVELOPMENT

Rabbi Mendel Ashkenazi
Yoni Ben-Oni
Rabbi Mendy Elishevitz
Mrs. Mushka Goldfarb
Mendel Grossbaum
Mrs. Mushkie Osdoba
Rabbi Aron Liberow
Mrs. Chana Weinbaum
ONLINE DIVISION

Mrs. Rachel Musicante
Mrs. Ya'akovah Weber
PROOFREADERS

Rabbi Levi Goldshmid
Rabbi Mendel Sirota
PRINTING AND DISTRIBUTION

Mrs. Shaina B. Mintz
Mrs. Shulamis Nadler
Ms. Chinkah Zirkind
ACCOUNTING

Ms. Chaya Mintz
Mrs. Shulamis Nadler
Mrs. Mindy Wallach
CONTINUING EDUCATION

JLI FLAGSHIP

Rabbi Yisrael Rice
CHAIRMAN

Rabbi Shmuly Karp
DIRECTOR

Mrs. Naomi Heber
PROJECT MANAGER

Jill Harkavy-Friedman, PhD
Kenneth Ginsburg, M.D., M.S. Ed
Madelyn S. Gould, PhD, M.P.H.
Lisa A. Horowitz, PhD, M.P.H
Lisa Jacobs, M.D., MBA
Thomas Joiner, PhD
E. David Klonsky, PhD
Lisa Miller, PhD
Laura H. Mufson, PhD
Tayyab Rashid, PhD
Sylvia J. Sandler, LMFT
Bella Schanzer, M.D.
Andrew Shatté, PhD
Arielle H. Sheftall, PhD
Jonathan Singer, PhD, LCSW
Casey Skvorc, PhD, JD
Darcy Wallen, LCSW, PC

JLI INTERNATIONAL

Rabbi Avrohom Sternberg
CHAIRMAN

Rabbi Dubi Rabinowitz
DIRECTOR

Rabbi Mendel Glazman
ADMINISTRATOR

Rabbi Eli Wolf
ADMINISTRATOR, JLI IN THE CIS
*In Partnership with the Federation
of Jewish Communities of the CIS*

Flor Setton
COORDINATOR,
CHABAD OF ARGENTINA

Rabbi Nochum Schapiro
REGIONAL REPRESENTATIVE, AUSTRALIA

Rabbi Avrohom Steinmetz
REGIONAL REPRESENTATIVE, BRAZIL

Rabbi Shevach Zlatopolsky
EDITOR, JLI IN THE CIS

Rabbi Shlomo Cohen
FRENCH COORDINATOR,
REGIONAL REPRESENTATIVE

Rabbi Avraham Golovacheov
REGIONAL REPRESENTATIVE, GERMANY

Rabbi Shlomo Koves
REGIONAL REPRESENTATIVE, HUNGARY

Rabbi Shmuel Katzman
REGIONAL REPRESENTATIVE,
NETHERLANDS

Rabbi Bentzi Sudak
REGIONAL REPRESENTATIVE,
UNITED KINGDOM

NATIONAL JEWISH RETREAT

Rabbi Hesh Epstein
CHAIRMAN

Mrs. Shaina B. Mintz
DIRECTOR

Bruce Backman
HOTEL LIAISON

Rabbi Menachem Klein
PROGRAM COORDINATOR

Rabbi Isaac Mintz
SHLUCHIM LIAISON

Rabbi Mendel Rosenfeld
LOGISTICS COORDINATOR

Ms. Mushka Majeski
Mrs. Aliza Scheinfeld
SERVICE AND SUPPORT

THE LAND & THE SPIRIT
Israel Experience

Rabbi Shmuly Karp
DIRECTOR

Rabbi Isaac Mintz
SHLUCHIM LIAISONS

Mrs. Shaina B. Mintz
ADMINISTRATOR

Rabbi Yechiel Baitelman
Rabbi Dovid Flinkenstein
Rabbi Chanoch Kaplan
Rabbi Levi Klein
Rabbi Mendy Mangel
Rabbi Sholom Raichik
STEERING COMMITTEE

SHABBAT IN THE HEIGHTS

Rabbi Shmuly Karp
DIRECTOR

Mrs. Shulamis Nadler
SERVICE AND SUPPORT

Rabbi Chaim Hanoka
CHAIRMAN

Rabbi Mordechai Dinerman
Rabbi Zalman Marcus
STEERING COMMITTEE

MYSHIUR
Advanced Learning Initiative

Rabbi Shmuel Kaplan
CHAIRMAN

Rabbi Shlomie Tenenbaum
ADMINISTRATOR

TORAHCAFE.COM
Online Learning

Rabbi Mendy Elishevitz
WEBSITE DEVELOPMENT

Moshe Levin
CONTENT MANAGER

Mendel Laine
FILMING

MACHON SHMUEL
The Sami Rohr Research Institute

Rabbi Zalman Korf
ADMINISTRATOR

Rabbi Moshe Miller, OBM
Rabbi Gedalya Oberlander
Rabbi Chaim Rapoport
Rabbi Levi Yitzchak Raskin
Rabbi Chaim Schapiro
RABBINIC ADVISORY BOARD

Rabbi Yakov Gershon
RESEARCH FELLOW

FOUNDING DEPARTMENT HEADS
Rabbi Mendel Bell
Rabbi Zalman Charytan
Rabbi Mendel Druk
Rabbi Menachem Gansburg
Rabbi Meir Hecht
Rabbi Levi Kaplan
Rabbi Yoni Katz
Rabbi Chaim Zalman Levy
Rabbi Benny Rapoport
Dr. Chana Silberstein
Rabbi Elchonon Tenenbaum
Rabbi Mendy Weg

JLI Chapter Directory

ALABAMA

BIRMINGHAM
Rabbi Yossi Friedman................................205.970.0100

MOBILE
Rabbi Yosef Goldwasser............................251.265.1213

ALASKA

ANCHORAGE
Rabbi Yosef Greenberg
Rabbi Mendy Greenberg............................907.357.8770

ARIZONA

CHANDLER
Rabbi Mendy Deitsch................................480.855.4333

FLAGSTAFF
Rabbi Dovie Shapiro................................928.255.5756

FOUNTAIN HILLS
Rabbi Mendy Lipskier..............................480.776.4763

ORO VALLEY
Rabbi Ephraim Zimmerman........................520.477.8672

PARADISE VALLEY
Rabbi Shlomo Levertov............................480.788.9310

PHOENIX
Rabbi Dovber Dechter..............................347.410.0785
Rabbi Zalman Levertov
Rabbi Yossi Friedman..............................602.944.2753

SCOTTSDALE
Rabbi Yossi Levertov..............................480.998.1410

SEDONA
Rabbi Mendel Kessler..............................928.985.0667

TUCSON
Rabbi Yehuda Ceitlin..............................520.881.7956

VAIL
Rabbi Yisroel Shemtov............................347.372.3092

ARKANSAS

LITTLE ROCK
Rabbi Pinchus Ciment..............................501.217.0053

CALIFORNIA

AGOURA HILLS
Rabbi Moshe Bryski................................818.516.0444

ALAMEDA
Rabbi Meir Shmotkin..............................510.640.2590

ARCADIA
Rabbi Sholom Stiefel..............................626.539.4578

BAKERSFIELD
Rabbi Shmuli Schlanger..........................661.834.1512

BEL AIR
Rabbi Chaim Mentz................................310.475.5311

BEL AIR WEST
Rabbi Mendy Mentz................................310.666.2302

BEVERLY HILLS
Rabbi Dovid Begun................................310.242.7750

BEVERLYWOOD
Rabbi Menachem Mendel Piekarski............310.597.0967

BURBANK
Rabbi Shmuly Kornfeld............................818.954.0070

CARLSBAD
Rabbi Yeruchem Eilfort
Mrs. Nechama Eilfort..............................760.943.8891

CERRITOS
Rabbi Mendel Lehrer..............................917.717.8704

CHATSWORTH
Rabbi Yossi Spritzer..............................818.307.9907

CHULA VISTA
Rabbi Mendy Begun................................347.587.0979

CONCORD
Rabbi Berel Kesselman............................925.326.1613

CONTRA COSTA
Rabbi Dovber Berkowitz..........................925.937.4101

CORONADO
Rabbi Eli Fradkin 619.365.4728

DANA POINT
Rabbi Eli Goorevitch 949.290.0628

DANVILLE
Rabbi Shmuli Raitman 213.447.6694

EMERYVILLE
Rabbi Menachem Blank 510.859.8808

ENCINO
Rabbi Aryeh Herzog 818.784.9986
Chapter founded by Rabbi Joshua Gordon, OBM

FOLSOM
Rabbi Yossi Grossbaum 916.608.9811

FREMONT
Rabbi Eli Landes 510.300.4090

GLENDALE
Rabbi Simcha Backman 818.240.2750

HIGHLAND PARK
Rabbi Mendel Korf 323.872.4876

HOLLYWOOD
Rabbi Zalman Partouche 818.964.9428

HUNTINGTON BEACH
Rabbi Aron David Berkowitz 714.846.2285

LAGUNA NIGUEL
Rabbi Mendy Paltiel 949.831.7701

LA JOLLA
Rabbi Baruch Shalom Ezagui 858.455.5433

LAKE BALBOA
Rabbi Eli Gurary 347.403.6734

LOMITA
Rabbi Sholom Pinson 310.326.8234

LONG BEACH
Rabbi Abba Perelmuter 562.773.1350

LOS ANGELES
Rabbi Yossi Elifort 310.515.5310
Rabbi Leibel Korf 323.660.5177
Rabbi Zalmy Labkowsky 213.618.9486
Rabbi Mendel Zajac 310.770.9051

MALIBU
Rabbi Levi Cunin 310.456.6588

MAR VISTA
Rabbi Shimon Simpson 646.401.2354

MARINA DEL REY
Rabbi Danny Yiftach-Hashem
Rabbi Dovid Yiftach 310.859.0770

MILL VALLEY
Rabbi Hillel Scop 415.336.3055

NEWHALL
Rabbi Choni Marosov 661.254.3434

NEWPORT BEACH
Rabbi Reuven Mintz 949.375.3707

NORTHRIDGE
Rabbi Eli Rivkin 818.368.3937

OJAI
Rabbi Mordechai Nemtzov 805.613.7181

PACIFIC PALISADES
Rabbi Zushe Cunin 310.454.7783

PALO ALTO
Rabbi Menachem Landa 415.418.4768
Rabbi Yosef Levin
Rabbi Ber Rosenblatt 650.424.9800

PASADENA
Rabbi Zushe Rivkin 626.788.3343

PLEASANTON
Rabbi Josh Zebberman 925.846.0700

PORTOLA VALLEY
Rabbi Mayer Brook 650.304.2098

POWAY
Rabbi Mendel Goldstein 858.208.6613

RANCHO CUCAMONGA
Rabbi Sholom Ber Harlig 909.949.4553

RANCHO MIRAGE
Rabbi Shimon H. Posner 760.770.7785

RANCHO PALOS VERDES
Rabbi Yitzchok Magalnic 310.544.5544

RANCHO S. FE
Rabbi Levi Raskin 858.756.7571

REDONDO BEACH
Rabbi Yossi Mintz
Rabbi Zalman Gordon 310.214.4999

RIVERSIDE
Rabbi Shmuel Fuss 951.329.2747

RESEDA
Rabbi Hershy Spritzer 818.881.1033

S. CLEMENTE
Rabbi Menachem M. Slavin 949.489.0723

S. CRUZ
Rabbi Yochanan Friedman 831.454.0101

S. DIEGO
Rabbi Rafi Andrusier 619.387.8770
Rabbi Yechiel Cagen 832.216.1534
Rabbi Motte Fradkin 858.547.0076

S. FRANCISCO
Rabbi Yakov Barber 424.499.9868
Rebbetzin Mattie Pil 415.933.4310
Rabbi Gedalia Potash 415.648.8000
Rabbi Shlomo Zarchi 415.752.2866

S. LUIS OBISPO
Rabbi Meir Gordon 347.675.3383

S. MATEO
Rabbi Yossi Marcus 650.341.4510

S. RAFAEL
Rabbi Yisrael Rice 415.492.1666

SHERMAN OAKS
Rabbi Nachman Abend 818.989.9539

SONOMA
Rabbi Mendel Wolvovsky 707.292.6221

SOUTH LAKE TAHOE
Rabbi Mordechai Richler 530.539.4363

SOUTH PASADENA
Rabbi Dovid Harlig 626.921.6256

STOCKHOLM
Rabbi Avremel Brod 209.952.2081

SUNNYVALE
Rabbi Yisroel Hecht 408.720.0553

TEMECULA
Rabbi Yonason Abrams 951.234.4196

TIBURON
Rabbi Levi Mintz 415.378.9364

TOPANGA
Rabbi Menachem Piekarski 858.335.7197

TUSTIN
Rabbi Yehoshua Eliezrie 714.508.2150

VACAVILLE
Rabbi Chaim Zaklos 707.592.5300

WEST HILLS
Rabbi Avi Rabin 818.337.4544

WEST HOLLYWOOD
Rabbi Mordechai Kirschenbaum 310.691.9988

WEST LOS ANGELES
Rabbi Mordechai Zaetz 424.652.8742

YORBA LINDA
Rabbi Dovid Eliezrie 714.693.0770

COLORADO

ASPEN
Rabbi Mendel Mintz 970.544.3770

DENVER
Rabbi Yossi Serebryanski 303.744.9699
Rabbi Mendel Popack 720.515.4337
Rabbi Mendy Sirota 720.940.3716

FORT COLLINS
Rabbi Yerachmiel Gorelik 970.407.1613

HIGHLANDS RANCH
Rabbi Avraham Mintz 303.694.9119

LONGMONT
Rabbi Yakov Borenstein 303.678.7595

VAIL
Rabbi Dovid Mintz 970.476.7887

WESTMINSTER
Rabbi Benjy Brackman 303.429.5177

CONNECTICUT

FAIRFIELD
Rabbi Shlame Landa 203.373.7551

GLASTONBURY
Rabbi Yosef Wolvovsky 860.659.2422

GREENWICH
Rabbi Yossi Deren
Rabbi Menachem Feldman 203.629.9059

GUILFORD
Rabbi Yossi Yaffe 203.645.4635

HAMDEN
Rabbi Moshe Hecht 203.635.7268

MILFORD
Rabbi Schneur Wilhelm 203.887.7603

NEW HAVEN
Rabbi Mendy Hecht 203.589.5375
Rabbi Chanoch Wineberg 203.479.0313

NEW LONDON
Rabbi Avrohom Sternberg 860.437.8000

ORANGE
Rabbi Hershy Hecht 203.464.7809

STAMFORD
Rabbi Yisrael Deren
Rabbi Levi Mendelow 203.3.CHABAD

WESTPORT
Rabbi Yehuda Kantor 561.460.3758

WEST HARTFORD
Rabbi Shaya Gopin 860.232.1116

SHELTON
Rabbi Schneur Brook 203.364.4149

DELAWARE

WILMINGTON
Rabbi Chuni Vogel 302.529.9900

DISTRICT OF COLUMBIA
Rabbi Levi Shemtov
Rabbi Yitzy Ceitlin 202.332.5600

FLORIDA

ALTAMONTE SPRINGS
Rabbi Mendy Bronstein 407.280.0535

AVENTURA
Rabbi Mendel Rosenblum 412.807.0584

BOCA RATON
Rabbi Zalman Bukiet 561.487.2934
Rabbi Arele Gopin 561.994.6257
Rabbi Moishe Denburg 561.526.5760
Rabbi Ruvi New 561.394.9770

BONITA SPRINGS
Rabbi Mendy Greenberg 239.949.6900

BOYNTON BEACH
Rabbi Sholom Ciment 561.732.4633
Rabbi Yosef Yitzchok Raichik 561.740.8738

BRADENTON
Rabbi Menachem Bukiet 941.388.9656

CAPE CORAL
Rabbi Yossi Labkowski 239.963.4770

CORAL GABLES
Rabbi Avrohom Stolik 305.490.7572

CORAL SPRINGS
Rabbi Hershy Bronstein 954.798.6023
Rabbi Yankie Denburg 954.471.8646

CUTLER BAY
Rabbi Yossi Wolff 305.975.6680

DAVIE
Rabbi Aryeh Schwartz 954.376.9973

DELRAY BEACH
Rabbi Yaakov Perman 561.666.2770

FISHER ISLAND
Rabbi Efraim Brody 347.325.1913

FLEMING ISLAND
Rabbi Shmuly Feldman 904.290.1017

FORT LAUDERDALE
Rabbi Yitzchok Naparstek 954.568.1190
Rabbi Schneur Kaplan 954.667.8000

HALLANDALE BEACH
Rabbi Mordy Feiner 954.458.1877

HOLLYWOOD
Rabbi Leibel Kudan 954.801.3367

JUPITER
Rabbi Berel Barash 561.317.0968

KENDALL
Rabbi Yossi Harlig 305.234.5654

KEY BISCAYNE
Rabbi Avremel Caroline 305.365.6744

LAUDERHILL
Rabbi Shmuel Heidingsfeld 323.877.7703

LONGWOOD
Rabbi Yanky Majesky 407.636.5994

MAITLAND
Rabbi Sholom Dubov
Rabbi Levik Dubov 470.644.2500
Rabbi Tzviki Dubov 407.529.8256

MARION COUNTY
Rabbi Yossi Hecht 352.330.4466

MIAMI
Rabbi Mendy Cheruty 305.219.3353
Rabbi Yakov Fellig 305.445.5444
Rabbi Chaim Lipskar 305.373.8303

MIAMI BEACH
Rabbi Yisroel Frankforter 305.534.3895
Rabbi Sholom Korf 786.423.6483
Rabbi Shmuel Mann 305.674.8400

N. MIAMI BEACH
Rabbi Eli Laufer 305.770.4412

NAPLES
Rabbi Fishel Zaklos 239.404.6993

ORLANDO
Rabbi Yosef Konikov 407.354.3660

ORMOND BEACH
Rabbi Asher Farkash 386.672.9300

PALM CITY
Rabbi Shlomo Uminer 772.485.5501

PALM BEACH
Rabbi Zalman Levitin 561.659.3884

PALM BEACH GARDENS
Rabbi Dovid Vigler 561.624.2223

PALM HARBOR
Rabbi Pinchas Adler 727.789.0408

PARKLAND
Rabbi Mendy Gutnick 954.600.6991

PEMBROKE PINES
Rabbi Mordechai Andrusier 954.874.2280

PENSACOLA
Rabbi Mendel Danow 850.291.9600

PLANTATION
Rabbi Pinchas Taylor 954.644.9177

PONTE VEDRA BEACH
Rabbi Nochum Kurinsky 904.543.9301

PORT ORANGE
Rabbi Mendel Niasoff 386.679.5756

ROYAL PALM BEACH
Rabbi Nachmen Zeev Schtroks 561.714.1692

S. AUGUSTINE
Rabbi Levi Vogel 904.521.8664

S. JOHNS
Rabbi Mendel Sharfstein 347.461.3765

S. PETERSBURG
Rabbi Alter Korf 727.344.4900

SARASOTA
Rabbi Chaim Shaul Steinmetz 941.925.0770
Rabbi Levi Steinmetz 941.928.9267

SATELLITE BEACH
Rabbi Zvi Konikov 321.777.2770

SINGER ISLAND
Rabbi Berel Namdar 347.276.6985

SOUTH PALM BEACH
Rabbi Leibel Stolik 561.889.3499

SOUTH TAMPA
Rabbi Mendy Dubrowski 813.922.1723

SOUTHWEST BROWARD COUNTY
Rabbi Aryeh Schwartz 954.252.1770

SUNNY ISLES BEACH
Rabbi Alexander Kaller 305.803.5315

SURFSIDE
Rabbi Dov Schochet 305.790.8294

TAMARAC
Rabbi Kopel Silberberg 954.882.7434

TAMPA
Rabbi Chaim Lipszyc 954.882.7434

VENICE
Rabbi Sholom Ber Schmerling 845.238.0770

VERO BEACH
Rabbi Motty Rosenfeld 772.245.6712

WATERWAYS
Rabbi Yisroel Brusowankin 786.663.8731

WESLEY CHAPEL
Rabbi Mendy Yarmush
Rabbi Mendel Friedman 813.731.2977

WEST DELRAY BEACH
Rabbi Yossi Schapiro 561.221.1618

WEST PALM BEACH
Rabbi Yoel Gancz 561.659.7770

WESTON
Rabbi Yisroel Spalter 954.349.6565

GEORGIA

ALPHARETTA
Rabbi Hirshy Minkowicz 770.410.9000

ATLANTA
Rabbi Yossi New
Rabbi Isser New 404.843.2464
Rabbi Alexander Piekarski 678.267.6418
Rabbi Ari Sollish 404.898.0434

ATLANTA: INTOWN
Rabbi Eliyahu Schusterman
Rabbi Chanan Rose 415.370.1333

AUGUSTA
Rabbi Zalman Fischer 706.836.1576

CUMMING
Rabbi Levi Mentz 310.666.2218

DUNWOODY
Rabbi Mendy Wineberg 347.770.2414

GAINESVILLE
Rabbi Nechemia Gurevitz 770.906.4970

GWINNETT
Rabbi Yossi Lerman 678.595.0196

MARIETTA
Rabbi Ephraim Silverman 770.565.4412

HAWAII

KAILUA-KONA
Rabbi Levi Gerlitzky 917.853.2787

KAPA'A
Rabbi Michoel Goldman 808.647.4293

IDAHO

BOISE
Rabbi Mendel Lifshitz 208.853.9200

ILLINOIS

ARLINGTON HEIGHTS
Rabbi Yaakov Kotlarsky 224.357.7002

CHAMPAIGN
Rabbi Dovid Tiechtel 217.355.8672

CHICAGO
Rabbi Mendy Benhiyoun 312.498.7704
Rabbi Meir Hecht 312.714.4655
Rabbi Dovid Kotlarsky 773.495.7127
Rabbi Mordechai Gershon 773.412.5189
Rabbi Yosef Moscowitz 773.772.3770
Rabbi Levi Notik 773.274.5123

ELGIN
Rabbi Mendel Shemtov 847.440.4486

GLENVIEW
Rabbi Yishaya Benjaminson 847.910.1738

GURNEE
Rabbi Sholom Tenenbaum 847.782.1800

HIGHLAND PARK
Mrs. Michla Schanowitz 847.266.0770

NAPERVILLE
Rabbi Mendy Goldstein 630.957.8122

NORTHBROOK
Rabbi Meir Moscowitz 847.564.8770

NORWOOD PARK
Rabbi Mendel Perlstein 312.752.8894

OAK PARK
Rabbi Yitzchok Bergstein 708.524.1530

PARK RIDGE
Rabbi Lazer Hershkovich 224.392.4442

PEORIA
Rabbi Eli Langsam 309.370.7701

SKOKIE
Rabbi Yochanan Posner 847.677.1770

VERNON HILLS
Rabbi Shimmy Susskind 718.755.5356

WILMETTE
Rabbi Dovid Flinkenstein 847.251.7707

INDIANA

INDIANAPOLIS
Rabbi Avraham Grossbaum
Rabbi Dr. Shmuel Klatzkin 317.251.5573

IOWA

BETTENDORF
Rabbi Shneur Cadaner 563.355.1065

KANSAS

OVERLAND PARK
Rabbi Mendy Wineberg 913.649.4852

KENTUCKY

LOUISVILLE
Rabbi Avrohom Litvin 502.459.1770

LOUISIANA

BATON ROUGE
Rabbi Peretz Kazen 225.267.7047

METAIRIE
Rabbi Yossie Nemes
Rabbi Mendel Ceitlin 504.454.2910

NEW ORLEANS
Rabbi Mendel Rivkin 504.302.1830

MAINE

BANGOR
Rabbi Chaim Wilansky 207.650.7223

PORTLAND
Rabbi Levi Wilansky 207.650.1783

MARYLAND

BALTIMORE
Rabbi Velvel Belinsky 410.764.5000
Classes in Russian

Rabbi Dovid Reyder 781.796.4204

BEL AIR
Rabbi Kushi Schusterman 443.353.9718

BETHESDA
Rabbi Sender Geisinsky 301.913.9777

CHEVY CHASE
Rabbi Zalman Minkowitz 301.260.5000

COLUMBIA
Rabbi Hillel Baron
Rabbi Yosef Chaim Sufrin 410.740.2424

FREDERICK
Rabbi Boruch Labkowski 301.996.3659

GAITHERSBURG
Rabbi Sholom Raichik 301.926.3632

OLNEY
Rabbi Bentzy Stolik 301.660.6770

OWINGS MILLS
Rabbi Nochum Katsenelenbogen 410.356.5156

POTOMAC
Rabbi Mendel Bluming 301.983.4200
Rabbi Mendel Kaplan 301.983.1485

ROCKVILLE
Rabbi Shlomo Beitsh 646.773.2675
Rabbi Moishe Kavka 301.836.1242

MASSACHUSETTS

ANDOVER
Rabbi Asher Bronstein 978.470.2288

ARLINGTON
Rabbi Avi Bukiet 617.909.8653

BOSTON
Rabbi Yosef Zaklos 617.297.7282

BRIGHTON
Rabbi Dan Rodkin 617.787.2200

CAPE COD
Rabbi Yekusiel Alperowitz 508.775.2324

CHESTNUT HILL
Rabbi Mendy Uminer 617.738.9770

LEXINGTON
Rabbi Yisroel New 646.248.9053

LONGMEADOW
Rabbi Yakov Wolff 413.567.8665

NEWTON
Rabbi Shalom Ber Prus 617.244.1200

PEABODY
Rabbi Nechemia Schusterman 978.977.9111

SUDBURY
Rabbi Yisroel Freeman 978.443.0110

SWAMPSCOTT
Rabbi Yossi Lipsker 781.581.3833

MICHIGAN

ANN ARBOR
Rabbi Aharon Goldstein 734.995.3276

BLOOMFIELD HILLS
Rabbi Levi Dubov 248.949.6210

GRAND RAPIDS
Rabbi Mordechai Haller 616.957.0770

TROY
Rabbi Menachem Caytak 248.873.5851

WEST BLOOMFIELD
Rabbi Elimelech Silberberg 248.855.6170

MINNESOTA

MINNETONKA
Rabbi Mordechai Grossbaum
Rabbi Shmuel Silberstein 952.929.9922

PLYMOUTH
Rabbi Nissan Naparstek 310.430.0960

S. PAUL
Rabbi Shneur Zalman Bendet 651.998.9298

MISSOURI

CHESTERFIELD
Rabbi Avi Rubenfeld 314.258.3401

S. LOUIS
Rabbi Yosef Landa 314.725.0400
Rabbi Yosef Abenson 314.448.0927

MONTANA

KALISPELL
Rabbi Shneur Wolf 406.885.2541

BOZEMAN
Rabbi Chaim Shaul Bruk 406.600.4934

NEVADA

LAS VEGAS
Rabbi Yosef Rivkin 702.217.2170

RENO
Rabbi Levi Sputz 347.262.4531

SUMMERLIN
Rabbi Yisroel Schanowitz
Rabbi Tzvi Bronchtain 702.855.0770

NEW JERSEY

BASKING RIDGE
Rabbi Mendy Herson
Rabbi Mendel Shemtov 908.604.8844

CHERRY HILL
Rabbi Mendel Mangel 856.874.1500

CLINTON
Rabbi Eli Kornfeld 908.623.7000

ENGLEWOOD
Rabbi Shmuel Konikov 201.519.7343

FAIR LAWN
Rabbi Avrohom Bergstein 201.794.3770

FANWOOD
Rabbi Avrohom Blesofsky 908.790.0008

FLANDERS
Rabbi Yaacov Shusterman 973.723.6868

FORT LEE
Rabbi Meir Konikov 201.886.1238

GREATER MERCER COUNTY
Rabbi Dovid Dubov
Rabbi Yaakov Chaiton 609.213.4136

HASKELL
Rabbi Mendy Gurkov 201.696.7609

HOLMDEL
Rabbi Shmaya Galperin 732.772.1998

JACKSON
Rabbi Shmuel Naparstek 732.668.7702

MADISON
Rabbi Shalom Lubin 973.377.0707

MANALAPAN
Rabbi Boruch Chazanow
Rabbi Levi Wolosow 732.972.3687

MEDFORD
Rabbi Yitzchok Kahan 609.451.3522

MONTCLAIR
Rabbi Yaacov Leaf 862.252.5666

MORRISTOWN
Rabbi Moishe Gurevitz 973.216.8077

MOUNTAIN LAKES
Rabbi Levi Dubinsky 973.551.1898

MULLICA HILL
Rabbi Avrohom Richler 856.733.0770

OLD TAPPAN
Rabbi Mendy Lewis 201.767.4008

RANDOLPH
Rabbi Avraham Bekhor 718.915.8748

RED BANK
Rabbi Dovid Harrison 973.895.3070

ROCKAWAY
Rabbi Asher Herson
Rabbi Mordechai Baumgarten 973.625.1525

RUTHERFORD
Rabbi Yitzchok Lerman 347.834.7500

SCOTCH PLAINS
Rabbi Avrohom Blesofsky 908.790.0008

SHORT HILLS
Rabbi Mendel Solomon
Rabbi Avrohom Levin 973.725.7008

SOUTH BRUNSWICK
Rabbi Levi Azimov 732.398.9492

TENAFLY
Rabbi Mordechai Shain 201.871.1152

TOMS RIVER
Rabbi Moshe Gourarie 732.349.4199

VENTNOR
Rabbi Avrohom Rapoport 609.822.8500

WEST ORANGE
Rabbi Mendy Kasowitz 973.325.6311

WOODCLIFF LAKE
Rabbi Dov Drizin 201.476.0157

NEW MEXICO

LAS CRUCES
Rabbi Bery Schmukler 575.524.1330

NEW YORK

ALBANY
Rabbi Mordechai Rubin................518.368.7886

BEDFORD
Rabbi Arik Wolf................914.666.6065

BENSONHURST
Rabbi Avrohom Hertz................718.753.7768

BINGHAMTON
Mrs. Rivkah Slonim................607.797.0015

BRIGHTON BEACH
Rabbi Dovid Okonov................718.368.4490

BRONXVILLE
Rabbi Sruli Deitsch................917.755.0078

BROOKVILLE
Rabbi Mendy Heber................516.626.0600

CEDARHURST
Rabbi Zalman Wolowik................516.295.2478

CLIFTON PARK
Rabbi Yossi Rubin................518.495.0772

COMMACK
Rabbi Mendel Teldon................631.543.3343

DELMAR
Rabbi Zalman Simon................518.866.7658

DOBBS FERRY
Rabbi Benjy Silverman................914.693.6100

EAST HAMPTON
Rabbi Leibel Baumgarten
Rabbi Mendy Goldberg................631.329.5800

ELLENVILLE
Rabbi Shlomie Deren................845.647.4450

FOREST HILLS
Rabbi Yossi Mendelson................917.861.9726

GLEN OAKS
Rabbi Shmuel Nadler................347.388.7064

GREAT NECK
Rabbi Yoseph Geisinsky................516.487.4554

ISLIP
Rabbi Shimon Stillerman................631.913.8770

KINGSTON
Rabbi Yitzchok Hecht................845.334.9044

LARCHMONT
Rabbi Mendel Silberstein................914.834.4321

LITTLE NECK
Rabbi Eli Shifrin................718.423.1235

LONG BEACH
Rabbi Eli Goodman................516.574.3905

LONG ISLAND CITY
Rabbi Zev Wineberg................347.218.2927

MANHASSET
Rabbi Mendel Paltiel................516.984.0701

MINEOLA
Rabbi Anchelle Perl................516.739.3636

MONTEBELLO
Rabbi Shmuel Gancz................845.746.1927

MELVILLE
Rabbi Yosef Raskin................631.276.4453

NEW HARTFORD
Rabbi Levi Charitonow................716.322.8692

NEW YORK
Rabbi Yakov Bankhalter................917.613.1678
Rabbi Nissi Eber................347.677.2276
Rabbi Berel Gurevitch................212.518.3122
Rabbi Daniel Kraus................917.294.5567
Rabbi Shmuel Metzger................212.758.3770

NYC TRIBECA
Rabbi Zalman Paris................212.566.6764

NYC UPPER EAST SIDE
Rabbi Uriel Vigler................212.369.7310

NYC WEST SIDE
Rabbi Shlomo Kugel................212.864.5010

OCEANSIDE
Rabbi Levi Gurkow................516.764.7385

OSSINING
Rabbi Dovid Labkowski................914.923.2522

OYSTER BAY
Rabbi Shmuel Lipszyc
Rabbi Shalom Lipszyc................347.853.9992

PARK SLOPE
Rabbi Menashe Wolf 347.957.1291

PORT WASHINGTON
Rabbi Shalom Paltiel 516.767.8672

PROSPECT HEIGHTS
Rabbi Mendy Hecht 347.622.3599

ROCHESTER
Rabbi Nechemia Vogel 585.271.0330

ROSLYN HEIGHTS
Rabbi Aaron Konikov 516.484.3500

SEA GATE
Rabbi Chaim Brikman 347.524.3214

SOUTHAMPTON
Rabbi Chaim Pape 917.627.4865

STATEN ISLAND
Rabbi Mendy Katzman 718.370.8953

STONY BROOK
Rabbi Shalom Ber Cohen 631.585.0521

SUFFERN
Rabbi Shmuel Gancz 845.368.1889

WEST BRIGHTON BEACH
Rabbi Moshe Winner 718.946.9833

YORKTOWN HEIGHTS
Rabbi Yehuda Heber 914.962.1111

NORTH CAROLINA

CARY
Rabbi Yisroel Cotlar 919.651.9710

CHAPEL HILL
Rabbi Zalman Bluming 919.357.5904

CHARLOTTE
Rabbi Yossi Groner
Rabbi Shlomo Cohen 704.366.3984

GREENSBORO
Rabbi Yosef Plotkin 336.617.8120

RALEIGH
Rabbi Pinchas Herman
Rabbi Mendy Wilschanski 919.847.8986

WILMINGTON
Rabbi Moshe Lieblich 910.763.4770

WINSTON-SALEM
Rabbi Levi Gurevitz 336.756.9069

OHIO

BEACHWOOD
Rabbi Moshe Gancz 216.647.4884

CINCINNATI
Rabbi Yisroel Mangel 513.793.5200

COLUMBUS
Rabbi Yitzi Kaltmann 614.294.3296

DAYTON
Rabbi Nochum Mangel 937.643.0770

OKLAHOMA

OKLAHOMA CITY
Rabbi Ovadia Goldman 405.524.4800

TULSA
Rabbi Yehuda Weg 918.492.4499

OREGON

PORTLAND
Rabbi Mordechai Wilhelm 503.977.9947

SALEM
Rabbi Avrohom Yitzchok Perlstein 503.383.9569

TIGARD
Rabbi Menachem Orenstein 971.329.6661

WEST LINN
Rabbi Shimon Wilhelm 503.753.4744

PENNSYLVANIA

AMBLER
Rabbi Shaya Deitsch 215.591.9310

BALA CYNWYD
Rabbi Shraga Sherman 610.660.9192

CLARKS SUMMIT
Rabbi Benny Rapoport 570.587.3300

DOYLESTOWN
Rabbi Mendel Prus 215.340.1303

FREEDOM
Rabbi Yosef Feller 612.275.6438

GLEN MILLS
Rabbi Yehuda Gerber 484.620.4162

LAFAYETTE HILL
Rabbi Yisroel Kotlarsky 484.533.7009

LANCASTER
Rabbi Elazar Green 717.723.8783

LEWISBURG
Rabbi Yisroel Baumgarten 631.880.2801

MECHANICSBURG
Rabbi Nissen Pewzner 717.798.0053

MONROEVILLE
Rabbi Mendy Schapiro 412.372.1000

NEWTOWN
Rabbi Aryeh Weinstein 215.497.9925

PHILADELPHIA
Rabbi Berel Paltiel 718.288.8574

PHILADELPHIA: CENTER CITY
Rabbi Yochonon Goldman 215.238.2100

PITTSBURGH
Rabbi Yisroel Altein .... 412.422.7300 EXT. 269

PITTSBURGH: SOUTH HILLS
Rabbi Mendy Rosenblum 412.278.3693

READING
Rabbi Yosef Lipsker 610.334.3218

RYDAL
Rabbi Zushe Gurevitz 267.536.5757

UNIVERSITY PARK
Rabbi Nosson Meretsky 814.863.4929

WYNNEWOOD
Rabbi Moishe Brennan 610.529.9011

PUERTO RICO

CAROLINA
Rabbi Mendel Zarchi 787.253.0894

RHODE ISLAND

WARWICK
Rabbi Yossi Laufer 401.884.7888

SOUTH CAROLINA

BLUFFTON
Rabbi Menachem Hertz 843.301.1819

COLUMBIA
Rabbi Hesh Epstein
Rabbi Levi Marrus 803.782.1831

GREENVILLE
Rabbi Leibel Kesselman 864.534.7739

MYRTLE BEACH
Rabbi Doron Aizenman 843.448.0035

TENNESSEE

CHATTANOOGA
Rabbi Shaul Perlstein 423.910.9770

KNOXVILLE
Rabbi Yossi Wilhelm 865.588.8584

MEMPHIS
Rabbi Levi Klein 901.754.0404

NASHVILLE
Rabbi Yitzchok Tiechtel 615.646.5750

TEXAS

AUSTIN
Rabbi Mendy Levertov 512.905.2778

BELLAIRE
Rabbi Yossi Zaklikofsky 713.839.8887

CYPRESS
Rabbi Levi Marinovsky 832.651.6964

DALLAS
Rabbi Zvi Drizin 214.632.2633
Rabbi Mendel Dubrawsky
Rabbi Moshe Naparstek 972.818.0770

EL PASO
Rabbi Levi Greenberg 347.678.9762

FORT WORTH
Rabbi Dov Mandel 817.263.7701

HOUSTON
Rabbi Dovid Goldstein
Rabbi Zally Lazarus 281.589.7188
Rabbi Moishe Traxler 713.774.0300

HOUSTON: RICE UNIVERSITY AREA
Rabbi Eliezer Lazaroff 713.522.2004

LEAGUE CITY
Rabbi Yitzchok Schmukler 281.724.1554

PLANO
Rabbi Eli Block 214.620.4083
Rabbi Mendel Block 972.596.8270

ROCKWALL
Rabbi Moshe Kalmenson 469.350.5735

ROUND ROCK
Rabbi Mendel Marasow 512.387.3171

S. ANTONIO
Rabbi Chaim Block
Rabbi Levi Teldon 210.492.1085
Rabbi Tal Shaul 210.877.4218

SOUTHLAKE
Rabbi Levi Gurevitch 817.451.1171

SUGAR LAND
Rabbi Mendel Feigenson 832.758.0685

THE WOODLANDS
Rabbi Mendel Blecher 281.865.7242

UTAH

LEHI
Rabbi Chaim Zippel 801.674.4566

PARK CITY
Rabbi Yehuda Steiger 435.714.8590

SALT LAKE CITY
Rabbi Benny Zippel 801.467.7777

S. GEORGE
Rabbi Mendy Cohen 862.812.6224

VERMONT

BURLINGTON
Rabbi Yitzchok Raskin 802.658.5770

MANCHESTER
Rabbi Menachem Andrusier 518.506.8678

WATERBURY CENTER
Rabbi Boruch Simon 518.360.7337

VIRGINIA

ALEXANDRIA/ARLINGTON
Rabbi Mordechai Newman 703.370.2774

FAIRFAX
Rabbi Leibel Fajnland 703.426.1980

GAINESVILLE
Rabbi Shmuel Perlstein 571.445.0342

LOUDOUN COUNTY
Rabbi Chaim Cohen 248.298.9279

NORFOLK
Rabbi Aaron Margolin
Rabbi Levi Brashevitzky 757.616.0770

RICHMOND
Rabbi Shlomo Pereira 804.740.2000

WINCHESTER
Rabbi Yishai Dinerman 540.324.9879

WASHINGTON

BAINBRIDGE ISLAND
Rabbi Mendy Goldshmid 206.397.7679

BELLINGHAM
Rabbi Yosef Truxton 360.224.9919

KIRKLAND
Rabbi Chaim S. Rivkin 425.749.8512

LYNNWOOD
Rabbi Berel Paltiel 425.286.7465

MERCER ISLAND
Rabbi Elazar Bogomilsky 206.527.1411
Rabbi Nissan Kornfeld 206.851.2324

NORMANDY PARK

Rabbi Moshe Wolff 206.946.2477

OLYMPIA

Rabbi Yosef Schtroks 360.867.8804

SEATTLE

Rabbi Yoni Levitin 206.851.9831

Rabbi Shnai Levitin 347.342.2259

SPOKANE COUNTY

Rabbi Yisroel Hahn 509.443.0770

WISCONSIN

BAYSIDE

Rabbi Cheski Edelman 414.439.5041

BROOKFIELD

Rabbi Levi Brook 925.708.4203

KENOSHA

Rabbi Tzali Wilschanski 262.359.0770

MADISON

Rabbi Avremel Matusof 608.335.3777

MEQUON

Rabbi Menachem Rapoport 262.242.2235

MILWAUKEE

Rabbi Levi Emmer 414.277.8839

Rabbi Mendel Shmotkin 414.961.6100

WYOMING

LARAMIE

Rabbi Yaakov Raskin 307.920.2613

ARGENTINA

BAHIA BLANCA

Rabbi Shmuel Freedman 347.300.2779

BUENOS AIRES

Rabbi Abraham Benchimol 54.11.6048.5333

Rabbi Yossi Birman 54.11.5334.6606

Mrs. Chani Gorowitz 54.11.4865.0445

Rabbi Menachem M. Grunblatt 54.911.3574.0037

Rabbi Mendy Gurevitch 55.11.4545.7771

Rabbi Mendel Levy 54.11.3687.8258

Rabbi Shlomo Levy 54.11.4807.2223

Rabbi Yosef Levy 54.11.4504.1908

Rabbi Yosef Yitzjok Levy 54.11.6292.4125

Rabbi Tzvi Lipinsky 54.11.5249.2693

Rabbi Yossi Ludman 54.11.3935.0214

Rabbi Yoel Migdal 54.11.4963.1221

Rabbi Mendi Mizrahi 54.11.4963.1221

Rabbi Shiele Plotka 54.11.4634.3111

Rabbi Itzjak Safranchik 54.11.3699.3977

Rabbi Shniur Zalmen Schvetz 54.11.3552.5208

Rabbi Shloimi Setton 54.11.4982.8637

Rabbi Pinhas Sudry 54.1.4822.2285

CORDOBA

Rabbi Menajem Turk 54.351.233.8250

ROSARIO

Rabbi Shlomo Tawil 54.93.4152.0039

SALTA

Rabbi Rafael Tawil 54.387.421.4947

S. MIGUEL DE TUCUMÁN

Rabbi Ariel Levy 54.381.473.6944

AUSTRALIA

NEW SOUTH WALES

BELLEVUE HILL

Mrs. Chaya Kaye 614.3342.2755

DOUBLE BAY

Rabbi Yanky Berger 612.9327.1644

DOVER HEIGHTS

Rabbi Motti Feldman 614.0400.8572

MAROUBRA

Rabbi Schneur Goldstein 614.3476.0722

NEWTOWN

Rabbi Eli Feldman 614.0077.0613

NORTH SHORE
Rabbi Nochum Schapiro
Rebbetzin Fruma Schapiro 612.9488.9548

SYDNEY
Rabbi Levi Wolff 614.2162.2622

TASMANIA

SOUTH LAUNCESTON
Mrs. Rochel Gordon 614.2055.0405

QUEENSLAND

BRISBANE
Rabbi Levi Jaffe 617.3843.6770

VICTORIA

EAST S. KILDA
Rabbi Sholem Gorelik 614.5244.8770

MOORABBIN
Rabbi Elisha Greenbaum 614.0349.0434

WESTERN AUSTRALIA

PERTH
Rabbi Shalom White 618.9275.2106

AZERBAIJAN

BAKU
Mrs. Chavi Segal 994.12.597.91.90

BELARUS

BOBRUISK
Mrs. Mina Hababo 375.29.104.3230

MINSK
Rabbi Shneur Deitsch
Mrs. Bassie Deitsch 375.29.330.6675

BELGIUM

ANTWERP
Rabbi Mendel Gurary 32.48.656.9878

BRUSSELS
Rabbi Shmuel Pinson 375.29.330.6675

BRAZIL

CURITIBA
Rabbi Mendy Labkowski 55.41.3079.1338

S. PAULO
Rabbi Avraham Steinmetz 55.11.3081.3081

CANADA

ALBERTA

CALGARY
Rabbi Mordechai Groner 403.281.3770

EDMONTON
Rabbi Ari Drelich
Rabbi Mendy Blachman 780.200.5770

BRITISH COLUMBIA

COQUITLAM
Rabbi Benzti Shemtov 250.797.7877

NANAIMO
Rabbi Mordechai Gurevitz 604.787.5667

RICHMOND
Rabbi Yechiel Baitelman 604.277.6427

VANCOUVER
Rabbi Dovid Rosenfeld 604.266.1313
Rabbi Shmuel Yeshayahu 604.738.7060

VICTORIA
Rabbi Meir Kaplan 250.595.7656

MANITOBA

WINNIPEG
Rabbi Shmuel Altein 204.339.8737

ONTARIO

BAYVIEW
Rabbi Levi Gansburg 416.551.9391

GREATER TORONTO REGIONAL OFFICE & THORNHILL
Rabbi Yossi Gansburg 905.731.7000

KINGSTON
Rabbi Yisroel Simon 613.770.1884

MAPLE
Rabbi Yechezkel Deren 647.883.6372

MISSISSAUGA
Rabbi Yitzchok Slavin 905.820.4432

NORTH YORK
Rabbi Sruli Steiner 647.501.5618

OTTAWA
Rabbi Menachem M. Blum 613.843.7770
Rabbi Moshe Caytak 613.902.4394

RICHMOND HILL
Rabbi Mendel Bernstein 905.303.1880

TORONTO
Rabbi Sholom Lezell 416.809.1365
Rabbi Shmuel Neft 647.966.7105
Rabbi Moshe Steiner 416.635.9606

WATERLOO
Rabbi Moshe Goldman 226.338.7770

WHITBY
Rabbi Tzali Borenstein 905.447.8215

QUEBEC

CÔTE S.-LUC
Rabbi Levi Naparstek 438.409.6770

DOLLARD-DES ORMEAUX
Rabbi Leibel Fine 514.777.4675

HAMPSTEAD
Rabbi Moshe New
Rabbi Berel Bell 514.739.0770

MONTREAL
Rabbi Ronnie Fine
Pesach Nussbaum 514.738.3434

MONTREAL WEST
Rabbi Mendy Marlow 514.632.9649

OLD MONTREAL/GRIFFINTOWN
Rabbi Nissan Gansbourg
Rabbi Berel Bell 514.800.6966

S. LAURENT
Rabbi Schneur Zalmen Silberstein 514.747.1199

S. LAZARE
Rabbi Nochum Labkowski 514.436.7426

TOWN OF MOUNT ROYAL
Rabbi Moshe Krasnanski
Rabbi Shneur Zalman Rader 514.342.1770

SASKATCHEWAN

SASKATOON
Rabbi Raphael Kats 306.384.4370

CAYMAN ISLANDS

GEORGE TOWN
Rabbi Berel Pewzner 717.798.1040

COLOMBIA

BOGOTA
Rabbi Chanoch Piekarski 57.1.635.8251

COSTA RICA

S. JOSÉ
Rabbi Hershel Spalter
Rabbi Moshe Bitton 506.4010.1515

CROATIA

ZAGREB
Rabbi Pinchas Zaklas 385.1.4812227

DENMARK

COPENHAGEN
Rabbi Yitzchok Loewenthal 45.3316.1850

DOMINICAN REPUBLIC

S. DOMINGO
Rabbi Shimon Pelman 829.341.2770

ESTONIA

TALLINN
Rabbi Shmuel Kot 372.662.30.50

FRANCE

BOULOGNE
Rabbi Michael Sojcher 33.1.46.99.87.85

DIJON
Rabbi Chaim Slonim 33.6.52.05.26.65

LA VARENNE-S.-HILAIRE
Rabbi Mena'hem Mendel Benelbaz 33.6.17.81.57.47

MARSEILLE
Rabbi Eliahou Altabe 33.6.11.60.03.05
Rabbi Mena'hem Mendel Assouline 33.6.64.88.25.04
Rabbi Emmanuel Taubenblatt 33.4.88.00.94.85

PARIS
Rabbi Yona Hasky 33.1.53.75.36.01
Rabbi Acher Marciano 33.6.15.15.01.02
Rabbi Avraham Barou'h Pevzner 33.6.99.64.07.70

PONTAULT-COMBAULT
Rabbi Yossi Amar 33.6.61.36.07.70

VILLIERS-SUR-MARNE
Rabbi Mena'hem Mendel Mergui 33.1.49.30.89.66

GEORGIA

TBILISI
Rabbi Meir Kozlovsky 995.32.2429770

GERMANY

BERLIN
Rabbi Yehuda Tiechtel 49.30.2128.0830

DUSSELDORF
Rabbi Chaim Barkahn 49.173.2871.770

HAMBURG
Rabbi Shlomo Bistritzky 49.40.4142.4190

HANNOVER 49.511.811.2822
Chapter founded by Rabbi Binyamin Wolff, OBM

GREECE

ATHENS
Rabbi Mendel Hendel 30.210.323.3825

GUATEMALA

GUATEMALA CITY
Rabbi Shalom Pelman 502.2485.0770

HUNGARY

BUDAPEST
Rabbi Shlomo Kovesh 361.268.0183

ISRAEL

ASHKELON
Rabbi Shneor Lieberman 054.977.0512

BALFURYA
Rabbi Noam Bar-Tov 054.580.4770

CAESAREA
Rabbi Chaim Meir Lieberman 054.621.2586

EVEN YEHUDA
Rabbi Menachem Noyman 054.777.0707

GANEI TIKVA
Rabbi Gershon Shnur 054.524.2358

GIV'ATAYIM
Rabbi Pinchus Bitton 052.643.8770

JERUSALEM
Rabbi Levi Diamond 055.665.7702
Rabbi Avraham Hendel 054.830.5799

KARMIEL
Rabbi Mendy Elishevitz 054.521.3073

KFAR SABA
Rabbi Yossi Baitch 054.445.5020

KIRYAT BIALIK
Rabbi Pinny Marton 050.661.1768

KIRYAT MOTZKIN
Rabbi Shimon Eizenbach 050.902.0770

KOCHAV YAIR
Rabbi Dovi Greenberg 054.332.6244

MACCABIM-RE'UT
Rabbi Yosef Yitzchak Noiman 054.977.0549

NESS ZIONA
Rabbi Menachem Feldman 054.497.7092

NETANYA
Rabbi Schneur Brod 054.579.7572

RAMAT GAN-KRINITZI
Rabbi Yisroel Gurevitz 052.743.2814

RAMAT GAN-MAROM NAVE
Rabbi Binyamin Meir Kali 050.476.0770

RAMAT YISHAI
Rabbi Shneor Zalman Wolosow 052.324.5475

RISHON LEZION
Rabbi Uri Keshet 050.722.4593

ROSH PINA
Rabbi Sholom Ber Hertzel 052.458.7600

TEL AVIV
Rabbi Shneur Piekarski 054.971.5568

JAMAICA

MONTEGO BAY
Rabbi Yaakov Raskin 876.452.3223

JAPAN

TOKYO
Rabbi Mendi Sudakevich 81.3.5789.2846

KAZAKHSTAN

ALMATY
Rabbi Shevach Zlatopolsky 7.7272.77.59.49

KYRGYZSTAN

BISHKEK
Rabbi Arye Raichman 996.312.68.19.66

LATVIA

RIGA
Rabbi Shneur Zalman Kot
Mrs. Rivka Glazman 371.6720.40.22

LITHUANIA

VILNIUS
Rabbi Sholom Ber Krinsky 370.6817.1367

LUXEMBOURG

LUXEMBOURG
Rabbi Mendel Edelman 352.2877.7079

MEXICO

PUERTO VALLARTA
Rabbi Shneur Hecht 52.32.2141.7279

S. MIGUEL DE ALLENDE
Rabbi Daniel Huebner 52.41.5181.8092

NETHERLANDS

ALMERE
Rabbi Moshe Stiefel 31.36.744.0509

AMSTERDAM
Rabbi Yanki Jacobs 31.644.988.627
Rabbi Jaacov Zwi Spiero 31.652.328.065

EINDHOVEN
Rabbi Simcha Steinberg 31.63.635.7593

HAGUE
Rabbi Shmuel Katzman 31.70.347.0222

HEEMSTEDE-HAARLEM
Rabbi Shmuel Spiero 31.23.532.0707

MAASTRICHT
Rabbi Avrohom Cohen 32.48.549.6766

NIJMEGEN
Rabbi Menachem Mendel Levine 31.621.586.575

ROTTERDAM
Rabbi Yehuda Vorst 31.10.265.5530

PANAMA

PANAMA CITY
Rabbi Ari Laine
Rabbi Gabriel Benayon 507.223.3383

RUSSIA

ASTRAKHAN
Rabbi Yisroel Melamed 7.851.239.28.24

BRYANSK
Rabbi Menachem Mendel Zaklas 7.483.264.55.15

CHELYABINSK
Rabbi Meir Kirsh 7.351.263.24.68

MOSCOW
Rabbi Aizik Rosenfeld 7.906.762.88.81
Rabbi Mordechai Weisberg 7.495.645.50.00

NIZHNY NOVGOROD
Rabbi Shimon Bergman 7.920.253.47.70

NOVOSIBIRSK
Rabbi Shneur Zalmen Zaklos 7.903.900.43.22

OMSK
Rabbi Osher Krichevsky 7.381.231.33.07

PERM
Rabbi Zalman Deutch 7.342.212.47.32

ROSTOV
Rabbi Chaim Danzinger 7.8632.99.02.68

S. PETERSBURG
Rabbi Shalom Pewzner 7.911.726.21.19
Rabbi Zvi Pinsky 7.812.713.62.09

SAMARA
Rabbi Shlomo Deutch 7.846.333.40.64

SARATOV
Rabbi Yaakov Kubitshek 7.8452.21.58.00

TOGLIATTI
Rabbi Meier Fischer 7.848.273.02.84

UFA
Rabbi Dan Krichevsky 7.347.244.55.33

VORONEZH
Rabbi Levi Stiefel 7.473.252.96.99

SINGAPORE

SINGAPORE
Rabbi Mordechai Abergel 656.337.2189
Rabbi Netanel Rivni 656.336.2127
Classes in Hebrew

SOUTH AFRICA

JOHANNESBURG
Rabbi Dovid Masinter
Rabbi Ari Kievman 27.11.440.6600

SWEDEN

STOCKHOLM
Rabbi Chaim Greisman 46.70.790.8994

SWITZERLAND

LUZERN
Rabbi Chaim Drukman 41.41.361.1770

THAILAND

BANGKOK
Rabbi Yosef C. Kantor 6681.837.7618

UKRAINE

BERDITCHEV
Mrs. Chana Thaler 380.637.70.37.70

DNEPROPETROVSK
Rabbi Dan Makagon 380.504.51.13.18

NIKOLAYEV
Rabbi Sholom Gotlieb 380.512.37.37.71

ODESSA
Rabbi Avraham Wolf
Rabbi Yaakov Neiman 38.048.728.0770 EXT. 280

ZAPOROZHYE
Mrs. Nechama Dina Ehrentreu 380.957.19.96.08

ZHITOMIR
Rabbi Shlomo Wilhelm 380.504.63.01.32

UNITED KINGDOM

BOURNEMOUTH
Rabbi Bentzion Alperowitz 44.749.456.7177

CHEADLE
Rabbi Peretz Chein 44.161.428.1818

ESSEX

EPPING
Rabbi Yossi Posen 44.749.650.4345

LEEDS
Rabbi Eli Pink 44.113.266.3311

LONDON
Rabbi Moshe Adler 44.771.052.4460
Rabbi Boruch Altein 44.749.612.3342
Rabbi Mendel Cohen 44.736.640.8244
Rabbi Mechel Gancz 44.758.332.3074
Rabbi Chaim Hoch 44.753.879.9524
Rabbi Mendel Kalmanson 44.758.592.0195
Rabbi Dovid Katz 44.207.625.2682
Mrs. Esther Kesselman 44.794.432.4829
Rabbi Mendy Korer 44.794.632.5444
Rabbi Baruch Levin 44.208.905.4141
Rabbi Eli Levin 44.754.046.1568

Mrs. Chanie Simon 44.208.458.0416
Rabbi Bentzi Sudak 44.781.211.1890
Rabbi Shneur Wineberg 44.745.628.6538

MANCHESTER
Rabbi Levi Cohen 44.161.792.6335
Rabbi Shmuli Jaffe 44.161.766.1812

NOTTINGHAM
Rabbi Mendy Lent 44.759.005.1261

RADLETT, HERTFORDSHIRE
Rabbi Alexander Sender Dubrawsky 44.794.380.8965

NOTES

NOTES

The Jewish Learning Multiplex

Brought to you by the Rohr Jewish Learning Institute

In fulfillment of the mandate of the Lubavitcher Rebbe, of blessed memory, whose leadership guides every step of our work, the mission of the Rohr Jewish Learning Institute is to transform Jewish life and the greater community through the study of Torah, connecting each Jew to our shared heritage of Jewish learning.

While our flagship program remains the cornerstone of our organization, JLI is proud to feature additional divisions catering to specific populations, in order to meet a wide array of educational needs.

THE ROHR JEWISH LEARNING INSTITUTE

A subsidiary of Merkos L'Inyonei Chinuch,
the adult education arm of the Chabad-Lubavitch movement

Torah Studies provides a rich and nuanced encounter with the weekly Torah reading.

 Jewish teens forge their identity as they engage in Torah study, social interaction, and serious fun.

 The Rosh Chodesh Society gathers Jewish women together once a month for intensive textual study.

 TorahCafe.com provides an exclusive selection of top-rated Jewish educational videos.

 Participants delve into our nation's past while exploring the Holy Land's relevance and meaning today.

 This yearly event rejuvenates mind, body, and spirit with a powerful synthesis of Jewish learning and community.

 Equips youths facing adulthood with education and resources to address youth mental health.

 Select affiliates are invited to partner with peers and noted professionals, as leaders of innovation and excellence.

 MyShiur courses are designed to assist students in developing the skills needed to study Talmud independently.

 This rigorous fellowship program invites select college students to explore the fundamentals of Judaism.

 A crash course that teaches adults to read Hebrew in just five sessions.

 Machon Shmuel is an institute providing Torah research in the service of educators worldwide.